NetBeans™ IDE Field Guide

NetBeans™ IDE Field Guide

Developing Desktop, Web, Enterprise, and Mobile Applications

Patrick Keegan
Ludovic Champenois
Gregory Crawley
Charlie Hunt
Christopher Webster

Sun Microsystems Press
A Prentice Hall Title

Prentice Hall Professional Technical Reference

Upper Saddle River, NJ • Boston • Indianapolis • San Francisco
New York • Toronto • Montreal • London • Munich • Paris • Madrid
Capetown • Sydney • Tokyo • Singapore • Mexico City

The publisher offers excellent discounts on this book when ordered in quantity for bulk purchases or special sales, which may include electronic versions and/or custom covers and content particular to your business, training goals, marketing focus, and branding interests. For more information, please contact U.S. Corporate and Government Sales, (800) 382-3419, corpsales@pearsontechgroup.com.

For sales outside the U.S., please contact International Sales, international@pearsoned.com.

Visit us on the Web: www.phptr.com

This Book Is Safari Enabled

The Safari® Enabled icon on the cover of your favorite technology book means the book is available through Safari Bookshelf. When you buy this book, you get free access to the online edition for 45 days.

Safari Bookshelf is an electronic reference library that lets you easily search thousands of technical books, find code samples, download chapters, and access technical information whenever and wherever you need it.

To gain 45-day Safari Enabled access to this book:

• Go to http://www.awprofessional.com/safarienabled
• Complete the brief registration form
• Enter the coupon code CJF9-VCPG-VOGK-RNG3-KMFW

If you have difficulty registering on Safari Bookshelf or accessing the online edition, please e-mail customer-service@safaribooksonline.com.

Library of Congress Cataloging-in-Publication Data:
NetBeans IDE field guide : developing Desktop, Web, Enterprise, and Mobile applications / Patrick Keegan ... [et al.].
   p. cm.
    Includes bibliographical references and index.
    ISBN 0-13-187620-1 (pbk. : alk. paper)
  1. Java (Computer program language) 2. Computer programming. I. Keegan, Patrick.
    QA76.73.J38N463 2005
    005.2'762—dc22

                                           2005012197

ISBN 0-13-187620-1
Text printed in the United States on recycled paper at Courier in Stoughton, Massachusetts.
First printing, June 2005

Contents

Chapter 4   Editing and Refactoring Code   **71**

Foreword

By James Gosling

The NetBeans IDE has really come a long way in the last few years. Since the first book was written, NetBeans has progressed from a tool with promise (from a small, young company in the Czech Republic) to one of the market leaders in the open source IDE tools space. It's been like watching a child grow and mature over the years and blossom in ways you could have never predicted.

It's a bit like watching Java grow. At first it was a language for the Internet and browsers. It was so versatile, people started using it in many ways. It developed into a great language for writing multi-tier applications. And then with J2EE, it created a whole new ecosystem of enterprise applications. Later, J2ME conquered the phone and mobility market.

NetBeans has been through a similar, multifaceted growth. With NetBeans IDE 4.1, one tool can manage the range of Java development. The IDE now adds J2EE EJB and web services development to the rich suite of development capabilities that service J2SE and J2ME.

I use NetBeans for all my Java development. The exciting new language features in J2SE 5.0 are fun to use and easy to develop with. One of the things that's nice for me personally is that with each release, once I download it, it is ready to go. I don't have go on a treasure hunt and assemble a particular set of plug-ins for me to begin development—as soon as I install NetBeans, I'm ready to start coding.

The PR people at Sun like to call me "the Father of Java." Given that, NetBeans must be my first techno-grandchild. Enjoy all that NetBeans IDE 4.1 provides and the worlds it opens for you. Happy programming.

James Gosling
May 2005

Foreword

By Bill Shannon

The NetBeans IDE was the first free and open source tool to provide support for building J2EE web tier applications five years ago. With the 4.1 release, the NetBeans IDE has advanced even further to include full support for building complete J2EE 1.4 applications, including Enterprise JavaBeans (EJB) components, as well as supporting the key new capability of J2EE 1.4—web services.

EJB components have been a core strength of the J2EE platform from the beginning. The NetBeans IDE now provides support for creating and using EJB components. Developers can create EJB session beans to contain their transactional business logic, and use message-driven beans to create event-driven applications. Developers can also use the powerful database support in the NetBeans IDE to map existing database tables to EJB entity beans, or to create new object models using EJB entity beans and map them to database tables.

The use of web services in the enterprise is expanding rapidly and forms the core of a Service-Oriented Architecture (SOA). A developer using the NetBeans IDE can easily create simple Java applications that are exposed as web services for others to use, without knowing all the details of web services protocols, Web Services Description Language (WSDL), etc. Similarly, given a WSDL description of a web service developed by someone else, a developer using the NetBeans IDE can easily make use of that web service in his or her J2EE application. Web services are incredibly important to enterprise applications, and the NetBeans IDE makes web services easy!

Deployment descriptors are key to enabling portable enterprise applications, but they can get in the way when developing simple applications. The NetBeans IDE removes the burden of dealing with deployment descriptors by completely managing them for the developer. Developers never need to think about deployment descriptors when developing and deploying J2EE applications. The NetBeans IDE will automatically and transparently create and manage the deployment descriptors that are needed for the J2EE application being developed.

The NetBeans IDE, when used with the J2EE SDK, provides a complete environment for creating, packaging, deploying, and debugging J2EE applications. The NetBeans IDE uses the J2EE application server from the J2EE SDK, and completely manages the application server for the developer. With a single click the NetBeans IDE will start the application server, deploy the application, and run the application in a mode ready for debugging!

The complexity of managing deployment descriptors is one of the problems recognized by J2EE 5.0, whose major goal is to significantly simplify development of J2EE applications. Version 4.1 of the NetBeans IDE delivers much of that simplification today. Future versions of the NetBeans IDE will further simplify J2EE application development, taking advantage of the improvements in J2EE 5.0.

The success of the J2EE platform is greatly enhanced by tools such as the NetBeans IDE, and J2EE developers will find that they're even more successful with the NetBeans IDE. We look forward to working with the NetBeans IDE team to provide great tools support to deliver on the promise of J2EE 5.0!

Bill Shannon
May 2005

Preface

This book is designed both as an introduction to NetBeans IDE and as a task reference, something that you can pick up from time to time to get an answer to a question or to find new ways to take advantage of the IDE's possibilities. Whether NetBeans is your first IDE or your fifth, this book can help you make the most of the IDE.

What Is NetBeans IDE?

NetBeans IDE is a free-of-charge integrated development environment (IDE) primarily focused on making it easier to develop Java applications. It provides support for all types of Java applications, from rich desktop clients to multi-tier enterprise applications to applications for Java-enabled hand-held devices.

NetBeans IDE has a modular architecture that allows for plug-ins. However, the range of features in the basic installation is so rich that you can probably can start using the IDE for your work without worrying about plug-ins at all.

The IDE itself is written in Java, so you can run it on any operating system for which there is a Java 2 Standard Edition JDK (Version 1.4.2, Version 5.0, or later) available. Click-through installers are generally available for Microsoft Windows, Solaris, Linux, Mac OS, and OpenVMS systems. You can also download the IDE as a .zip or .tar file if you want to install it on an operating system other than the ones listed above.

The IDE's basic job is to make the edit-compile-debug cycle much smoother by integrating the tools for these activities. For example, the IDE:

- Identifies coding errors almost immediately and marks them in the Source Editor.

- Helps you code faster with code completion, word matching, abbreviation expansion, and fix import features.

- Provides visual navigation aids, such as the Navigator window and "code folding," as well as numerous keyboard navigation shortcuts designed especially for Java programmers.

- Can display documentation for a class as you are typing in the Source Editor.

- Hot-links compilation errors in the Output window, so you can jump straight to the source by double-clicking the line or pressing F12.

- Manages package names and references to other classes. When you rename or move classes around, the IDE identifies places in the code that are affected by these changes and enables you to have the IDE generate the appropriate changes to those files.

- Has many debugging features that provide a comprehensive view of the way your code is working as it runs. You can set breakpoints, which persist from session to session and keep your code free of clutter, such as `println` statements.

- Helps you integrate other parts of your workflow, such as checking sources into and out from a version control system.

You can also download the NetBeans Profiler to augment the traditional edit-compile-debug cycle with performance testing.

What Makes NetBeans IDE Special

When you use NetBeans IDE, you get the benefits of a top-shelf IDE without the negatives that you might associate with moving your development to a single environment.

Like other integrated development environments, NetBeans IDE provides a graphical user interface for command line tools that handle the compiling, debugging, and packaging of applications.

Unlike other IDEs, NetBeans IDE does not force a build structure on you with project metadata that you need to reverse engineer if you are to use build the project outside of the IDE. NetBeans IDE builds on existing open standards to help you automate your development process without locking you in.

NetBeans IDE bases its whole project system on Ant, which is the de facto standard build tool for Java applications. The project metadata that NetBeans IDE produces is in the form of XML and properties files that can be used by Ant outside of the IDE. Thus developing a project in NetBeans IDE does not lock you or co-developers into NetBeans IDE.

You can use NetBeans IDE to create large projects with sophisticated build parameters. Where you already have such projects in place, you can adapt NetBeans IDE to work with them without necessarily changing the project's structure. If you are generally more comfortable with command line tools because of their transparency and the level of control they allow you over your projects, NetBeans IDE could become the first IDE that you love.

NetBeans IDE is also consistently ahead of the curve in providing support for new and evolving standards, such as the new language features that were introduced in the J2SE 5 JDK and new specifications in all areas of Java technology.

NetBeans IDE provides an astonishing array of features right out of the box. NetBeans has a fully featured J2EE development environment built in. All the editor, debugger and project support that is available for Java application development is also available for J2EE development. In addition, NetBeans IDE provides access to the Java BluePrints Solutions Catalog and the ability to install them as NetBeans projects.

The Mobility Pack, available as a free download, enables J2ME developers to design, develop and debug J2ME MIDlets from within NetBeans IDE. Providing one of the most powerful sets of mobile development tools, the Mobility Pack includes a flow designer to visually layout the application logic, a screen designer to create the user interface, an integrated device fragmentation solution, and tools for building client server applications.

What Comes with NetBeans IDE

Besides providing support for coding, NetBeans IDE comes bundled with other tools and libraries that you might already use in your production environment. The IDE integrates these tools into the IDE workflow, but you can also use them at the command line.

Out of the box with NetBeans IDE 4.1, you get:

- Apache Ant 1.6.2
- Tomcat 5.5.7
- JUnit 3.8.1
- Java BluePrints Solutions Catalog

If you download the Mobility Modules pack, you also get the Wireless Toolkit.

You can also get NetBeans IDE in a bundle with the J2SE JDK or the Sun Java System Application Server Platform Edition.

If you download the NetBeans Profiler, you also get a full-featured, nonintrusive Java profiler that is based on the JFluid profiling technology.

What This Book Will Do for You

This book was written with both new and existing NetBeans IDE users in mind.

If you are new to NetBeans IDE (or IDEs in general), this book will quickly guide you through the basics and advantages of using NetBeans IDE. Learn how to take advantage of the IDE's layout and feature integration to tighten up the basic edit-compile-debug cycle. Learn how to take advantage of the IDE's support for increasingly popular advanced technologies such as web services and J2EE technology to add new capabilities to your applications.

If you are already familiar with NetBeans IDE, this book will provide a new perspective on what you already know and possibly point you to useful features that you have not yet discovered. Learn how you can customize the IDE to work with complex build structures. If you are looking to move from client-server web applications to multi-tier transactional enterprise applications, this book will help you make that jump.

This book does not teach the Java programming language. Much of the material in this book is meaningful only if you have some experience with programming Java applications. However, this book could be a useful companion if you are expanding your Java technology palette into J2EE technology and other advanced areas.

How to Use This Book

There is a lot to write about NetBeans IDE, which is overflowing with features. *NetBeans™ IDE Field Guide* sorts out the essentials so that you can get productive quickly and then adds a generous selection of tips and advanced information.

This book is primarily designed as a task-reference with short topics on accomplishing specific tasks. If you wish, you can read the book from cover to cover, but most likely you will want to keep it near your computer to ask pressing questions or simply to read up on ways to get more out of your work with the IDE. The topics are written in a way that allows you to skip all over the book to get answers to the specific questions you have without having to follow long end-to-end examples.

Chapter 1 provides the information you need to get NetBeans IDE and to open your first project.

Chapter 2 provides an overview of the IDE environment and the basic tasks for developing general Java projects. If you have never used NetBeans IDE, you will probably want to read this chapter from end to end.

Chapter 3 provides in-depth information on setting up and configuring projects. Though this chapter is mostly geared toward general Java applications, a working knowledge of the information in this chapter will be useful for developing J2EE and J2ME applications as well.

Chapter 4 (editing) and Chapter 5 (debugging) provide useful tips and tricks for making your day-to-day coding and troubleshooting more productive.

Chapter 6 covers development of Web applications, with a focus on developing with the Tomcat Web server.

Several chapters are devoted to J2EE topics. You should begin with Chapter 7, Introduction to J2EE Development in NetBeans IDE, to get information on setting up your environment and learning how to leverage the Java BluePrints Solutions catalog in J2EE development.

If you are familiar with Web application development and would like to learn how to extend it into using J2EE Enterprise JavaBeans components, you should read Chapter 8, Extending Web Applications with Business Logic: Introducing Enterprise Beans.

If you are interested in learning how to extend your J2EE applications to include Web services, you should read Chapter 9, Extending J2EE Applications with Web Services.

Chapter 10, Developing Full Scale J2EE Applications, contains in-depth information on developing entity beans, assembling applications, verifying J2EE compliance, and other topics.

Chapter 11 covers special IDE features for using the NetBeans Mobility Pack to develop J2ME applications for handheld devices.

Chapter 12 provides information for taking advantage of NetBeans IDE's unique Ant integration to use the IDE with existing intricate build environments.

NetBeans As Platform and Open-Source Project

Besides being an IDE, NetBeans is also a 100% pure Java open-source platform. You can develop plug-in modules for NetBeans IDE or create an entirely different application built on top of a small core of the modules that make up the IDE. Because NetBeans is 100% pure Java, any platform that supports a Java Virtual Machine will run NetBeans. Hence, any plug-in module or application that extends NetBeans and that is 100% pure Java will also execute on any platform for which there is a Java Virtual Machine. However, you should note that this book covers use of the IDE only to develop Java applications.

See http://platform.netbeans.org for information on creating plug-in modules for NetBeans IDE and for information on using the NetBeans platform as an application framework.

About the Authors

Patrick Keegan is the lead technical writer for NetBeans IDE. He has been writing about the IDE since May 1999, when NetBeans was a small Czech company yet to be acquired by Sun Microsystems. He lives in Prague, Czech Republic.

Ludovic Champenois is a senior architect at Sun Microsystems, and has been with Sun for the last ten years. He is currently the tech lead and architect for NetBeans J2EE support, working with the Application Server group (J2EE 1.4 and J2EE 5.0) and the Tools organization to make sure that the NetBeans Open Source IDE is actively tracking the changes in the Java Platform (J2ME, J2SE, and J2EE). He is a civil engineer from L'Ecole Nationale Supérieure des Mines, Saint-Etienne, France.

Gregory Crawley conceptualized and implemented the Mobility device fragmentation solution for NetBeans IDE 4.0. He continues to be an avid NetBeans IDE user and developer of J2ME games in association with Cotopia Wireless.

Charlie Hunt is a NetBeans Technology Evangelist at Sun Microsystems. He has been working with Java since 1997 and has held many positions at Sun Microsystems, including Java Architect and Java Performance Engineer.

Christopher Webster, a member of the Java Studio Enterprise development team, focuses on service-oriented architecture (SOA) tools. Before joining Sun, Chris was a computer scientist at the Lawrence Livermore National Laboratory. Chris holds a B.S. in computer science from the University of Hawaii and an M.S. in computer science from Baylor University.

Acknowledgments

Patrick Keegan

First of all, I'd like to thank everybody who made my participation in this book possible, especially David Lindt, my manager, and John Jullion-Ceccarrelli, who assumed many of my lead duties and still managed to make enormous content contributions to the NetBeans IDE 4.1 release. The book itself would not have been possible without the support of Tim Cramer and efforts of Larry Baron, who pulled together the resources to make it happen. Thank you to everybody who so enthusiastically supported the book with a combination of small contributions, reviews, suggestions, and moral support. In particular, I would like to cite Vincent Brabant and David Coldrick.

Other people whose insight and sharp eyes greatly added to the quality of the book: Gregg Sporar, Geertjan Wielenga, Marian Petras, Maros Sandor, Karel Zikmund, Lubomir Cincura, David Konecny, Roman Stroubl, Milan Kubec, Jiri Prazak, Maros Sandor, and Adam Sotona. On the editorial and production side, thanks to Greg Doench, Tyrrell Albaugh, and Kathy Simpson for their guidance and flexibility. Last and possibly most, I'd like to thank Tim Boudreau, who goaded me into taking on this project.

Ludovic Champenois

First and foremost, my special thanks and love to my family—Vannina, my wife, and Elio, Flora, Lucas, Bianca, my four children—for supporting me during the last year. Bianca still believes Java is an island like Corsica, and she is right! Vannina reviewed parts of the book, and while having no knowledge at all of the domain, she gave me precious feedback: Keep it simple stupid! I love you. Love to Gaspard and Stan: *Je pense à vous si souvent*.

This book is about NetBeans, and NetBeans is a fantastic community—the people in Prague, the people in the U.S., many people from Sun Microsystems . . .

Jesse Glick, who trained me on the internals of NetBeans, back in 1999. Jeet Kaul and Jeff Jackson helped me tremendously in my quest to move J2EE support from Sun Studio products to the open source world. My thanks to the engineers from Studio—Nam Nnguyen, Rico Cruz, and Chris Webster—who changed their focus and invested all their time in the success of NetBeans IDE 4.1. Along with the engineers from the Sun Application Server organization—Vince Kraemer, Rochelle Raccah, Peter Williams, Nitya Doraisamy, Rajeshwar Patil, and Anil Gaur—they did most of the foundation work. Thanks, this was incredible cross-organizational teamwork! The foundation is finally there; let's have some rest before J2EE 5.0.

Gregory Crawley

Thanks to Martin Ryzl and the entire mobility team for their support throughout this entire process.

Charlie Hunt

I thank Tim Cramer, the director of NetBeans, for suggesting I contribute to this book. I have been blessed to work with a great team of coauthors who made the book writing an enjoyable experience: Patrick Keegan, Ludovic Champenois, Chris Webster, and Greg Crawley. I wish to extend a special thanks to Patrick Keegan for leading the writing effort. I also want to thank James Gosling and Bill Shannon for writing the forewords. Finally, I want to thank my wife, Barb Hunt, for her encouragement to contribute to the book and for putting up with me while I wrote.

Christopher Webster

I would like to thank Ludo for his leadership skills. I would also like to acknowledge the hard work from the Java Studio Enterprise team, the Application Server team, and the NetBeans J2EE team. Finally, I would also like to thank the early adopters of NetBeans IDE 4.1, whose feedback has been invaluable.

## CHAPTER 1

Download, Installation, and First Project

- Downloading the IDE
- Installing the IDE
- Setting a Proxy
- First NetBeans IDE Project

THIS CHAPTER PROVIDES THE BASIC INFORMATION that you need to get NetBeans IDE running on your system and then runs you through creation of a very simple project to get you started. Additional basic information follows in Chapter 2, NetBeans IDE Fundamentals.

Downloading the IDE

You can download NetBeans IDE from the netbeans.org web site or the java.sun.com site. Visit http://www.netbeans.org/downloads/index.html for a list of and links to all downloads.

NetBeans IDE 4.1 is available in the following distributions:

- The basic IDE distribution. This distribution includes support for developing general Java libraries, rich client applications, web applications, and enterprise tier applications. You can get this distribution as an installer (for Microsoft Windows, Solaris, Linux, and Mac OS systems) or as an archive distribution (.zip file or .tar file).

  Use this distribution if you already have the JDK installed on your system (must be version 1.4.2, 5.0, or compatible) and you do not need to download the Sun Java System Application Server (either because you already have it or because you do not need it for the applications you are developing).

- The basic IDE distribution bundled with the Sun Java System Application Server Platform Edition.

  This is the most convenient download if you want to start developing and deploying applications to an application server (and you do not yet have the Sun Java System Application Server).

- The basic IDE distribution bundled with J2SE JDK 5.0.

  This is a convenient download if you do not already have the JDK installed on your system. Both the JDK and the IDE are installed at the same time.

 Having just the Java Runtime Environment (JRE) installed on your system is not sufficient for running NetBeans IDE. You need to have the JDK, which includes a copy of the JRE. The IDE relies on development tools provided by the JDK, such as the `javac` compiler, and takes advantage of other parts of that download, such as the JDK sources that it includes. You can go to http://java.sun.com/j2se/index.jsp to find and download the latest version of the JDK.

In addition, there are the following optional add-on installers for NetBeans IDE:

- NetBeans Mobility Pack. This installer adds support for developing applications based on J2ME technology for mobile devices.
- NetBeans Profiler. This pack adds the ability to profile your application's performance using dynamic bytecode instrumentation.

As the name "add-on" implies, these installers work only if you have a compatible version of NetBeans IDE already installed on your system.

Installing the IDE

Installing the IDE is simple and is basically composed of these steps:

1. Make sure that you have a suitable JDK version installed on your system. For NetBeans IDE 4.1, the JDK version must be 1.4.2 or higher. If you do not have a suitable JDK version on your system, install that first or download a JDK/NetBeans IDE bundle.
2. If you are running on the Solaris or Linux operating system, change the permissions on the installer file to make it executable (if necessary).
3. Double-click the installer (or, on Solaris or Linux, launch the installer from the command line) and then step through the installer wizard.

That's pretty much all you have to do. The installer guides you through selecting a JDK on your system to run the IDE on and (optionally) creates desktop icons and Start menu items for the IDE.

See Configuring the IDE for J2EE Development in Chapter 7 for information on setting up the Sun Java System Application Server.

Setting a Proxy

It is useful for the IDE to have a web connection. The IDE periodically checks the web to see if new or updated modules are available. Also, some IDE functions such as Validate XML might rely on resources on the web. In addition, some Help menu items are links to documentation on the web.

If you work behind a firewall, you might need to configure the IDE to use a proxy for HTTP connections to the web. The IDE attempts to use your system's proxy. If that does not work, you can set the proxy manually.

To set a proxy manually in the IDE:

1. Choose Tools | Setup Wizard.
2. In the Web Proxy section of the wizard page, select the Use HTTP Proxy radio button, and fill in values for the proxy host and port.

First NetBeans IDE Project

Once you have started the IDE, you are presented with a "welcome" window and some other empty windows. To help get you started, this section provides a quick run-through of setting up, compiling, and running a "Hello World" project.

To set up the project:

1. Choose File | New Project (or press Ctrl-Shift-N).
2. In the New Project wizard, expand the General node, select Java Application, and click Next (as shown in Figure 1-1).

   The Java Application template sets up a basic project and includes a main class.
3. In the Name and Location page of the wizard (as shown in Figure 1-2), type HelloWorld as the project name.
4. In the Create Main Class field, change helloworld.Main to com.mydomain. myproject.HelloWorld. (When you enter a fully qualified class name in this field, the IDE generates directories for each level of the package structure.)
5. Click Finish.

Once you have finished the wizard, the IDE will run a scan of the classpath that has been set for the project to enable features such as code completion to work.

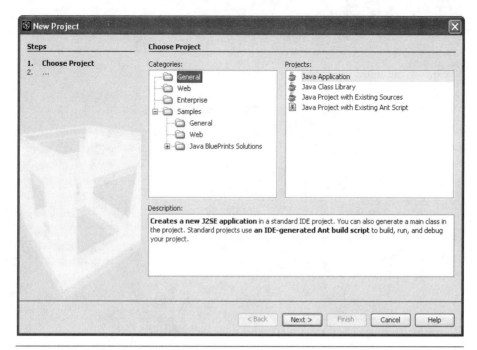

Figure 1-1   New Project wizard, Choose Project page

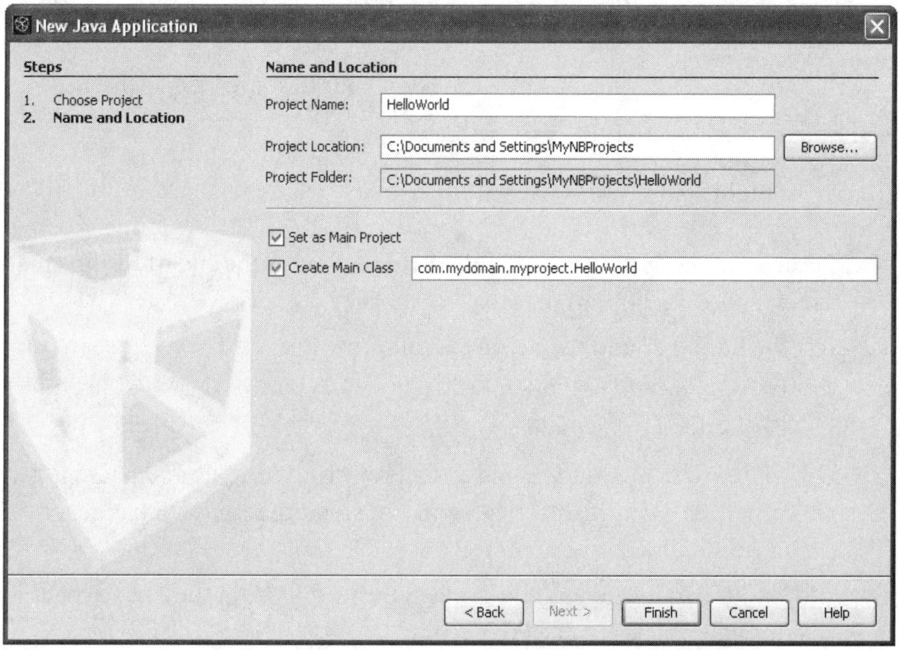

Figure 1-2   New Project wizard, Name and Location page

The following windows then get populated:

- ▪ The Projects window, which provides access to your sources, any tests you might have, and your classpath (represented through the Libraries and Test Libraries nodes). See Figure 1-3.

Figure 1-3   Projects window with nodes for the HelloWorld project

- ▪ The Navigator window, which provides an easy way for you to view and access members of the currently selected class. It also makes browsing the inheritance tree of a class easy.
- ▪ The Source Editor, where a tab for the HelloWorld source file opens. See Figure 1-4.

To modify, build, and run the project:

1. In the Source Editor, click within the main method at the end of the line that reads // TODO code application logic here.
2. Press the Enter key and then type the following line:
   ```
   System.out.println("Hello World!");
   ```
3. Press Ctrl-S to save the application.
4. Press F11 (or choose Build | Build Main Project) to compile and package the application. This command triggers an Ant script that the IDE has generated and maintained for the project.

   The Output window opens and displays the output from the Ant script as it runs through its targets. See Figure 1-5.
5. Press F6 (or choose Run | Run Main Project) to run the project.

   The Output window should display a combination of Ant output and the "Hello World!" message from your application. See Figure 1-6.

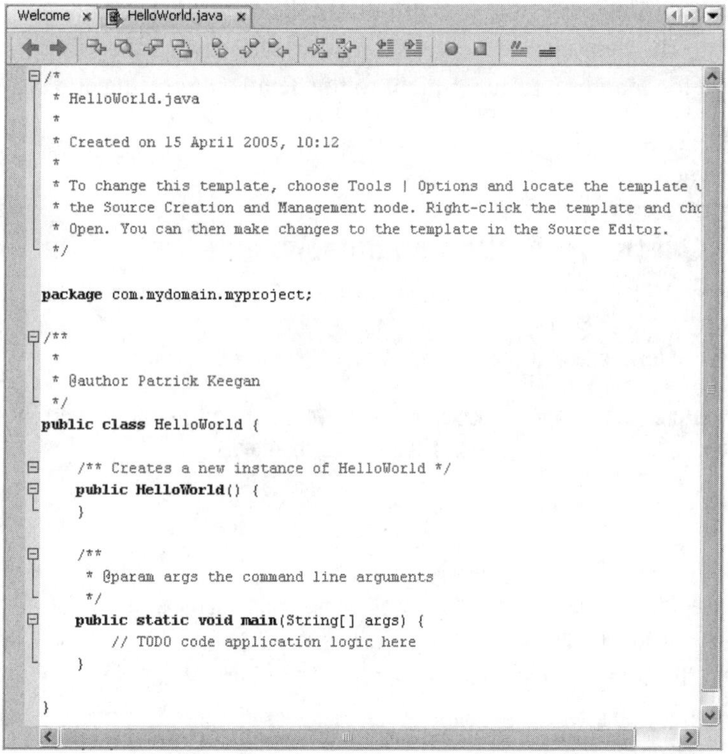

```
/*
 * HelloWorld.java
 *
 * Created on 15 April 2005, 10:12
 *
 * To change this template, choose Tools | Options and locate the template t
 * the Source Creation and Management node. Right-click the template and cho
 * Open. You can then make changes to the template in the Source Editor.
 */

package com.mydomain.myproject;

/**
 *
 * @author Patrick Keegan
 */
public class HelloWorld {

    /** Creates a new instance of HelloWorld */
    public HelloWorld() {
    }

    /**
     * @param args the command line arguments
     */
    public static void main(String[] args) {
        // TODO code application logic here
    }

}
```

Figure 1-4　Source Editor with HelloWorld.java open

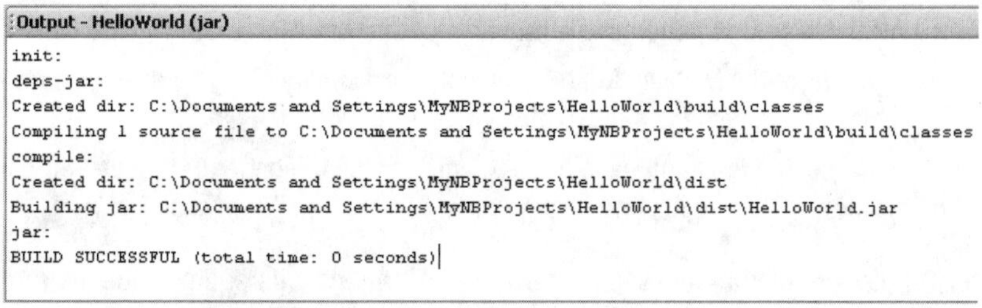

```
Output - HelloWorld (jar)
init:
deps-jar:
Created dir: C:\Documents and Settings\MyNBProjects\HelloWorld\build\classes
Compiling 1 source file to C:\Documents and Settings\MyNBProjects\HelloWorld\build\classes
compile:
Created dir: C:\Documents and Settings\MyNBProjects\HelloWorld\dist
Building jar: C:\Documents and Settings\MyNBProjects\HelloWorld\dist\HelloWorld.jar
jar:
BUILD SUCCESSFUL (total time: 0 seconds)
```

Figure 1-5　Output window showing successful building of the HelloWorld project

```
Output - HelloWorld (run)
init:
deps-jar:
compile:
run:
Hello World!
BUILD SUCCESSFUL (total time: 0 seconds)
```

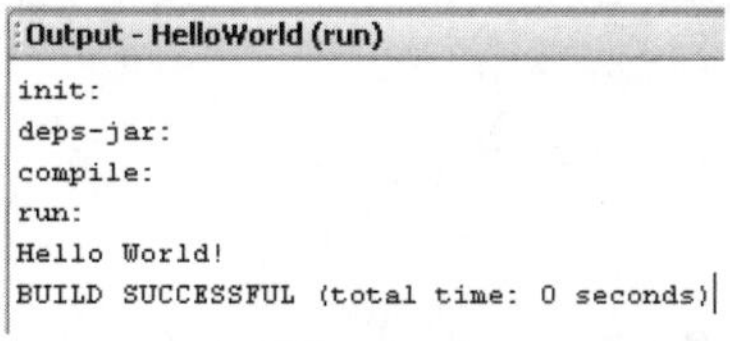

Figure 1-6　Output window showing the successful running of the HelloWorld project

With that, you have created and run an application in the IDE. You can now move on to the next chapter to get a broader overview of the IDE. Or you can skip ahead to Chapter 3 to cut straight to the details of creating and customizing projects.

Trying Out NetBeans IDE with Sample Code

If you want to check out the features of NetBeans IDE on working code without touching your existing projects, or if you just want to see what a working project looks like in the IDE, you can open one of the sample projects that come with the IDE.

When you create a sample project, the sample code is copied into a directory of your choosing, and all necessary project metadata is generated.

To create a sample project:

1. Choose File | New Project.
2. In the New Project wizard, expand the Samples folder; choose a template from one of the categories; and click Next.
   - The General category contains a simple J2SE application.
   - The Web category contains several examples designed to run on the Tomcat server.
   - The BluePrints Solutions category contains examples of useful design patterns for J2EE applications. These examples accompany the BluePrints Solutions Catalog, which is available from the Help menu and which provides documentation for these design patterns in a problem/solution format.
   - If you have the Mobility Modules installed, a Mobility category also appears and includes samples from the J2ME Wireless Toolkit.
3. On the Name and Location page of the wizard, check the generated values for name and location of the project and change them, if you wish. Then click Finish.

Once you have created a new sample project, you can view its source code and project structure and then build and run that application within the IDE.

## CHAPTER 2

NetBeans IDE Fundamentals

- Creating a Project
- Configuring the Classpath
- Creating a Subproject
- Creating and Editing Files
- Setting Up and Modifying Java Packages
- Compiling and Building
- Viewing Project Metadata and Build Results
- Navigating to the Source of Compilation Errors
- Running
- Creating and Running Tests
- Debugging the Application
- Integrating Version Control Commands
- Managing IDE Windows

THIS CHAPTER PROVIDES A GENERAL OVERVIEW of both the workflow in the IDE and the key parts of the IDE. Once you finish this chapter, you should have a solid understanding of the IDE's principles and be able to take advantage of the IDE's central features.

If you are already familiar with NetBeans IDE (4.0 or higher), you can probably skim this chapter or skip it altogether. Subsequent chapters will revisit most of this material in greater depth to answer more involved questions and provide additional details that you can use to squeeze more productivity out of your work with the IDE.

Creating a Project

Before you can do any serious work in the IDE, you need to set up a project. The project essentially sets up a context for you to write, compile, test, and debug your application. This context includes the classpath; folders for your sources and tests; and a build script with targets for compiling the application, running tests, and building JAR files (or other types of distributable archive files).

You can choose among a variety of project template categories, which are grouped according to the technology you are basing your application on (for example, general Java, J2EE web tier, J2EE enterprise tier, and J2ME).

Within the template categories, you have templates for new applications and for setting up an IDE project for existing applications you are working on. The New Project wizard provides a description for each template.

The With Existing Sources templates in each category enable you to set up standard IDE projects around applications that you have been developing in a different environment.

The With Existing Ant Script templates in each category, unlike the With Existing Sources templates and other standard project templates, take that a step further and enable you to set up a project based entirely on any existing Ant script. This approach requires some manual configuration to get some IDE features (such as debugging) to work with the Ant script, but the payoff is that you can get the IDE to work with any project structure, even if it does not adhere to the conventions of a standard IDE project. See Chapter 12 for information on creating a project with a With Existing Ant Script template.

To set up a project:

1. Choose File | New Project.
2. In the wizard, select a template for your project, and complete the wizard.

   The fields that you are asked to fill in depend on the template. Typically, you need to specify a location for the project (or, in the case of projects that use existing sources, where the sources are located). Web, Enterprise, and Mobility projects also include fields relevant for those specific types of applications. Figure 2-1 shows the Name and Location page of the wizard for a new Web Application project.

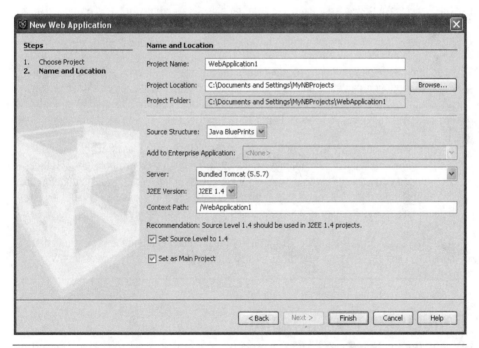

Figure 2-1   New Project wizard, Web Application template, Name and Location page

When you create a project, typically, the IDE does the following things for you:

- Creates a source tree with a skeleton class inside.
- Creates a folder for unit tests.

- Creates an Ant build script (`build.xml`), which contains the instructions that the IDE uses when you perform commands on your project, such as compiling source files, running the application, running tests, debugging, compiling Javadoc documentation, and building JAR files.

You can find more information on setting up standard projects in Chapter 3. You can find more information on setting up free-form projects (those using the With Existing Ant Script template) in Chapter 12.

Projects Window

The Projects window is essentially the command center for your work. It is organized as a tree view of nodes that represent parts of your project. It provides an entry point for your files as well as configuration options for the application you are developing.

In addition to displaying nodes for the files in the application that you are developing, the Projects window provides a representation of your classpath. The Libraries node for each project shows the version of the JDK you are developing against, as well as any other libraries you are basing your project on.

The Projects window presents your project in "logical" form—that is, it represents the units of your application conceptually (rather than literally). For example, Java sources are grouped into packages without nodes for each level of file hierarchy. Files that you do not normally need to view, such as compiled Java classes and project metadata files, are hidden. This makes it easier to access the files you most regularly work with.

If you want to browse the physical structure of the project, including the project metadata, compiled classes, JAR files, and other files created in builds, open the Files window.

Configuring the Classpath

When you create a project, the IDE sets up a default classpath for you based on the project template you are using. If you have other things to add to the classpath, you can do so through the Libraries node of the project.

In fact, the IDE distinguishes among several types of classpaths, depending on project type, such as compilation classpath, test compilation classpath, running classpath, and test running classpath. The compilation classpath typically serves as a base for the other classpaths (for example, other classpaths inherit what is in the compilation classpath).

To add an item to the compilation classpath (and, thus, the other classpaths as well), right-click the project's Libraries node and choose Add JAR/Folder (see Figure 2-2).

Figure 2-2   Projects window, adding a JAR file to the classpath

When you right-click the Libraries node, you also can choose Add Project or Add Library. When you add a project, you add the project's output (such as a JAR file) to the classpath.

If you choose Add Library, you can add one of the "libraries" recognized by the IDE's Library Manager. In the Library Manager, libraries are essentially just a convenient grouping of one or more JAR files, sources, and/or Javadoc documentation. Designating libraries in the Library Manager is useful for several IDE features. For example, designating a JAR file and its sources as a library ensures that you can step through that JAR file's code when debugging.

You can manage existing libraries and designate new ones in the Library Manager, which you can open by choosing Tools | Library Manager.

You can edit other classpaths in the Properties dialog box for a project. To open the Project Properties dialog box, right-click the project's node in the Projects window and choose Properties. In the dialog box, click the Libraries node and use the customizer in the right panel to specify the different classpaths (see Figure 2-3).

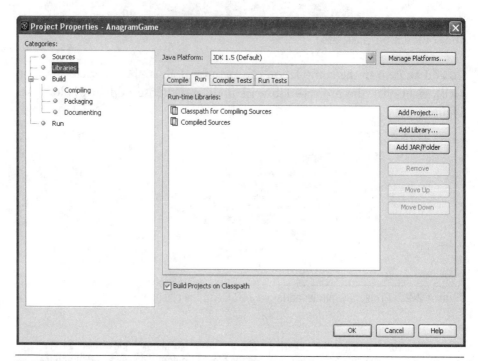

Figure 2-3   Project Properties dialog box, Libraries page

Creating a Subproject

Though there is no explicit distinction in the IDE between a project and a sub-project, you can create a hierarchy of projects by specifying dependencies between projects. For example, you might create an umbrella Web Application project that relies on one or more Java Class Library projects. For larger applications, you might have several layers of project dependencies.

To set dependencies between projects:

1. Right-click the project's Libraries node and choose Add Project.
2. In the file chooser that appears, navigate to the folder for the project you want to depend on, and click Add Project. Project folders are designated with the ![icon] icon.

Once you have established this dependency, the distributed outputs (such as JAR files) of the "added" project become part of the other project's classpath.

There is no visual project/subproject distinction in the IDE, but there is a concept of "main" project. The main project in the IDE is simply the one that the IDE treats as the entry point for the primary commands such as Build Main Project and Run Main Project. The current main project is indicated with bold font in the Projects window (see Figure 2-4).

There can be only one main project set at a time, though it is possible to have multiple projects open at the same time (including umbrella projects that serve as entry points for other applications you are developing).

You can make a project the main project by right-clicking its node in the Projects window and choosing Set Main Project.

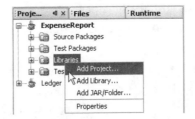

Figure 2-4 Projects window, making one project depend on another

Creating and Editing Files

Once you have a project set up, you can add files to your project and start editing. You can add files to a project by creating them from the New File wizard.

To open the New File wizard, do one of the following:

- In the Projects window, right-click the Source Packages node (or one of the package nodes underneath it) and choose one of the templates from the New submenu. If none of the templates there suits you, choose File/Folder (as shown in Figure 2-5) to open a wizard with a complete selection of available templates.
- Choose File | New File to open the New File wizard.

In the New File wizard, you can name the file and specify a folder. For Java classes, you can designate a period-delimited package name (as opposed to a slash-delimited folder name).

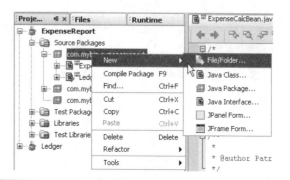

Figure 2-5   Projects window, creating a new file

Once you complete the wizard, the file opens up in a tab in the area of the IDE to the right of the Projects window. For most templates, a Source Editor tab opens.

About the Source Editor

The Source Editor is the central area of the IDE where you write and generate code. The Source Editor is actually a collection of different types of editors with different purposes. There are text editors for different types of files, such as Java, JSP (as shown in Figure 2-6), XML, HTML, and plain-text files. These editors all share a base of features (such as a set of common keyboard shortcuts). The individual editors have features unique to that file type, such as syntax highlighting, additional keyboard shortcuts, code completion, special navigation shortcuts, and so on. See Chapter 4 for a survey of Source Editor features.

There are also visual editors for AWT and Swing forms, deployment descriptors, and other types of files, though it is possible to edit the source of these types of files directly.

For example, GUI templates such as JPanel Form and JFrame Form open in a visual design area (as shown in Figure 2-7) along with Palette, Inspector, and Properties windows. You can click the Source button in the design area's toolbar to access the file's source.

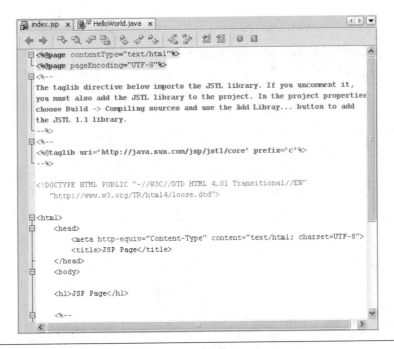

Figure 2-6   Source Editor window with a JSP file open

Setting Up and Modifying Java Packages

You can set up a Java package in the New Project and New File wizards.

To create a new package, right-click the Source Packages node within your project and choose New | Java Package. In the wizard, fill in a period-delimited package name (for example, com.mybiz.myapp).

You can then move classes into this package by cutting and pasting or by dragging their nodes.

 When you move classes, the Refactor Code for Moved Class dialog box opens and offers to update the rest of the code in the project to reflect the changed location of the class. Click Next to see a preview of the changes in the Refactoring window. Then click Do Refactoring to make the changes.

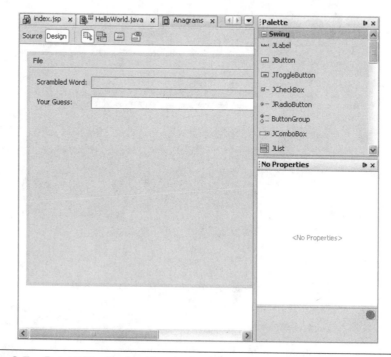

Figure 2-7   Form Editor Design View in the Source Editor window

Compiling and Building

When you set up a project, the IDE provides a default classpath and compilation settings, so the project should be ready to compile as soon as you have added some classes to the project.

You can compile an individual file or package by right-clicking its node and choosing Compile. But more typically, you will "build" the entire project. Building, depending on project type, typically consists of compiling projects and subprojects and of creating outputs such as JAR files for each of those projects.

To build your project, right-click the project's node in the Projects window and choose Build Project. If that project is currently designated as the main project (the project name is bold in the Projects window), you can choose Build | Build Main Project or press F11. If you want to delete the products of previous builds before building again, choose Build | Clean and Build Main Project or press Shift-F11.

When you initiate a build, the IDE tracks the progress of the build in the Output window in the form of Ant output.

You can specify compiler options in the Project Properties dialog box. Right-click the project's node in the Projects window and choose Properties. Then click the Build | Compiling node to enter the options.

See Chapter 3 for more detailed information on building your project.

Viewing Project Metadata and Build Results

In the Files window, you can view the physical structure of your project, including compiled class files, output JAR files, your build script, and other project metadata.

Project-related commands (such as Build Project) are not available from nodes in the Files window, but other "explorer"-type commands like Open, Cut, and Paste are available.

The Files window is useful if you want to customize the build script for your project or you want to browse your project's outputs. You can also examine the contents of JAR files created by your project.

Figure 2-8 shows the structure of the HelloWorld application you created in Chapter 1.

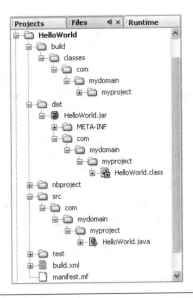

Figure 2-8   Files-window "physical" view of the HelloWorld project

Navigating to the Source of Compilation Errors

If any compilation errors are reported when you compile or build, you can navigate straight to the source of the error by double-clicking the hyperlinked error in the Output window (as shown in Figure 2-9) or by pressing F12.

If you have multiple errors, you can use F12 (Next Error) and Shift-F12 (Previous Error) to navigate between the locations of the errors.

Figure 2-9   Output window with compiler error showing

Running

You can run the application you are developing from within the IDE by right-clicking the project's node and choosing Run Project or by pressing F6.

You can run an individual file by right-clicking the file in the Source Editor or the file's node in the Projects window and choosing Run File or pressing Shift-F6.

You can stop a running application by opening the Runtime window, expanding the Processes node, right-clicking the node for the running process, and choosing Terminate Process.

If you need to specify a main class for the project or you want to run the project with some arguments, you can specify these in the Project Properties dialog box. Right-click the project's node in the Projects window, choose Properties, and select the Run node in the Project Properties dialog box. You can then use the Main Class, Arguments, and VM Options fields.

Creating and Running Tests

IDE project templates are set up with unit testing in mind. Most project types set up a folder for unit tests next to the folder containing your sources for unit tests. You can have the IDE generate skeleton code for a class's unit test and place it within the test folder with a package structure corresponding to that of the class to be tested.

To generate unit test code for a class:

1. In the Projects window, right-click the class you want to create a test for and choose Tools | JUnit Tests | Create Tests.

2. In the Create Tests dialog box, set a class name and location, and specify the code generation options for the test.

   By default, the class name is filled in for you and corresponds to the name of the class being tested with `Test` appended to the name. The test class is placed in a test folder that has the same package structure as your sources.

   If you later add some new methods to your class, you can choose the Create Tests command again. Test methods for the new methods will be added to the existing test class.

   To run the selected project's tests, press Alt-F6 or choose Run | Test `"ProjectName"`.

3. To run a test for a specific file, select the file in the Source Editor or Projects window and press Ctrl-F6 or choose Run | Run File | Test `"Filename"`.

Debugging the Application

The IDE's debugger enables you to pause execution of your program at strategic points (*breakpoints*) and check the values of variables, the status of threads, and so on. Once you have paused execution at a breakpoint, you can step through code line by line.

To start debugging a program:

1. Make sure that the program you want to debug is currently set as the IDE's main project.

The name of the main project is shown in bold font in the Projects window. You can make a project the main project by right-clicking its node and choosing Set Main Project.

2. Determine the point in your code where you want to start debugging and set a breakpoint at that line by clicking in the left margin of that line.

The ▣ icon appears in the left margin to mark the breakpoint. In addition, the whole line is highlighted in pink.

3. Start the debugger by choosing Run | Debug Main Project or pressing F5.

The IDE builds (or rebuilds) the application and then opens the Debugger Console in the bottom-left portion of the IDE and the Watches, Call Stack, and Local Variables windows in the lower-right portion.

4. Click the Local Variables window (as shown in Figure 2-10) to view the values of any of the variables of the program that are currently in scope.

See Chapter 5 for a more in-depth look at the IDE's debugging features.

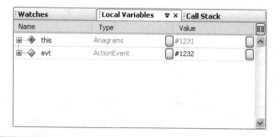

Figure 2-10   Debugger windows, with the Local Variables window in focus

Integrating Version Control Commands

If you already use a version control system for your sources, you can easily integrate that system's commands into the IDE workflow. The IDE provides support for working with various version control systems.

The IDE acts as a graphical interface for the version control client application you are already using. When you call version control commands from the IDE, the IDE passes those commands to the version control client, which then carries out the commands. The IDE also displays any output generated by the version control client.

In NetBeans IDE 4.1, setting up the IDE to work with versioned sources is separate from project setup. If you want to make version control commands available within the IDE for a project, you need to register the versioned working directory with the IDE.

 If you are using a post-4.1 version of the IDE, this process might be streamlined so that the registration of the version control system in the IDE is coupled with the creation of the project.

To set up the IDE to work with your version control system:

1. Choose Versioning | Versioning Manager.
2. In the Versioning Manager dialog box, click Add.
3. Select the version control system you are using from the Profile combo box and point to the location of the working directory.

   If you have several projects within the same working directory, you can select the root directory to register version control for all of those projects at the same time.

4. Verify the server settings that the IDE fills in and add any missing settings.

   If you are using CVS as your version control system, you have the option of using a client built into the IDE instead of a separate CVS executable.

5. If the working directory you have specified does not yet contain sources, use the Checkout page of the wizard to check out the sources.
6. Click Finish to exit the wizard and then click Close to exit the Versioning Manager.
7. If you have not already done so, create an IDE project (or IDE projects) for your sources through the New Project wizard so that you can further develop these sources in the IDE.

 If no profile is available in the wizard for the version control system you are using, you might be able to find a profile online at http://vcsgeneric.netbeans.org/profiles/index.html.

You can also create your own profile by choosing the Empty profile in the Versioning Manager and then customizing it to work with your version control system. See http://vcsgeneric.netbeans.org/doc/profiles/index.html for information on creating a profile for your version control system.

See Setting up a Project to Work with Version Control on page 50 for more information on using version control with the IDE, including information on versioning your project metadata.

Once you have set up a version control working directory in this manner, the Versioning window appears in the area occupied by the Projects window. You can run version control commands on the files from this window. However, you cannot run project-related commands or do explorer-type things with files, such as open, copy, or paste.

If you already have set up an IDE project for those sources, a submenu with version control commands appears in the right-click menu of all of that project's nodes in the Projects window.

Managing IDE Windows

The IDE's window system is designed to provide a coherent and unobtrusive layout of the various windows you need while enabling you to adjust the layout effortlessly as you work. These are some of the things you can do as you work:

- Resize windows by clicking on a window border and dragging it to the width or height you prefer.
- Maximize a window within the IDE by double-clicking on its tab. (You can revert to the previous window layout by again double-clicking on the tab.) You might find this feature particularly useful in the Source Editor.
- Move a window to a different part of the IDE by clicking on its tab and dragging it to a different part of the IDE.
- Use drag and drop on a tab in the window to split the window.
- Make a window "sliding" by clicking its ◀▯ button. When you click this button, the window is minimized, with a button representing that window placed on one of the edges of the IDE. You can mouse over the button to display the window temporarily, or you can click the button to open the window.

## CHAPTER 3

IDE Project Fundamentals

- Introduction to IDE Projects
- Choosing the Right Project Template
- Creating a Project from Scratch
- Importing a Project Developed in a Different Environment
- Navigating Your Projects
- Working with Files Not in the Project
- Creating Packages and Files in the Project
- Configuring the Project's Classpath
- Changing the Version of the JDK That Your Project Is Based On
- Changing the Target JDK for a Standard Project
- Referencing JDK Documentation (Javadoc) from the Project
- Adding Folders and JAR Files to the Classpath
- Making External Sources and Javadoc Available in the IDE
- Structuring Your Projects
- Displaying and Hiding Projects
- Setting Up a Project to Work with Version Control
- Compiling a Project
- Running a Project
- Writing Your Own Manifest for Your JAR File
- Filtering Contents Packaged into Outputs
- Running a Project from Outside of the IDE
- Customizing the IDE-Generated Build Script
- Running a Specific Ant Target from the IDE
- Completing Ant Expressions
- Making a Menu Item or Shortcut for a Specific Ant Target

NETBEANS IDE HAS A COMPREHENSIVE PROJECT SYSTEM that provides a structure for your sources, tests, and outputs and that simplifies your workflow. This project system is based on the Ant build tool, which provides added flexibility in the way you configure your projects.

This chapter provides an overview of the project system and how you can leverage it for your projects. In Chapter 12, you can learn some more advanced techniques, which are particularly useful if you are developing applications with specific requirements that are not addressed in standard IDE projects.

This chapter focuses on general issues for general Java projects (with some information specific for web projects added in). However, most of the information is relevant for all project categories. If you need project-related information that is specific to Enterprise or Mobility projects, see the corresponding chapters in this book.

Introduction to IDE Projects

The starting point for most work in the IDE is through the creation of a project. When you create a project, the IDE typically does the following things for you (depending on project type):

- Creates a source tree with a skeleton class inside.
- Creates a folder for unit tests.
- Sets classpaths for compilation, running, and (depending on type of project) testing. (The compilation classpath also determines the classes that the Source Editor is aware of, for example, when you use code completion features.)
- Sets the Java platform that the project is to run on. By default, it is the same platform that the IDE runs on.
- Creates an Ant build script (`build.xml`), which contains the instructions that the IDE uses when you perform commands on your project, such as compiling source files, running the application, running tests, debugging, compiling Javadoc documentation, and building JAR files. In addition, you can use this build script to run Ant targets on your project from outside of the IDE.

You can have multiple projects open at the same time, and the projects can be linked through dependencies. Project-specific commands in the Build and Run

What Is Ant, and Do I Need to Know Anything About It?

Ant is the tool that NetBeans IDE uses for running project-related commands. If you have no interest in Ant as such, you can completely ignore it, much as you would never bother decoding project metadata in another IDE. However, if Ant is already the lifeblood of your build process, you can set up NetBeans IDE to accommodate your existing build process, either by overriding specific Ant targets that the IDE generates or by providing your own Ant script.

Ant was developed by the Apache Software Foundation to automate routine developer tasks, such as compiling, testing, and packaging your application. Ant is similar to Make but Ant has the advantage of being written in Java, so it works across multiple platforms. You can also use Ant to invoke other processes, such as checking out sources from version control, obfuscating classes, and so on. In addition, you can write Java classes to extend Ant's functionality. On big development efforts, Ant is often used as a production tool to compile and package the whole application for distribution.

Ant scripts themselves are written in XML. They are divided into high-level *targets*, which are collections of tasks that are run for specific purposes, such as cleaning the build directory, compiling classes, and creating packaged outputs.

Other IDEs provide integration with Ant to support writing and running of build scripts. NetBeans IDE takes this a step further by making Ant the backbone for all project-related commands in the IDE. When you create an IDE project, the IDE generates an Ant script for you with targets for, among other things, compiling, running, debugging, and packaging your application. When you run project commands in the IDE (such as Build Main Project or Run Main Project), the IDE itself is calling an Ant script.

The fact that the IDE's project system is based on Ant provides another advantage: Other developers do not have to use NetBeans IDE to build the project. It is possible to run an IDE-generated Ant script from another IDE or the command line, which could be particularly useful for doing production builds of your team's application.

menus act on the currently designated main project. The main project is marked in bold, as shown in Figure 3-1.

Unlike in 3.x versions of NetBeans IDE, explicit creation of an IDE project is a primary step in your workflow in NetBeans IDE 4.1. In NetBeans IDE 3.x versions, "projects" were a peripheral paradigm with a limited feature scope.

Also, as opposed to the filesystem concept in NetBeans IDE 3.x, the folders included in the Projects and Files windows do not necessarily represent the classpath. In fact, it is OK to have multiple projects open, even if they have no relationship to the main project you are working with. Likewise, a project you are working on can depend on projects that you currently do not have open.

Figure 3-1   Projects window

Choosing the Right Project Template

When you open the New Project wizard (File | New Project), you are presented with several templates, the use of which might not be immediately apparent.

Depending on the distribution of the IDE that you have, you might have several categories of templates. See Table 3-1 for the list:

Table 3-1   Project Template Categories

Template Category	Description
General	For desktop applications or Java libraries based on Java 2 Standard Edition.
Web	For web applications based on Java 2 Enterprise Edition.
Enterprise	For enterprise tier applications, such as those that include Enterprise JavaBeans components (EJBs) and web services, based on Java 2 Enterprise Edition.
MIDP	For applications targeted toward handheld devices, based on Java 2 Micro Edition.
Samples	Sample applications that are ready to build and run from the IDE.

For each category, the IDE provides various templates based on the structure of the project and whether you already have sources and/or a fixed Ant script in place.

Standard project templates (all of the templates with the exception of With Existing Ant Script templates) provide maximum integration with the IDE's user interface. However, the use of those templates assumes that your project:

- Is designed to produce one distributable output (for example, a JAR or WAR file)
- Will use the Ant script that the IDE has generated for you (though you can customize this Ant script)

If either of those things is not true of your project, you can do one or more of the following:

- Restructure your sources to fit into this model.
- Create individual projects for each output and declare dependencies between the projects.
- Modify the generated Ant script to add or override targets.
- Use a With Existing Ant Script (or free-form) template (marked with a 🏃 icon to create your project).

The free-form templates offer you more flexibility in structuring your project. However, when you use a free-form template, you have to do some extra configuration and write build targets to get some IDE functionality (like debugging) to work. See Chapter 12 for more information on free-form projects.

This chapter mainly covers general Java projects created from standard templates. There is also some information on web projects, though web projects are covered in more detail in Chapter 6. See Chapter 8 for information on setting up EJB projects, Chapter 9 for web service projects, Chapter 10 for J2EE application projects, and Chapter 11 for J2ME projects.

Creating a Project from Scratch

If you want to start developing an application from scratch, start with the base template for the type of application you are developing. Below are procedures for creating a general Java application and a web application.

For a Java desktop application or a standard Java library to be used by other applications, do the following:

1. Choose File | New Project (Ctrl-Shift-N).

2. In the Categories tree, select the General folder.

3. Select Java Application (as shown in Figure 3-2) or Java Class Library.

   The Java Application template includes skeleton code for a main class. Use this template if you want this project to contain the entry point for your application.

   The Java Library template contains no main class. Use this template if you want to create a library that is used by other applications.

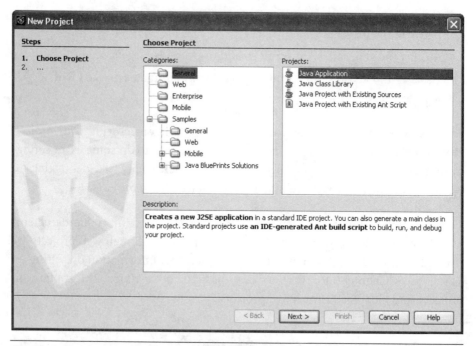

Figure 3-2   New Project wizard, Choose Project page

4. Click Next.

5. Optionally, fill in the following fields on the Name and Location page of the wizard:

Project Name. The name by which the project is referred to in the IDE's user interface.

Project Location. The location of the project on your system.

The resulting Project Folder field shows the location of the folder that contains folders for your sources, test classes, compiled classes, packaged library or application, and so on.

6. Optionally, deselect the Set As Main Project checkbox if you have another project open that you want the IDE's main project commands (such as Build Main Project) to apply to.

7. Set the main class, using the fully qualified class name but without the .java extension (for example, com.mycompany.myapp.MyAppMain).

8. Click Finish.

The generated project is viewable in both the Projects window and the Files window.

The Projects window provides a "logical" view of your sources and other files you are likely to edit often (such as web pages in web application projects). Project metadata (including the project's Ant build script) and project outputs (such as compiled classes and JAR files) are not displayed here.

Java source files are grouped by package instead of by folder hierarchy.

The Files window represents all of the files that are in your project in folder hierarchies as they appear on your system.

For web applications, do the following:

1. Choose File | New Project (Ctrl-Shift-N).

2. In the Categories tree, select the Web folder.

3. Select Web Application and click Next.

4. Fill in the following fields (or verify the generated values) in the Name and Location panel of the wizard (as shown in Figure 3-3):

    Project Name. The name by which the project is referred to in the IDE's user interface.

    Project Location. The location of the project on your system.

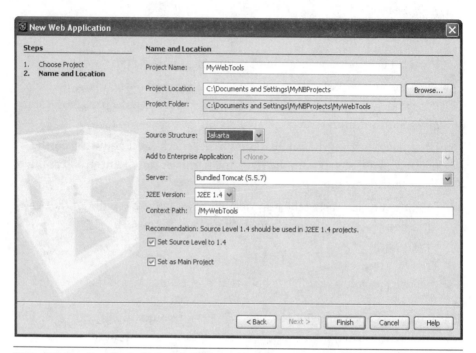

Figure 3-3   New Project wizard, Name and Location page for Web Application project

The resulting Project Folder field shows the location of the folder that contains folders for your sources, test classes, compiled classes, packaged library or application, and so on.

Source Structure. Sets some conventions that will be used for structuring your application. If you will be deploying to Tomcat, you should choose Jakarta. If you will be deploying to Sun Java System Application Server, choose Java BluePrints.

Server. The server on which you plan to deploy the application. Only servers that are registered in the IDE's Server Manager are available in the combo box. You can add additional servers (or server instances) there by choosing Tools | Server Manager in the main menu.

5. Optionally, deselect the Set As Main Project checkbox if you have another project open that you want the IDE's main project commands (such as Build Main Project) to apply to.

6. Optionally, adjust the following:

J2EE Version. The version of the J2EE platform that your application will run against. Version 1.4 is preferable if you are starting from scratch, as it supports several constructs that are not recognized in Version 1.3, such as tag files. However, you might need to use Version 1.3 if you are setting up a project with existing sources already developed against that level.

Context Path. The URL namespace that the web application uses. For example, if the context property value is `MyWebApp`, the web application is accessed from a file within `http://HostName:PortNumber/MyWebApp/`.

7. Click Finish.

For more information specific to developing web applications, see Chapter 6.

If the application you are developing requires multiple outputs, you can create multiple IDE projects to accommodate them. You can connect projects by declaring dependencies in a project's Project Properties dialog box. See Creating Subprojects on page 49.

Importing a Project Developed in a Different Environment

If you have a project that you have been working on in a different development environment, you can "import" the project into NetBeans IDE using a "With Existing Sources" project template.

When you import a project, you point the IDE to the folders for your sources and your tests (they are not copied), and create a folder that holds metadata for the project. Below are procedures for importing a general Java application and importing a web application. If you want to import a project developed in Eclipse, you can use the Eclipse Project Importer. See Appendix A.

To import a Java application that was created in a different environment:

1. Choose File | New Project (Ctrl-Shift-N).
2. In the Categories tree, select the General folder.
3. Select Java Project with Existing Sources and click Next.

4. On the Name and Location page of the wizard, fill in the following fields (or verify the generated values):

   Project Name. The name by which the project is referred to in the IDE's user interface.

   Project Folder. The location of the project's metadata. By default, the IDE places this folder with your project sources, but you can designate a different location.

5. Optionally, deselect the Set As Main Project checkbox if you have another project open that you want the IDE's main project commands (such as Build Main Project) to apply to.

6. On the Existing Sources page of the wizard (as shown in Figure 3-4), enter the location of your sources by clicking the Add Folder button next to the Source Package Folders field and navigating to the root of your sources. For example, the root folder might be called src.

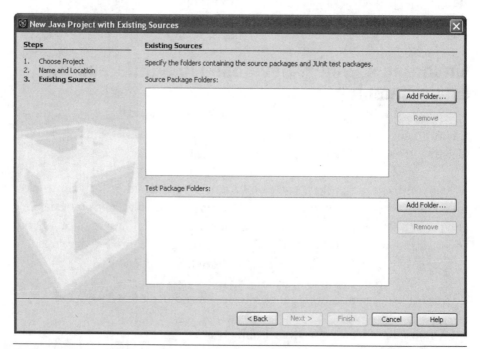

Figure 3-4 New Project wizard, Existing Sources page for Java project with existing sources

If you have multiple source root folders, repeat this step for each source root. Note, however, that sources added in this manner can be added to only one project (though this limitation might disappear after NetBeans IDE 4.1).

7. In the Test Packages Folder field, enter the folder that contains the default package of your unit tests (for example, the folder might be called `tests`).

   If you have multiple test root folders, repeat this step for each source root. You can leave this field blank if you have no unit tests.

8. Click Finish.

To import a web application that you have begun developing in a different environment:

1. Choose File | New Project (Ctrl-Shift-N).

2. In the Categories tree, select the Web folder.

3. Select Web Application with Existing Sources and click Next.

4. On the Name and Location page of the wizard, fill in the following fields (or verify the generated values):

   Location. The folder that contains your web pages and sources. If you have multiple source roots, you can fill those in later.

   Project Name. The name by which the project is referred to in the IDE's user interface.

   Project Folder. The location of the project's metadata.

   Server. The server that you plan to deploy the application to. Only servers that are registered in the IDE's Server Manager are available in the combo box. You can add additional servers (or server instances) there by choosing Tools | Server Manager in the main menu.

5. Optionally, deselect the Set As Main Project checkbox if you have another project open that you want the IDE's main project commands (such as Build Main Project) to apply to.

6. Optionally, adjust the following:

   J2EE Version. The version of the J2EE platform that your application will run against. Version 1.4 is preferable if you are starting from scratch, as it supports several constructs that are not recognized in Version 1.3, such as tag files. However, you might need to use Version 1.3 if you are setting up a project with existing sources already developed against that level.

Context Path. The URL namespace that the web application uses. For example, if the context property value is MyWebApp, the web application is accessed from a file within http://HostName:PortNumber/MyWebApp/.

7. Click Next.

8. In the Existing Sources and Libraries page (as shown in Figure 3-5), fill in or verify the contents of the following fields:

Web Pages Folder. The folder that contains your web pages. This field should be filled in automatically, based on what you specified in the Location field of the wizard's Name and Location page.

Libraries Folder. The (optional) folder that contains any libraries specifically for this project, such as tag libraries.

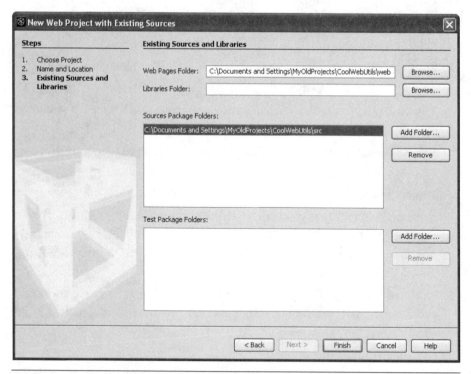

Figure 3-5 New Project wizard, Existing Sources and Libraries page for Web Application with Existing Sources template

Source Package Folders. The folder (or folders) that contains your sources. This field should be filled in automatically, based on what you specified in the Location field of the wizard's Name and Location page and should contain the default Java package for the project (for example, the folder might be called src). You can click Add Folder to add additional source roots. However, you can add each source root to only one NetBeans IDE 4.1 project.

Test Package Folders. The folder (or folders) that contains any unit tests that you have written for your sources. You can click Add Folder to add additional test roots.

9. Click Finish.

For more complex projects that require a lot of classes, it might work best to use the web application project as the main project and configure it to depend on Java Library projects that handle most of the processing in your application. For applets and tag libraries, it is necessary to use Java Library projects to get them to work within your web app. See Chapter 6.

Navigating Your Projects

Once the project is set up, your files are accessible from both the Projects window and the Files window.

Projects Window

The Projects window (shown in Figure 3-6) is designed to be the center of operations for file creation, project configuration, and project building. The Projects window displays only the files that are likely to be regularly edited in a project, such as Java source files, web pages, and tests. Build outputs and project metadata are ignored.

Java sources are displayed according to package structure, which generally makes it easier to navigate to files because you do not have to navigate through nested folder hierarchies.

The main node for each project has commands on its contextual (right-click) menu for compiling, running, debugging, creating Javadoc, and performing other project-related actions.

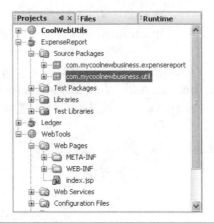

Figure 3-6   Projects window

Files Window

The Files window displays your files organized according to file hierarchy, much as they appear in a file manager on your system. (One exception to this is that the .form files that are used to generate the design view of GUI classes that you create in the IDE's Form Editor are not displayed; just the .java file is displayed.) In addition to your sources, tests, and web files, project metadata and files produced when you build the project appear. See Figure 3-7.

Figure 3-7   Files window

The Files window is useful if you need to browse the physical structure of your project, such as the contents of the JAR file (or other archive file) produced by the project. The Files window also provides direct access to project metadata files if you need to customize them. Otherwise, it is probably best to work in the Projects window, because project-related commands are not available in the Files window.

If you prefer a physical view of your files but do not want to see the top levels of the file hierarchy that are necessitated by the Java package structure, you can use the Favorites window. See Working with Files Not in the Project later in this chapter.

You can also set the Projects window to display files according to file hierarchy instead of by package. Choose Tools | Options. Then expand the IDE Configuration | Look and Feel node and select the Package View node. In the Package View Type property, select Tree View from the combo box.

Fast Navigation Between the Projects and Files Windows

If you are working with a node in one window but want to switch to that node in a different window, there are several keyboard shortcuts available to speed navigation. For example, if you have been working in the Projects window and now want to inspect the build script (which, in standard projects, is viewable through the Files window), you can jump straight to the project's node in the Files window without having to scroll to the node. See Table 3-2 for some of the shortcuts that are particularly useful for navigating between the "explorer"-style windows.

You can also use these shortcuts in the Source Editor when you want to jump to the node for that file.

Table 3-2   Shortcuts to Select the Current File's Node in a Different Window

Keyboard Shortcut	Action
Ctrl-Shift-1	Open the Projects window and display the node that corresponds to the currently selected file, package, or folder.
Ctrl-Shift-2	Open the Files window and display the node that corresponds to the currently selected file, package, or folder.
Ctrl-Shift-3	Open the Favorites window and display the node that corresponds to the currently selected file, package, or folder.
Ctrl-Shift-8	Open the Versioning window and display the node that corresponds to the currently selected file, package, or folder. This command works only if you have set up the IDE to use version control for that project.

Physical Structure of IDE Projects

The Projects window provides a "logical" view of projects that is oriented toward coding activities and does not include all files in the project. For example, output files (such as compiled classes and JAR files), project metadata, and version control metadata files (if you are using version control) are hidden.

If you want to see the actual files created in the project, open the Files window (by clicking the Files tab above the Projects window).

When you create a general project (using a standard template), the IDE creates the following folders and files:

- `nbproject` folder, which includes files that store data about your project and are used to create the build script for your project.
- `src` folder, which holds your source files (assuming that the IDE project was not created with existing sources). This folder corresponds with the Source Packages node that appears in the Projects window.
- `test` folder, which holds any unit tests that you create for your project. This folder corresponds with the Test Packages node that appears in the Projects window.
- `build.xml` file, which is the Ant build script that is used when compiling, cleaning, running, and debugging your project. This file actually imports the `build-impl.xml` file, which is generated in the `nbproject` folder.

When you build your project, the following folders are added:

- `build` folder, which holds the compiled class files
- `dist` folder, which holds the packaged output for the project (a JAR file)

For web applications created from standard templates, the IDE creates the following folders and files:

- `nbproject` folder, which includes files that store data about your project and are used to create the build script for your project
- `src` folder, which holds Java source files
- `web` folder, which typically holds the WEB-INF and META-INF folders, as well as any HTML pages, JSP pages, custom tag libraries, and other files for the web application

- `build.xml` file, which is the Ant build script that is used when compiling, cleaning, running, and debugging your project

When you build your project, the following folders are added:

- `build` folder, which holds the compiled class files
- `dist` folder, which holds the compiled application in distributable form (a WAR file)

Working with Files Not in the Project

When you set up a project in the IDE, only the files most likely to need hand editing (such as your source files) are exposed in the Projects window. You can access all files in your project using the Files window, but sometimes there are other files you might want to access. If there are other files on your system that you want to regularly have access to, you can display them in the Favorites window.

To use the Favorites window:

1. Choose Window | Favorites (Ctrl-3) to open the Favorites window as a tab in the area occupied by the Projects window.
2. In the Favorites window, right-click the Favorites node and choose Add Favorites.
3. In the file chooser, select the root folder that you want to add to Favorites.

You can add multiple folders to the Favorites window, and you can add folders at any level of a file hierarchy. This provides a lot of flexibility in what files you make visible. For example, if you have a deep package hierarchy, you can save a lot of time on folder expansion by adding folders that directly contain your files.

You can run most IDE commands on nodes in the Favorites window. However, project-specific commands (such as Build Main Project) are not available in Favorites, so you must choose those commands in the Projects window, through the main menu, or through keyboard shortcuts.

 If you merely want to open a file in the IDE one time, you can use the File | Open command.

Creating Packages and Files in the Project

Once the project is set up, you can create packages and files from the Projects window or the Files window. Right-click the node for the package or folder where you would like to add a class or package and choose New | File/Folder (Ctrl-N) to open the New File wizard. Or you can directly choose one of the templates below the File/Folder menu item.

To create a Java package:

1. Right-click the Source Packages node in the Projects window and choose New | Java Package.

   If Java Package is not one of the choices in the New submenu, choose New | File/Folder instead. In the New File wizard, select the Java Classes node, select Java Package, and click Next.

2. In the Package Name field of the wizard, type the name of the package, delimiting levels of the package with periods (for example, `com.mydo-main.myproject`), and then click Finish.

> When creating subpackages, you can save yourself a few keystrokes by choosing New | Java Package from a package node. The base package name is already filled in for you, so you just need to add the last part of the new package name.
>
> You can also enter a new package when using the New File wizard to create a new Java class.

To create a file:

1. Right-click the Source Packages node in the Projects window and choose New | File/Folder (Ctrl-N).

2. In the New File wizard, browse the templates available, select the one you want, and click Finish.

> You can also select a template straight from the New submenu, where a short list of templates commonly used for the selected project type is displayed. The list of files that are available there is updated to reflect the templates that you commonly use.

See Chapter 4 for more information on editing Java files.

File Templates

File creation in the IDE begins with templates. The templates that are available depend on the features that you have installed in the IDE. Following are some of the available categories:

Java Classes

Several templates that provide skeleton code for basic types of classes, such as main classes, interfaces, and exceptions.

Java GUI Forms

Swing and AWT templates for developing visual desktop applications. When you create a file from one of these templates, the Form Editor opens, which enables you to build forms visually (dragging and dropping components from a palette to the Form Designer, changing properties in the Component Inspector, and so on).

JavaBeans Objects

Various templates for classes that adhere to the JavaBeans component architecture. Included are templates for a bean with a skeleton getter and setter, BeanInfo classes, a property editor, and a customizer class.

JUnit

Templates that provide skeleton code for unit tests of Java classes.

XML

XML-related templates for XML documents, XML schemata, DTDs, XSL stylesheets, and cascading stylesheets.

Ant Build Scripts

Provides a simple template for a simple skeleton for an Ant script and a template for a custom Ant task with detailed comments. These scripts could be useful if you want to extend the default behavior of the IDE's project system but are not necessary if the IDE's project system already provides all of the features you need.

Web

Provides templates that are useful for web applications, including JSP files, HTML files, tag library files, and tag library descriptors (TLD files). Also provides Java class templates for servlets, filters, tag handlers, and web application listeners. See Chapter 6 for more information on working with these types of files.

Other

Provides templates for HTML, properties, and empty files.

Starting with a Blank File

If you want to start with a completely blank file without a predetermined file extension, you can use the Other | Empty File template. If you give the file an extension that the IDE recognizes, the IDE will treat it as that type of file in the editor (complete with syntax highlighting and other Source Editor features).

Configuring the Project's Classpath

You can manage the classpath for your application through the Libraries node of the project's Project Properties dialog box. To get there, right-click the project's node in the Projects window, choose Properties, and then select the Libraries node in the dialog box that appears.

The IDE enables you to have different classpaths for compiling, testing, and running your application. When you set the compilation classpath, those items are automatically added to the other classpaths. Then you can add items specific to compiling tests, running the application, and running tests on the application.

The compilation classpath also affects some editor features, such as which classes are available in the code completion feature.

See the following topics for instructions on specific tasks.

Changing the Version of the JDK That Your Project Is Based On

By default, IDE projects use the same JDK that the IDE runs on. To set up a project to run on a different JDK, you need to:

1. Add the JDK in the Java Platform Manager.
2. Specify the JDK for the project to use in the project's Project Properties dialog box.

By default, the IDE includes only the version of the JDK that the IDE is running on in the Java Platform Manager.

To make another JDK version available for projects in the IDE:

1. Choose Tools | Java Platform Manager.
2. Click Add Platform.
3. In the file chooser, navigate to and select the JDK version that you want to add to the Java Platform Manager.
   The JDK folder should be marked with the icon in the file chooser.
4. Close the Java Platform Manager.

To switch the JDK that a project uses:

1. Right-click the project's main node in the Projects window and choose Properties.
2. Select the Libraries node.
3. Select the JDK that you want to use in the Java Platform combo box.
4. If the version of the JDK that you want does not appear in the list, click Manage Platforms to open the Java Platform Manager and click Add Platform to add a JDK to the list of those recognized by the IDE.

> If you want to change the JDK that the IDE itself runs on, you can do so in the netbeans.conf file in the IDE's installation directory. In a file manager on your system, navigate to the IDE's installation directory, expand *NetBeansHome*/etc, and open netbeans.conf in a text editor. Below the #netbeans_jdkhome="/path/to/jdk" comment line, type the netbeans_jdkhome option with the path to the JDK.
>
> For example:
>
> netbeans_jdkhome="C:/j2sdk1.4.2_07"
>
> The Default choice, which appears anywhere that you can set the Java platform, then is changed to refer to the JDK you have switched to.

Changing the Target JDK for a Standard Project

If you want to have the sources for your project compiled for a lower version of the JDK than the project is using, you can set a lower source level in the Project Properties dialog box.

To change the target JDK for your project:

1. Right-click the project's main node in the Projects window and choose Properties.
2. Select the Sources node.
3. In the Source Level combo box, select the source level that you want to compile to.

Referencing JDK Documentation (Javadoc) from the Project

When you are coding in the IDE, it is often useful to have Javadoc documentation handy for the classes you are using. When you have Javadoc documentation on your system, you can freely browse it from within the IDE by jumping to a browser from the class you have currently selected in your code (Alt-F1).

The JDK documentation is not included with the standard JDK download. If you do not have the JDK documentation on your system, you can get it from http://java.sun.com (for JDK 5.0, go to http://java.sun.com/j2se/1.5.0/download.jsp).

To make JDK documentation viewable in the IDE:

1. Choose Tools | Java Platform Manager.
2. Select the Javadoc tab.
3. Click the Add ZIP/Folder button. Then navigate to and select the JDK documentation .zip file or folder on your system.
4. Close the Java Platform Manager.

 You do not need to have the JDK's Javadoc on your system to see Javadoc when you are using code completion. The code completion box gets Javadoc comments straight from the JDK source code.

Adding Folders and JAR Files to the Classpath

If your project relies on prebuilt binaries or classes that are not part of a NetBeans IDE project, you can add these to your classpath as well.

To add a JAR file or a set of classes to your project classpath:

1. Expand the project's node in the Projects window.
2. Right-click the project's Libraries node and choose Add JAR/Folder. In the file chooser, navigate to and select the folder or JAR file and click Open.

 If the JAR file that you want to add to the classpath is built from another project in the IDE, you can link the project so that that JAR is rebuilt each time you build your current project. See Structuring Your Projects on page 48.

Making External Sources and Javadoc Available in the IDE

You might want to associate documentation and source with classes that your project depends on. This is useful if you want to do any of the following:

- As you are debugging, see the source when stepping into a class that your project depends on.
- Jump to the source of a referenced class from the Source Editor (Alt-O).
- Jump to the Javadoc documentation of a source file from within the IDE (Alt-F1).

The IDE has a Library Manager feature that enables you to declare these associations, which you can then take advantage of for all of your projects.

To create a library:

1. Choose Tools | Library Manager and then click the New Library button.
2. In the New Library dialog box, type a display name for the library and click OK.
3. In the Class Libraries list, select the new library.
4. Select the Classpath tab and click Add JAR/Folder. Then select the JAR file or the folder that contains the classes and click Add JAR/Folder.
5. If you want to associate sources with the library, select the Sources tab and click Add JAR/Folder. Then select the JAR file or the folder that contains the sources and click Add JAR/Folder.

6. If you want to associate Javadoc documentation with the library, select the Javadoc tab and click Add JAR/Folder. Then select the JAR file or the folder that contains the documentation and click Add ZIP/Folder.

7. Click OK to close the Library Manager.

To add a library to your project:

1. Expand the project's node in the Projects window.

2. Right-click the project's Libraries node and choose Add Library.

When a library with a JAR file, sources, and documentation is designated in the Library Manager, the IDE recognizes the association of those elements, even if you only add the JAR file to your project.

If the library you have designated consists of more than one JAR file, the other JARs are not duplicated on the classpath if you have added them to the classpath individually.

Structuring Your Projects

Standard IDE projects are essentially modular. If your application needs to be built into just one JAR file, you can build it with a single project. If your application exceeds that scope, you can build your application from multiple IDE projects that are linked together with one of those projects declared as the main project.

Setting the Main Project

The main project is the one that project-specific commands (such as Build Main Project) in the main menu always act on. When an application is composed of many related projects, the main project serves as the entry point for the application for purposes of compiling, running, testing, and debugging. You can have only one main project set at a time.

To make a project the main project, right-click that project's node and choose Set Main Project.

If you find that your main project inadvertently gets changed from time to time, it might be because some project templates contain an option to make the new project the main project. If you create a new project that you do not want to be a main project, make sure to deselect the Set As Main Project checkbox in the New Project wizard.

Creating Subprojects

For more complex applications, you might need to create multiple IDE projects, where one project is the application entry point that depends on other projects. (Any project that has another project depending on it functions as a subproject, though it is not specifically labeled as such in the IDE.)

Each IDE project can create one distributable output (such as a JAR file), which in turn might be used by other projects. There is no particular limit to how long a chain of dependencies can be, though the chain must not be circular. (For example, if project A depends on classes in project B, project B cannot depend on classes in project A.)

 Though it might be a hassle at first, reorganizing your code to eliminate circular dependencies will probably pay off in the long run by making your code easier to maintain and extend.

To make one project dependent on another project:

1. Expand the project's node in the Projects window.
2. Right-click the project's Libraries node and choose Add Project. In the file chooser that appears, navigate to the IDE project folder. All project folders are marked with the ![icon] icon in the file chooser.

 When you add a project to another project's classpath, all sources and Javadoc documentation are recognized by the other project as well.

Displaying and Hiding Projects

You can have multiple IDE projects open at the same time, whether or not they are connected to one another in any way. However, the only projects that you *need* to have open at any given time are the main project (which serves as an entry point for building, running, and debugging) and the projects that you are currently editing. Even if your main project depends on other projects (subprojects), these projects do not need to be open if you are not actively working on them. Any dependencies that you have set up in the Project Properties dialog box are honored whether the subprojects are open or closed.

To hide a project, right-click the project's node in the Projects window and choose Close Project.

To display a project, choose File | Open Project (Ctrl-Shift-O).

To open all of the projects that a project depends on, right-click the project's node in the Projects window and choose Open Required Projects.

Setting Up a Project to Work with Version Control

For projects of any size, using a version control (source control) system offers several advantages:

- You can save the history of versions of your files, which enables you to revisit previous versions of your files to help diagnose and fix problems in your programs.
- Multiple developers can work on the same source files and quickly incorporate changes that others make.
- Multiple users can work with the same project metadata and quickly incorporate changes that others make to the project metadata.

NetBeans IDE provides a user interface for the CVS, PVCS, and Visual Source Safe version control systems (VCSs). If you have one of these VCSs installed on your system, you can call version control commands on your files from within the IDE.

 If your project uses a version control system other than those named above, you can check http://vcsgeneric.netbeans.org/profiles/index.html to see if there is a profile for your VCS and download it.

Though version control features are not tightly coupled with the IDE's project system, working with VCSs in the IDE is straightforward:

- Use the Versioning Manager to point the IDE to the version control project (or, in CVS terminology, working directory).
- Call version control commands on the files from the various "explorer" windows (Projects, Files, Versioning, and Favorites).
- Call IDE project commands from nodes in the Projects window. (You have to explicitly set up an IDE project.)

 When you create an IDE project, the IDE does not automatically recognize whether you are using version control. Likewise, when you set up a version control project in the IDE, the IDE does not set up an IDE project.

To start working with version-controlled sources:

1. Choose Versioning | Versioning Manager.
2. In the Versioning Manager dialog box, click Add.
3. Select one of the version control systems offered in the Profiles combo box and then fill in the requested information about your version control project, including where the version-controlled sources are located and where the executable for the version control system is located.

   If CVS is your version control system, you can have the IDE use a CVS executable that you have on your system or the IDE's own built-in CVS client.

Once you have your VCS set up with the IDE, the Versioning window opens as a tab in the space also occupied by the Projects and Files windows. In the Versioning window, you can run any available version control commands, though other IDE commands are not available there.

You probably will do most of your work in the Projects window, where project-related commands are available. Version control commands are available in file nodes in the Projects window, but you need to use the Files window or Versioning window if you want to run a version control command on a folder.

Versioning and Sharing Project Metadata

If you are part of a team that is developing an application for which, in addition to sharing sources, you share a build environment, you can put the project metadata under version control. For example, you could change a project's dependencies, check in those changes to your version control system, and have others on your team update those changes.

The metadata for NetBeans IDE projects is stored in XML and properties files, which makes it fairly easy to include in your version control project and share with other users.

To put your IDE project metadata under version control, add the following to your VCS repository:

- The project's `nbproject` folder and the files within it, such as `project.xml`, `build-impl.xml`, and `project.properties`. (The `private` folder, which holds settings specific to your local copy of the IDE, is automatically ignored.)
- The project's `build.xml` file.

Both the nbproject folder and the build.xml file are visible from the Files window. You can add them by right-clicking the nodes for those files and choosing the appropriate command for your version control system. For CVS, this would be CVS | Add followed by CVS | Commit.

If the project metadata files are in the same directory as your sources, you can simply add them within your current VCS setup. (For example, in CVS, you would merely run the Add and Commit commands.)

If the project metadata files are in a different directory (as they typically are when you create a project using existing sources) or not everybody on your team is using NetBeans IDE, you might need to create to a new area for them in your VCS repository (for example, in CVS, you would probably create a new CVS module).

 If you create an IDE project within an existing VCS working directory that you have registered in the Versioning Manager and then establish dependencies in that project to other projects and libraries that are also within the VCS working directory, the IDE assumes that all other people working on these projects will be accessing all of these resources from the same relative location. As a result, the IDE stores all references to the locations of these resources as relative paths in the project.properties file, which makes this information sharable among all users who check out the projects from the VCS. This saves users who check out these projects from having to set these classpath dependencies themselves.

If the projects (including sources and nbproject folder) are not all within a VCS working directory, the references are stored as absolute paths in the private.properties file, which is excluded from the VCS. Anybody who does a VCS checkout of such a project (and then uses the File | Open Project command) is then prompted to use the Resolve Reference Problems command to set the references to the resources manually.

Resolving Merge Conflicts in Project Metadata Files

If your project's properties are modified by two or more developers simultaneously, merge conflicts can occur when you update your project from your version control system.

If merge conflicts occur in project.xml or project.properties, you should be able to resolve them manually in the Source Editor.

Should a merge conflict occur in your build-impl.xml file (which itself would probably be a result of a merge conflict in the project.xml file), do the following:

1. Resolve the merge conflict in the `project.xml` file and commit the change.

2. Delete the `build-impl.xml` file.

3. In the Projects window, right-click the project's main node and choose Close Project.

4. Reopen the project by choosing New | Open Project. The `build-impl.xml` file will be regenerated when you reopen the project.

Compiling a Project

Once you have set up your project, created your source files, and set up any necessary dependencies, you can compile your project by choosing Build | Build Main Project (F11).

By default, when you build a standard Java project in the IDE, the following occurs:

- All modified files in the project are saved.

- Any uncompiled files (or files that have been modified since they were last compiled) under the Source Packages node are compiled.

- A JAR file (or other archive, depending on the project category) is created with your classes and other resources.

- Any projects that the main project depends on are built. (In fact, these projects are built first.)

When you build your project, output on the progress of the Ant script is printed to the Output window.

 If you merely want to compile your project (without building JAR files or running any other postcompile steps), you can create a shortcut to the `compile` target in the project's build script. Open the Files window and expand the `build.xml` node. Right-click the `compile` target and choose Create Shortcut. In the wizard, you can designate a menu item, toolbar button, and a keyboard shortcut for the target. The shortcut works only for that particular project.

Setting Compiler Options

You can set compiler options in the Project Properties dialog box for a project.

1. Right-click the project's node and choose Properties.

2. In the Project Properties dialog box, select the Build | Compile node.

3. Select the checkbox for any options that you want to have included.

4. For options that are not covered by a checkbox, type the option in the Additional Compiler Options field as you would when compiling from the command line.

Compiling Selected Files or Packages

If you have a larger project, you might want to be able to compile a few files without rebuilding the entire project.

To compile a single file, right-click the file's node and choose Compile File (F9).

To compile a package, right-click the package's node in the Projects window and choose Compile Package (F9).

Doing a Fresh Build

The Build Project command produces its outputs incrementally. When you rebuild a project, any files that have changed or have been added are recompiled, and the JAR file (or other output file) is repackaged with these changed classes. As your project evolves, sometimes you need to explicitly erase your compiled classes and distributables, particularly if you have removed or renamed some source files. Otherwise, classes that are no longer part of your sources might linger in your compiled outputs and cause problems with running your program.

To clean your project, right-click the node for your project in the Projects window and choose Clean Project. This command deletes the `build` and `dist` folders in your project.

To do a fresh build, choose Build | Clean and Build Main Project (Shift-F11).

Stopping a Build

If you start a build and want to halt it before it completes, choose Build | Stop Building. The build will terminate, but any artifacts created by the build will remain.

Changing the Location of Compiled Classes and JAR Files

By default, the compiled class files and the packaged distributable (for example, a JAR or WAR file) are placed in folders (named `build` and `dist`, respectively) parallel to the `src` folder in your project. If you would like the outputs to appear elsewhere or simply would like to change the names of the folders, you can do so in the `project.properties` file.

 If you want to have your class files placed in the same directory as their source files, you need to override the project's `clean` target so that only class files are deleted from the directory when the Clean command is run. You also need to adjust the IDE's Ignored Files property. See Compiling Classes into the Same Directories As Your Sources on page 56.

To access the `project.properties` file:

1. Open the Files window by clicking the Files tab (or pressing Ctrl-2).
2. Expand the project's `nbproject` folder and open the `project.properties` file.

Table 3-3 lists properties that determine where your outputs are created for general Java and web projects.

Table 3-3 Ant Properties for Build Outputs in Standard Projects

Property	Specifies the Directory...
`build.classes.dir`	Where compiled class files are created. You can change the name of the output folder here.
`build.test.classes.dir`	Where unit test files are created (for general Java and web projects).
`build.test.results.dir`	Where unit test results are stored (for general Java and web projects).
`build.generated.dir`	Where the IDE places various temporary files, such as servlet source and class files generated by the IDE when you run the Compile JSP command. These files are not included in the WAR file.
`build.web.dir`	Where the WEB-INF folder and other key folders are placed in the built web application (for web projects).

(continued)

Table 3-3   Ant Properties for Build Outputs in Standard Projects (*Continued*)

Property	Specifies the Directory . . .
build.dir	Where the above directories for the previously listed properties are placed. You can also change the value of this property. If you remove this property from the values of other properties, you must also override any targets that use this property (such as the clean target).
dist.jar	Where the project's JAR file is created. Also specifies the name of the JAR file (for general Java projects).
dist.war	Where the project's WAR file is created. Also specifies the name of the WAR file (for web projects).
dist.javadoc.dir	Where Javadoc for the project is generated when you run the Generate Javadoc for Project command.
dist.dir	Where the generated Javadoc documentation and the project's JAR file or WAR file are placed.

If you move either the build folder or the dist folder outside of the project's folder, it will no longer be visible in the Files window. You can remedy this by setting up the Favorites window to display the folder. Choose Window | Favorites (Ctrl-3). Then right-click the Favorites node and choose Add to Favorites. Navigate to the folder that you want to display and click Add.

Compiling Classes into the Same Directories As Your Sources

If your build environment requires that you compile your classes into the same directories as your sources, you must:

- Modify the properties that represent any build outputs that you want to have moved

- Override the IDE's do-clean target so that it deletes only the class files in your source directory and not your sources as well

- Optionally, update the IDE's Ignore Files property so that compiled class files are not displayed in the Projects window

Here is the step-by-step procedure for having your classes compiled into the same directories as your sources for a general Java project:

1. Open the Files window by clicking the Files tab (or pressing Ctrl-2).

2. Expand the project's nbproject folder and open the project.properties file.

3. Change the build.classes.dir property to point to your source directory.

4. Open the build-impl.xml file and copy the do-clean target.

5. Paste the do-clean target into your build.xml file.

6. In the build.xml file modify the do-clean target so that only class files are deleted. For example, you might replace

```
<delete dir="${build.dir}"/>
```

with

```
<delete includeEmptyDirs="true">
    <fileset dir=".">
        <include name="${build.classes.dir}/**/*.class"/>
    </fileset>
</delete>
```

7. If you do not want compiled class files to display in the Projects and Files windows, choose Tools | Options, expand IDE Configuration | System, and select the System Settings node. Select the Ignored Files property and add to the regular expression to designate the files to ignore. For example, you might add |class$ to the end of the expression.

Investigating Compilation Errors

If you get an error when compiling a class, you can jump to the source of the error by double-clicking the hyperlinked error line in the Output window or by pressing F12. If there are multiple errors, you can cycle through them by pressing F12 (next error) or Shift-F12 (previous error).

Saving Build Output

You can save build output to a file by right-clicking in the Output window and choosing Save As.

By default, every command that you run in the IDE that uses Ant re-uses the same tab in the Output window; thus, the output from the previous command is cleared every time you run a new build command. If you would like to preserve the Ant output in the UI, you can configure the IDE to open up a new tab every time you run a build command.

To preserve the output from all build commands in the IDE:

1. Choose Tools | Options; then navigate to and select the Building | Ant Settings node.
2. Deselect the Reuse Output Tabs property.

Running a Project

Once you have set up your project, created your source files, and set up any necessary dependencies, you can run your project in the IDE by choosing Run | Run Main Project (F6).

By default, when you run a general Java project in the IDE, the following occurs:

- All modified files in the project are saved.
- Any uncompiled files (or files that have been modified since they were last compiled) under the Source Packages node are compiled.
- A JAR file with your classes and other resources is created (or updated).
- Any projects that the main project depends on are built. (In fact, these projects are built first.)
- The project is run inside of the IDE. For general Java projects, the IDE uses the designated main class as the entry point.

When you build your project, output on the progress of the Ant script is printed to the Output window.

Setting or Changing the Project Main Class

To run a general Java project, you have to have an executable class designated as the entry point. You can designate the main class:

- In the New Project wizard when creating your project from the Java Application project template.
- In the project's Project Properties dialog box. (In the Projects window, right-click the project's node and choose Properties. Then select the Run node and fill in the Main Class field with the fully qualified name of the main class, without the .java extension.)

If you try to run a project that has no main class set, you will be prompted to choose one from a list of executable classes found within the project's source packages. If the class that you want to use as the main class is not among the project's sources (for example, if it is in a subproject or another JAR on your classpath), you can set that class in the Project Properties dialog box as detailed in the procedure above.

Setting Runtime Arguments

If you need to pass arguments to the main class when you are running your project, you can specify those arguments through the Project Properties dialog box:

1. Right-click the project's node in the Projects window and choose Properties.
2. Select the Run node and add the arguments as a space-separated list in the Arguments field.

Setting Java Virtual Machine Arguments

If you need to pass arguments to the Java virtual machine that is spawned to run the project in, you can do so through the Project Properties dialog box:

1. Right-click the project's node in the Projects window and choose Properties.
2. Select the Run node and add the arguments as a space-separated list in the VM Options field.

Setting the Runtime Classpath

By default, the classpath for running the project inherits the compilation classpath. If you need to alter the classpath just for runtime, you can make adjustments in the Running Project section of the project's Project Properties dialog box:

1. Right-click the project's node in the Projects window and choose Properties.
2. Select the Libraries node.
3. In the tabbed panel on the right side of the Project Properties dialog box, click the Run tab.
4. Use the Add Project (for other IDE projects), Add Library (for collections of JARs, sources, and Javadoc that you have designated in the Library Manager), or Add JAR/Folder buttons to make additions to your classpath.

Writing Your Own Manifest for Your JAR File

When you build a general Java project, a JAR file is created with a simple manifest with entries for Manifest-Version, Ant-Version, and Created-By. If the project has a main class designated, that main class is also designated in the JAR manifest.

If you have other entries that you would like to add to the manifest of a project created from the Java Application template or Java Project with Existing Sources template, you can add them directly in the manifest.mf file that sits next to the build.xml file. Go to the Files window and double-click the manifest.mf file's node to edit in the Source Editor.

You can also specify a different manifest file for the project to use. To specify a custom manifest:

1. Open the Files window by clicking the Files tab (or by pressing Ctrl-2).
2. Expand the project's nbproject folder and open the project.properties file.
3. In the manifest.file property, type the manifest's name. If the manifest is not in the same folder as the build.xml file, include the relative path from the build.xml file.

 You can write the manifest in the IDE's Source Editor by using the Empty File template. Open the Files window. Then right-click the project's main folder and choose New | Empty File.

For projects created from the Java Library template, a basic manifest is generated, but no editable copy of that manifest appears in the Files window. If you would like to specify a different manifest for a project created from the Java Library template, simply add the manifest.file property to the project's project.properties file and point it to the manifest that you have created.

Filtering Contents Packaged into Outputs

If you have any files that appear within your source packages but that you do not want packaged in the project's distributable, you can have those files filtered out of the project's distributable.

By default, .form files and .java files are filtered from the output JAR file of general Java projects. In web projects, .form, .java, and .nbattrs files are filtered out by default.

To change the filter for the JAR file contents of a general Java project:

1. Right-click the project's node in the Projects window and choose Properties.
2. Select the Build | Packaging node and modify the regular expression in the Exclude from JAR File field. (The name of this field depends on the type of project. For web projects, the field is called Exclude from WAR File.)

 .form files are created for classes that you create with the IDE's Form Editor. The IDE uses these files to regenerate the design view of those classes; however, they are not necessary for the packaged application. If you delete a .form file, the corresponding .java file remains, and you can edit the code, but you can no longer use the IDE's Form Editor to change the form.

.nbattrs files are files that NetBeans IDE creates to hold information about given directories. Projects created in NetBeans IDE 4.0 and later are unlikely to have these files, but legacy projects might.

Running a Project from Outside of the IDE

Because the IDE's project commands are based on Ant scripts and properties files, you can run these targets from outside of the IDE.

Assuming that you have Ant installed on your system, you simply can call the build.xml file or one of its targets from the command line by changing directories to the directory holding build.xml and typing ant.

If your project uses optional Ant tasks that are defined within the IDE, you might need to do some manual configuration. For example, if you have a target that depends on JUnit, you need to place the JUnit binary in your Ant classpath.

Setting Up a Headless Build Environment

If you have a large nested project structure that you want to run from outside of the IDE, such as when you are doing production builds of your application, you will probably need to make some adjustments to set up headless builds.

Following are the tasks you need to perform:

- Set up Ant (Version 1.6 or higher) on your system. You can either download Ant or use the Ant JAR file that is included with the IDE (*NBHome*/ide5/ant/lib/ant.jar in the IDE's installation directory). Visit http://ant.apache.org/ to download or get more information on Ant. NetBeans IDE 4.1 is bundled with Ant Version 1.6.2, so any standard projects that you set up will use that version. Also, make sure that the command-line version of Ant that you are using is running from the same version of the Java platform that your project is using.

- Make JUnit available to Ant. You can do this by adding the JUnit JAR file to *AntHome*/lib. You can use the IDE's copy of JUnit, which is located in *NBHome*/ide5/modules/ext and is named according to version number. (In NetBeans IDE 4.1, for example, it is junit3.8.1.jar.)

- Make sure that any libraries that the IDE uses when building your project are accessible from the build script that the build machine uses. These libraries are specified in the build.properties file that is located in your IDE user directory. You can find the IDE's user directory by choosing Help | About, clicking the Detail tab, and looking at the User Dir value.

Customizing the IDE-Generated Build Script

The build scripts that the IDE generates for you in standard projects are based on common scenarios that work for many development situations. But if the script does not do what you want it to do, you can add to, override parts of, or change the script entirely.

When you create a standard project, the IDE generates two build scripts: build-impl.xml and build.xml.

The build-impl.xml file is generated based on the type of project template you started with and is regenerated based on any changes that occur in the project's associated project.xml file. Do not edit build-impl.xml directly, because any changes you make there would be lost any time the file was regenerated.

The build.xml file serves as the master build script. By default, it has no targets of its own. It imports build-impl.xml. You can freely edit build.xml.

To help make sense of the Ant script, you can use the Ant Debugger to step through execution of the script so that you can quickly see the order in which the various targets are called. See Debugging Ant Scripts on page 366 for more information.

Adding a Target

To add a target to the build script of a standard project:

1. In the Files window, expand the project's main folder.
2. Double-click the `build.xml` file to open it in the Source Editor.
3. Below the `import` element, type any targets that you would like to add to the build script.

Adding a Subtarget

To make customization of build scripts easier, the generated build scripts include several empty targets that are called from main targets.

For example, the compile target depends on `pre-compile` and `post-compile` targets, which have nothing in them. If you need to add any steps to the build process just before or after compilation of your files, you can customize these targets without having to add to the `depends` attribute of the `compile` target.

To add to a target using one of the existing empty subtargets:

1. In the Files window, expand the project's `nbproject` folder and open the `build-impl.xml` file.
2. Copy the empty target that you want to use, paste it into the project's `build.xml` file, and then make your modifications to it there.

For example, you could call Ant's `rmic` task in the `post-compile` target to run the `rmic` compiler on all classes with names beginning with `Remote` (as shown in the snippet below):

```
<target name="-post-compile">
    <rmic base="${build.classes.dir}" includes="**/Remote*.class"/>
</target>
```

For further convenience, some of the main targets also include "-pre-pre" targets that handle some basic steps before the empty targets are called. For example, the -pre-pre-compile target, which creates the directory to hold the class files to be compiled, is called before the -pre-compile target.

Overriding an Existing Target

If adding subtargets to a main target is not sufficient for what you need to accomplish, you can completely override part of a build script.

To override a target in a standard project's build script:

1. In the Files window, expand the projects nbproject folder and open the build-impl.xml file.
2. Copy the target that you want to override, paste it into the project's build.xml file, and then make your modifications to it there.

When a target appears in both the build-impl.xml and build.xml files, the version in the build.xml file takes precedence.

If you are merely modifying the depends attribute of the target, you do not have to copy the whole body of the target. You can copy just the target element without its subelements. The subelements will be imported from the build-impl.xml file.

Inside the Generated Build Scripts

Here is a look at all of the pieces of the project metadata and how they work together.

When you create a standard project, the IDE creates the files listed in Table 3-4.

 There is also a build.properties file that is created in your IDE's user directory. This file holds properties for the location of libraries that are packaged with the IDE, any libraries that you specify with the IDE's Library Manager, and any versions of the Java platform that you register with the IDE's Java Platform Manager. The private.properties file references the build.properties file with its user.properties.file property.

Table 3-4 Metadata for a Standard Project

File	Description
build.xml	This script is the master build script for the project. When you call a project-related command from the IDE, the IDE calls a target in this file. You can freely edit this file if you want to make customizations to your build process. This file is generated when you create the project but is not regenerated afterward. Any configuration that you do in the IDE that is relevant to the build script is reflected in the build-impl.xml file, which is imported by build.xml. If a target with the same name appears in both build.xml and build-impl.xml, the target in build.xml takes precedence.
nbproject/build-impl.xml	Included in standard projects (but not free-form projects), this file contains the meat of the build script and is imported by build.xml. It is generated based on the type of project and the contents of that project's project.xml file. Do not edit this file.
nbproject/project.properties	Included in standard projects (but not free-form projects), this file contains values that the build script uses when building your project. These values include things such as the name and location of the directory for your compiled files and references to properties set elsewhere in the project. Changes that you make in your Project Properties dialog box are propagated here. You can also modify this file directly in the Source Editor.
nbproject/project.xml	Provides the basic metadata that determines how the project works in the IDE. For standard projects, this file determines how build-impl.xml and project.properties are generated. For free-form projects, this file serves as the glue between your build script and the IDE's user interface. This file is generally editable, but you are likely to need to edit it only for free-form projects.
nbproject/genfiles.xml	Used by the IDE to help keep track of the state of the build script (such as whether the build-impl.xml file needs to be regenerated). Do not edit this file.
nbproject/private/private.properties	Holds properties that are specific to your installation of the IDE. These properties are not to be versioned, but they can be used by headless builds run on your machine.

Running a Specific Ant Target from the IDE

You can run any Ant target within the IDE by expanding the build script's node in the Files window, right-clicking the target, and choosing Run Target.

You can stop the target by choosing Build | Stop Building.

Completing Ant Expressions

The IDE has a "completion" feature to reduce the number of keystrokes needed when editing an Ant script. When you use the completion feature, the Source Editor gives you a choice of how to complete the current word with a popup dialog box.

Activate the completion feature by typing the first few characters of an element or attribute and then pressing Ctrl-spacebar.

If there is only one possible completion, the missing characters from the word are filled in. (For attributes, =" is generated as well.)

If there are multiple possible matches, you can choose a completion by scrolling through the list and then pressing the Enter key once the correct word is selected. Keep typing to narrow the number of selections in the list.

The order of the selection list is generally *smart*, meaning that elements or attributes that are commonly used in the given context are put at the top.

For example, you can enter the following target

```
<target name="default" depends="dist,javadoc"
    description="Build whole project."/>
```

by doing the following:

1. Typing <t
2. Pressing Ctrl-spacebar and then Enter to select target
3. Pressing the spacebar
4. Pressing Ctrl-spacebar and then Enter to select name, as shown in Figure 3-8 (name=" is inserted into the script)

Figure 3-8   Code completion box for an Ant script

5. Typing `default"`

6. Pressing Ctrl-spacebar and then Enter to select `depends` (`depends="` is inserted into the script)

7. Typing `dist,javadoc"`

8. Pressing Ctrl-spacebar and then Enter to select `description` (`description="` is inserted into the script)

9. Typing `Build whole project."/>`

Making a Menu Item or Shortcut for a Specific Ant Target

If you have a target in your build script that you use often but that is not represented by a menu item or keyboard shortcut, you can create such a menu item and a shortcut:

1. In the Files window, expand the projects `nbproject` folder and expand the `build-impl.xml` node.

2. Right-click the target that you want to map and choose Create Shortcut.

A wizard opens that enables you to set a menu item, toolbar item, and a keyboard shortcut for the target. Because the IDE records these custom menu items and shortcuts as Ant files, you can customize the way the shortcuts are called by selecting the Customize Generated Ant Code checkbox in the wizard.

Shortcuts set in this way are not global. They apply only to the build script on which they are set.

The wizard prevents you from overriding existing custom shortcuts, but it does not prevent you from overriding standard IDE shortcuts. If you inadvertently use a key combination for your new shortcut that is used elsewhere in the IDE, your new shortcut takes precedence.

Removing a Custom Menu Item or Shortcut

If you have added a menu item or shortcut for an Ant target and would like to remove it, you can do so manually. The IDE stores these customizations in your user directory in small XML files that work as mini-Ant scripts.

To remove a shortcut to an Ant target:

1. In your IDE's user directory, expand the config folder. (If you are not sure where your IDE user directory is, choose Help | About and click the Details tab to find out.)

2. Look in the following subfolders (and possibly their subfolders) for an XML file with the name of the Ant target or the keyboard shortcut:
   - Menu (if you have created menu items)
   - Shortcuts (if you have created keyboard shortcuts)
   - Toolbar (if you have added a toolbar item)

3. Manually delete the XML file that represents the shortcut.

Changing a Custom Menu Item or Shortcut

You can change a custom menu item for an Ant target by doing one of the following:

- Deleting the mini Ant script for the target and creating a new shortcut.
- Editing the mini Ant script for the target. For example, you can change the build script that a shortcut applies to by changing the antfile attribute in the shortcut's script.

To manually edit the file for the custom menu item or shortcut:

1. In your IDE's user directory, expand the config folder. (If you are not sure where your user IDE directory is, choose Help | About and click the Details tab to find out.)

2. Look in the following subfolders (and possibly their subfolders) for an XML file with the name of the Ant target or the keyboard shortcut:
   - Menu (if you have created menu items)

- Shortcuts (if you have created keyboard shortcuts)
- Toolbar (if you have added a toolbar item)

3. Double-click the node for the menu item or shortcut to open it in the Source Editor.

## CHAPTER 4

Editing and Refactoring Code

- Opening the Source Editor
- Managing Automatic Insertion of Closing Characters
- Displaying Line Numbers
- Generating Code Snippets
- Handling Imports
- Displaying Javadoc Documentation While Editing
- Formatting Code
- Navigating within the Current Java File
- Navigating from the Source Editor
- Searching and Replacing
- Moving a Class to a Different Package
- Changing a Method's Signature
- Tracking Notes to Yourself in Your Code
- Comparing Differences Between Two Files
- Splitting the Source Editor
- Maximizing Space for the Source Editor
- Changing Source Editor Keyboard Shortcuts
- Building Rich Clients

NETBEANS IDE PROVIDES A LOT OF TOOLS TO SUPPORT JAVA application development, but it's the Source Editor where you will spend most of your time. Given that fact, a lot of attention has been put into features and subtle touches to make coding faster and more pleasurable.

Code generation and navigation features are available with keyboard shortcuts so that your hands rarely have to stray from the keyboard. Refactoring features enable you to make changes to the structure of your code and have those changes propagated throughout your project. In addition, there is a wide range of simple shortcuts for file navigation that, taken together, make coding much smoother.

Architecturally, the Source Editor is actually a collection of different types of editors, each of which contains features specific to certain kinds of files. For example, when you open up a Java file, there is a syntax highlighting scheme specifically for Java files, along with code completion, refactoring, and other features specific to Java files. Likewise, when you open up JSP, HTML, XML, .properties, deployment descriptor, and other types of files, you get a set of features specific to those files.

Perhaps most importantly, the Source Editor is tightly integrated with other parts of the IDE, which greatly streamlines your workflow. For example, you can specify breakpoints directly in the Source Editor and trace code as it executes. When compilation errors are reported in the Output window, you can jump to the source of those errors by double-clicking the error or pressing F12.

Opening the Source Editor

Before you start working in the Source Editor, you should have an IDE project set up. You can then open an existing file or create a new file from a template. See Chapter 3 for basic information on creating projects and files and for a description of the various file templates.

If you would like simply to create a file without immediately making it part of a project, you can use the Favorites window. The Favorites window enables you to make arbitrary folders and files on your system accessible through the IDE. The Favorites window is not designed for full-scale project development, but it can be useful if you just want to open and edit a few files quickly.

To use the Source Editor without creating a project:

1. Choose Window | Favorites to open the Favorites window.
2. Add the folder where you want the file to live (or where it already lives) by right-clicking the Favorites node, choosing Add to Favorites, and choosing the folder from the file chooser.
3. In the Favorites window, navigate to the file that you want to edit and double-click it to open it in the Source Editor.

   If you want to create a new file, right-click a folder node, choose New | Empty File, and enter a filename (including extension).

Managing Automatic Insertion of Closing Characters

When typing in the Source Editor, one of the first things that you will notice is that the closing characters are automatically inserted when you type the opening character. For example, if you type a quote mark, the closing quote mark is inserted at the end of the line. Likewise, parentheses(()), brackets ([]), and curly braces ({}) are completed for you.

While this might seem annoying at first, the feature was designed to not get in your way. If you type the closing character yourself, the automatically inserted character is overwritten. Also, you can end a line by typing a semicolon (;) to finish a statement. The semicolon is inserted at the end of the line after the automatically generated character or characters.

See the following subtopics for information on how to use the insertion of matching closing characters.

Finishing a Statement

When the Source Editor inserts matching characters at the end of the line, this would appear to force you to move the insertion point manually past the closing character before you can type the semicolon. In fact, you can just type the semicolon without moving the insertion point, and it will be placed at the end of the line automatically.

For example, to get the line

```
System.out.println("Testing");
```

you would only have to type

```
System.out.println("Testing;
```

Splitting a String Between Two Lines

If you have a long string that you want to split between two lines, the Source Editor adds the syntax for concatenating the string when you press Enter.

For example, to get the lines

```
String s = "Though typing can seem tedious, reading long" +
"and convoluted sentences can be even worse."
```

you could type

```
String s = "Though typing can seem tedious, reading long
and convoluted sentences can be even worse.
```

The final three quote marks and the plus sign (+) are added for you.

If you want to break the line without creating the concatenation, press Shift-Enter.

Displaying Line Numbers

By default, line numbers are switched off in the Source Editor to save space and reduce visual clutter. If you need the line numbers, you can turn them on by right-clicking in the left gutter of the Source Editor and choosing Show Line Numbers, as shown in Figure 4-1.

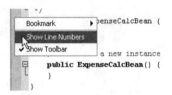

Figure 4-1 Activating line numbers

Generating Code Snippets

The Source Editor has several features for reducing the keystrokes needed for typing code. In addition to saving keystrokes, these features might save typos and help you find the right class and method names. This section concentrates on features for Java files, but many of the features (such as code completion and word matching) are also available for other types of files, such as JSP and HTML files.

Completing Java Statements

When you are typing Java identifiers in the Source Editor, you can use the IDE's code completion box to help you finish expressions, as shown in Figure 4-2. In addition, a box with Javadoc documentation appears and displays documentation for the currently selected option in the code completion box.

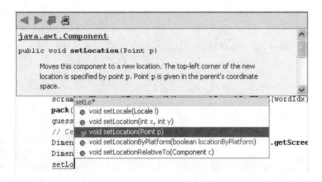

Figure 4-2   Code completion box with accompanying Javadoc popup

To open the code completion box, do one of the following:

- Type the first few characters of an expression and then press Ctrl-spacebar (or Ctrl-\).
- Pause after typing a period (.) in an expression.
- Type the new or import keyword, type a space, and then pause for a moment.

The code completion box opens with a selection of possible matches for what you have typed so far.

To narrow the selection in the code completion box, continue typing the expression.

To complete the expression and close the code completion box, do one of the following:

- Continue typing until there is only one option left and then press Enter.
- Scroll through the list, using the arrow keys or your mouse to select a value, and then press Enter.

To complete the expression and leave the code completion box open, select a completion and press Shift-Enter. This is useful if you are chaining methods. For example, if you want to type

```
getRootPane().setDefaultButton(defaultButton)
```

you might do the following:

1. Type getRo (which would leave only getRootPane() in the code completion box) and press Shift-Enter.
2. Type .setDef (which should make setDefaultButton(defaultButton) the selected method in the code completion box) and press Enter.

If the method that you choose in the code completion box has a parameter (as in the example above), a placeholder parameter is inserted. You can type over this placeholder with the parameter name that you want to use.

If the method takes multiple parameters, a placeholder for the first parameter is generated. When you enter a value and then a comma, a placeholder for the next value is entered.

Once you have finished typing parameter values, type a semicolon (;) to end the line. The semicolon is automatically inserted after the closing parenthesis.

To fill in text that is common to all of the remaining choices, press Tab. For example, if you are working on a Swing class, and you have typed addW, there will be three listener methods beginning with addWindow. Press Tab to extend addW to addWindow. Then type the next letter (F for addWindowFocusListener(1), L for addWindowListener(1), or S for addWindowStateListener(1)) and press Enter to complete the expression.

To close the code completion box without entering any selection, press Esc.

Disabling Automatic Appearance of the Java Code Completion Box

If you find the code completion box to be more of a nuisance than a help, you can disable automatic appearance of the code completion popup. Code completion will still work if you manually activate it by pressing Ctrl-spacebar or Ctrl-\.

You can also leave automatic appearance of the code completion popup enabled but disable the bulkier Javadoc code completion box. The Javadoc popup can be manually invoked with Ctrl-Shift-spacebar.

To disable automatic appearance of the code completion box:

1. Choose Tools | Options, expand the Editing | Editor Settings node, and select the Java Editor node.
2. Scroll down to the Expert section of the property sheet and deselect the Auto Popup Completion Window property.

To disable automatic appearance of the Javadoc popup when you use the code completion box:

1. Choose Tools | Options, expand the Editing | Editor Settings node, and select the Java Editor node.
2. Scroll down to the Expert section of the property sheet and deselect the Auto Popup Javadoc Window property.

 You can also merely adjust the amount of time that elapses before the code completion box appears. By default, the delay is 500 milliseconds. You can change this value in the Delay of Completion Window Auto Popup property.

Changing Shortcuts for Code Completion

If you prefer to use different shortcuts for code completion, you can change those shortcuts in NetBeans IDE:

1. Choose Tools | Options and select the Editing | Editor Settings node.
2. Click the […] button in the Global Key Bindings property to open the Global Key Bindings dialog box.
3. Select a key binding that you want to change, click Add, and type the shortcut that you want to use.

Relevant commands are Show Code Completion, Hide Code Completion, and Show the Javadoc Window.

Matching Other Words in a File

If you are typing a word that appears elsewhere in your file, you can use a keyboard shortcut to complete that word according to the first word found in the Source Editor that matches the characters you have typed. This word-match feature works for any text in the file.

To search backward from the cursor for a match, press Ctrl-K.

To search forward from the cursor for a match, press Ctrl-L.

For example, if you have defined the method `refreshCustomerInfo` on line 100 and now want to call that method from line 50, you can type `ref` and then press Ctrl-L. If there are no other words that start with `ref` between lines 50 and 100, the rest of the word `refreshCustomerInfo` will be filled in. If a different match is found, keep pressing Ctrl-L until the match that you want is filled in.

Generating Methods to Override from Extended Classes

When you extend a class, you have the extended methods available to override. To make overriding easier, you can generate the methods to be overridden in your new class and then modify the methods in your class.

To have methods that are to be overridden inserted into your code:

1. Choose Tools | Override Methods or press Ctrl-I.
2. In the Override and Implement Methods dialog box (shown in Figure 4-3), select the methods to be overridden. You can Ctrl-click items to select multiple methods.

   You can deselect the Generate Super Calls checkbox if you do not want to generate a call to the super implementation of the method.

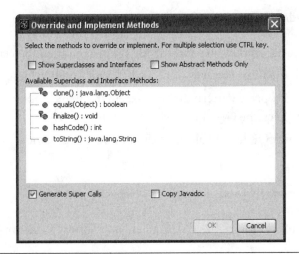

Figure 4-3   Override and Implement Methods dialog box

Generating Methods from Implemented Interfaces

When you create a class that implements an interface, you can use the IDE's Synchronize feature to generate that interface's methods in the class.

To generate methods in a class that implements an interface:

1. In your class declaration, type `implements` *InterfaceName.*
2. Choose Tools | Synchronize.

   The Synchronize dialog box appears and enables you to specify which of the interfaces you want to generate methods for.

You can also have the IDE automatically prompt you to generate an interface's methods after you declare that a class implements an interface. Choose Tools | Options. Expand Editing | Java Sources and select the Source Synchronization node. In the Properties pane of the window, select the Synchronization Enabled checkbox.

Generating Read/Write Properties

You can generate properties in accordance with the JavaBeans component model from scratch, or you can use the Encapsulate Fields feature to create a getter and setter for an existing field.

To create a read/write property from scratch:

1. In the Projects window, expand the file's node and then the class (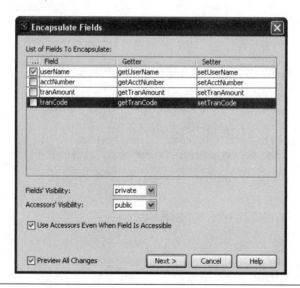) node.
2. Right-click the Bean Patterns node and choose Add | Property.
3. In the New Property Pattern dialog box, enter a name and type for the property. Then check the Generate Field checkbox.

   After you click OK, a field along with get and set methods for that field are generated.

To provide accessor methods for a given field:

1. In the Source Editor, right-click the field and choose Refactor | Encapsulate Fields.
2. In the Encapsulate Fields dialog box (shown in Figure 4-4), verify that the field you have selected is checked as the one to be encapsulated. Then set the visibility for the field and for the accessor methods (the getter and setter).
3. Click Next to preview the changes in the Refactoring window.
4. In the Refactoring window, verify the changes that are about to be made and click Do Refactoring.

Figure 4-4   Encapsulate Fields dialog box

Encapsulate Fields is one of several "refactoring" commands in the IDE. Refactoring commands provide a way for you to make naming and structural changes and to have those changes reflected in the rest of your project. See Refactoring Commands on page 104 for a summary of the refactoring commands.

Expanding Abbreviations

For commonly used keywords and identifiers, you can take advantage of abbreviations in the Source Editor to reduce the number of keystrokes. Abbreviations are expanded when you type the abbreviation and then press the spacebar.

If an abbreviation is the same as the text that you want to type (for example, you do not want it to be expanded into something else), press Shift-spacebar to keep it from expanding.

See Table 4-1 for a list of abbreviations for Java files. There are also abbreviations set for JSP files (see Chapter 6, Expanding Abbreviations for JSP Files).

Table 4-1 Java Abbreviations in the Source Editor

Abbreviation	Expands To
ab	abstract
bo	boolean
br	break
ca	catch (
cl	class
cn	continue
df	default:
En	Enumeration
eq	equals
Ex	Exception
ex	extends
fi	final
fa	false
fy	finally
fl	float

(continued)

Table 4-1 Java Abbreviations in the Source Editor (*Continued*)

Abbreviation	Expands To
ie	interface
im	implements
iof	instanceof
ir	import
le	length
Ob	Object
pst	printStackTrace();
pr	private
psf	private static final
psfb	private static final boolean
psfi	private static final int
psfs	private static final String
pe	protected
pu	public
Psf	public static final
Psfb	public static final boolean
Psfi	public static final int
Psfs	public static final String
re	return
st	static
St	String
serr	System.err.println("|");
sout	System.out.println("|");
sw	switch {
sy	synchronized
tds	Thread.dumpStack();
tw	throw
twn	throw new
th	throws
wh	while (

In the expansion of some of your abbreviations, it might be desirable to have the insertion point rest somewhere in the middle of the text. For example, the insertion point appears between the quote marks when `sout` is expanded to `System.out.println("")`; so that you can then type the string to be printed without having to move the cursor.

Use the pipe (|) character in the Expansion field of the abbreviation to mark where the insertion point should appear when the abbreviation is expanded.

Adding, Changing, and Removing Abbreviations

You can modify existing abbreviations (both the abbreviation and the expansion), create new ones, and delete abbreviations in the Abbreviations dialog box for a type of file.

1. Choose Tools | Options, expand the Editing | Editor Settings node, and select the node for type of editor you want to modify abbreviations for.
2. Click the ▢ button in the Abbreviations property to open the Abbreviations property editor.
3. Use the Add, Edit, and Remove buttons to modify the list of abbreviations.

Creating and Using Macros

You can record macros in the IDE to reduce what would normally involve a long set of keystrokes to one keyboard shortcut. In macros, you can combine the typing of characters in the Source Editor and the typing of other keyboard shortcuts.

To record a macro:

1. Put the insertion point in the part of a file in the Source Editor where you want to record the macro.
2. Click the ● button in the Source Editor's toolbar (or press Ctrl-J and then type s) to begin recording.
3. Record the macro using any sequence of keystrokes, whether it is the typing of characters or using keyboard shortcuts. Mouse movements and clicks (such as menu selections) are not recorded.
4. Click the ▣ button in the Source Editor's toolbar (or press Ctrl-J and then type e) to finish recording.

5. In the Recorded Macro dialog box that appears, click Add to assign a key-board shortcut to the macro.

6. In the Add Keybinding dialog box, press the keys that you want to use for the keyboard shortcut. (For example, if you want the shortcut Alt-Shift-Z, press the Alt, Shift, and Z keys.) If you press a wrong key, click the Clear button to start over.

   Be careful not to use a shortcut that is already assigned. If the shortcut you enter is an editor shortcut, a warning appears in the dialog box. However, if the key combination is a shortcut that applies outside of the Source Editor, you will not be warned.

Any macro that you record works only for the type of file in which it was recorded.

After you have recorded a macro, you can edit it by hand in the Recorded Macro dialog box.

The keyboard shortcuts that you include in a macro are indicated by their action names. You can get a list of these action names in the Key Bindings dialog box for the particular editor type, which you use when you assign or edit keyboard shortcuts.

Creating and Customizing File Templates

You can customize the templates that you create files from in the IDE and create your own templates. This might be useful if you need to add standard elements in all of your files (such as copyright notices) or want to change the way other elements are generated.

You can also create your own templates and make them available in the New File wizard.

There are several macros available for use in templates to generate text dynamically in the created files. These macros are identifiable by the double underscores that appear both before and after the macro name. See Table 4-2 for a list of the macros available.

To edit a template:

1. Choose Tools | Options, expand the Source Creation and Management | Templates node, and then expand the category node for the template that you want to edit.

2. Right-click the template's node and choose Open.

3. Edit the template and then save it.

 Not all of the templates listed under Source Creation and Management | Templates node represent objects that can be modified at the user level. In some cases, the templates are available in the New File wizard but do not represent file constructs (such as those in the Enterprise and Sun Resources categories). In others, the templates not related to file creation at all are exposed (such as those in the Filesystems and Privileged categories).

To create a new template:

1. Choose File | New File and select the template that you want to base your new template on.

2. Edit the file, incorporating any of the template macros that you want to use (see Table 4-2), and save it.

Table 4-2   Java File Template Macros

Macro	Substituted Information
__USER__	Your username. If you would like to change the value of __USER__, choose Tools | Options and select the Editing | Java Sources node. Then click the [...] button in the Strings Table property and change the value of USER.
__DATE__	The date the new file is created.
__TIME__	The time the new file is created.
__NAME__	The name of the class (without the file extension). It is best not to use this macro for the class and constructor name in the file (instead, use the filename).
__PACKAGE__	The name of the package where the class is created.
__PACKAGE_SLASHES__	The name of the class's package with slash (/) delimiters instead of periods (.).
__PACKAGE_AND_NAME__	The fully qualified name of the file (such as com.mydomain.mypackage.MyClass).
__PACKAGE_AND_NAME_SLASHES__	The fully qualified name of the file with slash (/) delimiters instead of periods (.).
__QUOTES__	A double quote mark ("). Use this macro if you want the substituted text to appear in quotes in the generated file. (If you place a macro within quote marks in the template, text is not substituted for the macro name in the created file.)

If the template is for a Java class, you can use the filename for the class name and constructor name. These are automatically adjusted in the files you create from the template.

3. In the Projects window, right-click the file's node and choose Save As Template from the contextual menu.

4. In the Save As Template dialog box, select the category to be used for the template in the New File wizard.

Handling Imports

The IDE has a pair of commands that you can use to manage import statements in your code:

- Fix Imports (Alt-Shift-F), which automatically inserts any missing import statements for the whole file. Import statements are generated by class (rather than by package). For rapid management of your imports, use this command.

- Fast Import (Alt-Shift-I), which enables you to add an import statement or generate the fully qualified class name for the currently selected identifier. This command is useful if you want to generate an import statement for a whole package or if you want to use a fully qualified class name inline instead of an import statement.

You can also have an import statement generated when you are using code completion. If you have the code completion box open, and you start typing a simple class name instead of the fully qualified class name (for example, you type Con and then select ConcurrentHashMap from the code completion box), the following import statement will be added:

```
import java.util.concurrent.ConcurrentHashMap;
```

Displaying Javadoc Documentation While Editing

The IDE gives you a few ways to access documentation for JDK and library classes.

To glance at documentation for the currently selected class in the Source Editor, press Ctrl-Shift-spacebar. A popup window appears with the Javadoc documentation for the class. This popup also appears when you use code completion. You can dismiss the popup by clicking outside of the popup.

To open a web browser on documentation for the selected class, right-click the class and choose Show Javadoc (or press Alt-F1).

To open the index page for a library's documentation in a web browser, choose View | Documentation Indices and choose the index from the submenu.

Documentation for some libraries is bundled with the IDE. However, you might need to register the documentation for other libraries in the IDE for the Javadoc features to work. See Making External Sources and Javadoc Available in the IDE in Chapter 3 for more information.

Paradoxically, JDK documentation is available through a popup in the Source Editor but not through a browser by default. This is because the Javadoc popup in the Source Editor picks up the documentation from the sources that are included with the JDK. However, the browser view of the documentation requires compiled Javadoc documentation, which you have to download separately from the JDK.

Formatting Code

When you type or have code generated in the Source Editor, your Java code is automatically formatted in the following ways by default:

- Members of classes are indented four spaces.
- Continued statements are indented eight spaces.
- Any tabs that you enter are converted to spaces.
- When you are in a block comment (starting with /**), an asterisk is automatically added to the new line when you press Enter.
- The opening curly brace is put on the same line as the declaration of the class or method.
- No space is put before an opening parenthesis.

If your file loses correct formatting (which is likely if you paste text into the file), you can reformat the whole file by pressing Ctrl-Shift-F. If you have any lines selected, the reformatting applies only to those lines.

Indenting Blocks of Code Manually

You can select multiple lines of code and then indent all of those lines by pressing Tab or Ctrl-T.

You can reverse indentation by selecting some lines and then pressing Shift-Tab or Ctrl-D.

Changing Formatting Rules

You can adjust the way your files are formatted using so-called indentation engines, which hold settings for number of spaces, placement of curly braces, and so on. By default, all Java files use the Java indentation engine. You can modify this indentation engine, set up Java files to use a different one, or create a new one entirely.

To adjust formatting rules for Java files:

1. Choose Tools | Options.
2. Expand Editing | Indentation Engines and select the Java Indentation Engine node.
3. Adjust the properties for the indentation engine to your taste.
4. Reformat each file to the new rules by opening the file and pressing Ctrl-Shift-F (with no text selected).

There are other preset indentation engines available, both generic (such as the "simple" and "line wrapping" indentation engines) and for other types of files (notably for JSP, HTML, and XML files).

To change the indentation engine that is used for Java files:

1. Choose Tools | Options.
2. Expand Editing | Editor Settings and select the Java Editor node.
3. Select the indentation engine from the Indentation Engine property's combo box.
4. Reformat each file to the new rules by opening the file and pressing Ctrl-Shift-F (with no text selected).

To create a new indentation engine:

1. Choose Tools | Options.
2. Expand Editing | Indentation Engines, right-click the node for the indentation engine you want to base your new indentation engine on, and choose Copy.
3. Right-click the Indentation Engines node and choose Paste | Copy.
4. Modify the name of the indentation inline and adjust the properties to your taste.
5. In the Options dialog box, expand Editing | Editor Settings and select the node for the editor (such as Java Editor or HTML Editor) that you want the indentation engine to apply to.

 Any changes that you make in formatting rules do not apply to code in the guarded blocks that is generated when you design AWT or Swing forms in the Form Editor.

Text Selection Shortcuts

To enable you to keep both hands on the keyboard, a number of shortcuts allow you to select text, deselect text, and change the text that is selected. See Table 4-3 for a selection of these shortcuts.

Table 4-3 Text Selection Shortcuts

Description	Shortcut
Selects the current identifier or other word that the insertion point is on.	Alt-J
Selects all the text between a set of parentheses, brackets, or curly braces. The insertion point must be resting immediately after either the opening or closing parenthesis/bracket/brace.	Ctrl-Shift-[
Selects the next (previous) character or extends the selection one character.	Shift-Right (Shift-Left)
Selects the next (previous) word or extends the selection one word.	Ctrl-Shift-Right (Ctrl-Shift-Left)
Creates or extends the text selection one line down (up).	Shift-Down (Shift-Up)
Creates or extends the text selection to the end (beginning) of the line.	Shift-End (Shift-Home)

(continued)

Table 4-3 Text Selection Shortcuts (*Continued*)

Description	Shortcut
Creates or extends the text selection to the end (beginning) of the document.	Ctrl-Shift-End (Ctrl-Shift-Home)
Creates or extends the text selection one page down (up).	Shift-Page Down (Shift-Page Up)

Changing Fonts and Colors

You can adjust the fonts that are used in the Source Editor and the way colors and background highlighting are used to represent syntactic elements of your code.

Fonts and colors are determined by the type of file that you are editing, so any adjustments that you make are per type of file.

To change font size for an editor type:

1. Choose Tools | Options.
2. Expand Editing | Editor Settings and select the node for the editor type (such as Java Editor or HTML Editor).
3. Change the Font Size property.

To change the color and highlighting scheme for a type of file:

1. Choose Tools | Options.
2. Expand Editing | Editor Settings and select the node for the editor type (such as Java Editor or HTML Editor).
3. Click the ▭ button in the Fonts and Colors property.
4. In the Fonts and Colors dialog box (shown in Figure 4-5), select an item from the Syntax column.
5. Change the scheme for that syntax element in the Font, Foreground Color, and Background Color fields. You can enter the values directly or click the ▭ button next to each field to bring up a font chooser or a color chooser.

   If you select the Inherit checkbox for any of the three settings, that item will use the setting from one of the other syntax elements, usually from the Default element.

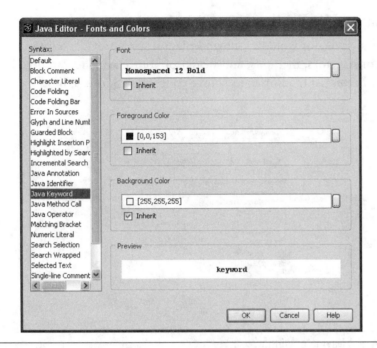

Figure 4-5   Fonts and Colors dialog box for Java Editor

Navigating within the Current Java File

The IDE provides several mechanisms to make it easier to view and navigate a given Java file:

- The Navigator window, which appears below the Projects window and provides a list of members (for example, constructors, fields, and methods) in the currently selected Java file.

- Bookmarks, which enable you to easily jump back to specific places in the file.

- The Alt-K and Alt-L "jump list" shortcuts, mentioned in Jumping Between Areas Where You Have Been Working later on page 95.

- Keyboard shortcuts to scroll the window. See Table 4-4 in the following section.

- The code folding feature, which enables you to collapse sections of code (such as method bodies, Javadoc comments, and blocks of import statements) thus making a broader section of your class visible in the window at a given time.

Viewing and Navigating Members of a Class

The IDE's Navigator window (shown in Figure 4-6) provides a list of all "members" (constructors, methods, and fields) of your class. You can double-click a member in this list to jump to its source code in the Source Editor.

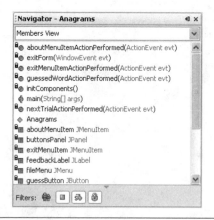

Figure 4-6   Navigator window

You can use the filter buttons at the bottom of the window to hide nonpublic members, static members, fields, and/or inherited members.

Moving the Insertion Point and Scrolling the Window

You can use a wide range of shortcuts for moving the insertion point around and scrolling the Source Editor without moving the insertion point. See Table 4-4 for a list of some of the most useful file navigation shortcuts.

Table 4-4   Cursor and Scrolling Shortcuts

Description	Shortcut
Moves the insertion point to the next word (previous word).	Ctrl-Right (Ctrl-Left)
Moves the insertion point to the top (bottom) of the file.	Ctrl-Home (Ctrl-End)
Scrolls up (down) without moving the insertion point.	Ctrl-Up (Ctrl-Down)
Scrolls the window so that the current line moves to the top of the window.	Alt-U, then T

Description	Shortcut
Scrolls the window so that the current line moves to the middle of the window.	Alt-U, then M
Scrolls the window so that the current line moves to the bottom of the window.	Alt-U, then B
Moves the insertion point to the parenthesis, bracket, or curly brace that matches the one directly before your insertion point.	Ctrl-[

Bookmarking Lines of Code

You can set bookmarks in files to make it easy to find an area of the file that you are working with frequently. You can then cycle through the file's bookmarks by pressing F2 (forward) or Shift-F2 (backward).

To bookmark a line in a file, click in the line and press Ctrl-F2. To remove a bookmark, also use Ctrl-F2.

Hiding Sections of Code

You can collapse (or *fold*) low-level details of code so that only one line of that block is visible in the Source Editor, leaving more room to view other lines. Methods, inner classes, import blocks, and Javadoc comments are all foldable.

Collapsible blocks of code are marked with the ⊟ icon in the left margin next to the first line of the block. The rest of the block is marked with a vertical line that extends down from the ⊟ icon. Collapsed blocks are marked with the ⊞ icon. You can click one of these icons to fold or expand the particular block that it represents. See Figure 4-7 for an example.

You can also collapse and expand single or multiple blocks of code with keyboard shortcuts and menu items in the Edit | Code Folds menu and the Code Folds submenu in the Source Editor. See Table 4-5 for a list of these commands and shortcuts.

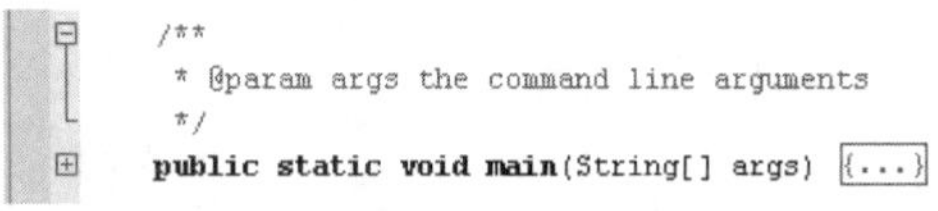

Figure 4-7   Examples of expanded and folded code in the Source Editor

Table 4-5 Code Folding Commands

Command	Shortcut
Collapse Fold	Ctrl-NumPad-Minus
Expand Fold	Ctrl-NumPad-Plus
Collapse All	Ctrl-Shift-NumPad-Minus
Expand All	Ctrl-Shift-NumPad-Plus
Collapse All Javadoc	none
Expand All Javadoc	none
Collapse All Java Code (collapses everything except Javadoc documentation)	none
Expand All Java Code (expands everything except Javadoc documentation)	none

By default, no code is folded. You can configure the Source Editor to fold code by default when you create a file or open a previously unopened file.

To configure the IDE to fold certain elements of code automatically:

1. Choose Tools | Options and select the Editing | Editor Settings | Java Editor node.
2. Click the ⬚ button in the Code Folding property.
3. Select the checkbox for any of the code elements that you would like to be folded by default (method, inner class, import, Javadoc comment, or initial comment).

Navigating from the Source Editor

The IDE includes handy shortcuts for navigating among files, different bits of code, and different windows. The more of these shortcuts that you can incorporate into your workflow, the less your fingers will have to stray from your keyboard to your mouse.

Switching Between Open Files

You can switch between open files with the Alt-Left and Alt-Right keyboard shortcuts.

Jumping to Related Code and Documentation

The shortcuts in Table 4-6 enable you to jump to parts of the current file or other files that are relevant to the selected identifier. The first five of these shortcuts are available from the Edit menu and the Go To submenu of the Source Editor's contextual (right-click) menu. The Show Javadoc command is available straight from the Source Editor's contextual menu.

Table 4-6 Java Class Navigation Shortcuts

Command	Shortcut	Description
Go to Source	Alt-O (or Ctrl-click)	Jumps to the source code for the currently selected class, method, or field, if the source is available. You can achieve this either by pressing Alt-O with the identifier selected or by holding down the Ctrl key, hovering the mouse over the identifier until it is underlined in blue, and then clicking it.
Go to Declaration	Alt-G	Jumps to the declaration of the currently selected class, method, or field.
Go to Super Implementation	Ctrl-B	Jumps to the super implementation of the currently selected method (if the selected method overrides a method from another class or is an implementation of a method defined in an interface).
Go to Line	Ctrl-G	Jumps to a specific line number in the current file.
Go to Class	Alt-Shift-O	Enables you to type a class name and then jumps to the source code for that class if it is available to the IDE.
Show Javadoc	Alt-F1	Displays documentation for the selected class in a web browser. For this command to work, Javadoc for the class must be made available to the IDE through the Java Platform Manager (for JDK documentation) or the Library Manager (for documentation for other libraries).

Jumping Between Areas Where You Have Been Working

When you are working on multiple files at once or in different areas of the same file, you can use the "jump list" shortcuts to navigate directly to areas where you have been working instead of scrolling and/or switching windows. The "jump list" is essentially a history of lines where you have done work in the Source Editor.

You can navigate back and forth between jump list locations with the Alt-K (back) and Alt-L (forward) shortcuts. Use Alt-Shift-K and Alt-Shift-L to navigate files in the jump list without stopping at multiple places in a file.

Jumping from the Source Editor to a File's Node

When you are typing in the Source Editor, you can jump to the node that represents the current file in other windows. This can be useful, for example, if you want to navigate quickly to another file in the same package or you want to browse versioning information for the current file.

See Table 4-7 for a list of available shortcuts.

Table 4-7 Shortcuts for Selecting the Current File in a Different Window

Command	Shortcut
Select the node for the current file in the Projects window.	Ctrl-Shift-1
Select the node for the current file in the Files window.	Ctrl-Shift-2
Select the node for the current file in the Favorites window.	Ctrl-Shift-3

Searching and Replacing

There are several types of searches in the IDE for different needs. You can

- Find and replace names of classes, methods, and fields in your project using the Find Usages command
- Find and replace specific character combinations in an open file by pressing Ctrl-F in the file
- Find files that match search criteria based on characters in the file, characters in the filename, file type, date, and/or version control status by right-clicking a folder or project node in the Projects window and choosing Find (or by pressing Ctrl-F)

Finding Occurrences of the Currently Selected Class, Method, or Field Name

When you are working in the Source Editor, you can quickly find out where a given Java identifier is used in your project using the Find Usages command.

Find Usages improves upon a typical Find command by being sensitive to the relevance of text in the Java language context.

The Find Usages command output displays lines in your project that contain

- A declaration of the class, interface, method, or field
- (For classes and interfaces) a declaration of a method or variable of the class or interface
- (For classes and interfaces) a usage of the type, such as at the creation of a new instance, importing a class, extending a class, implementing an interface, casting a type, or throwing an exception
- (For classes and interfaces) a usage of the type's methods or fields
- (For fields) the getting or setting of the field's value
- (For methods) the calling of the method
- (For methods) the overriding of the method
- Comments that reference the identifier

The Find Usages command does not match

- Parts of words
- Words that differ in case

To find occurrences of a specific identifier in your code:

1. In the Source Editor, move the insertion point to the class, method, or field name that you want to find occurrences of.
2. Right-click and choose Find Usages or press Alt-F7.
3. In the Find Usages dialog box, select the types of occurrences that you want displayed and click Next.

The results are displayed in the Usages window (shown in Figure 4-8), which appears in the bottom of the IDE.

You can navigate to a given occurrence of a class, method, or field name by double-clicking the occurrences line in the Usages window.

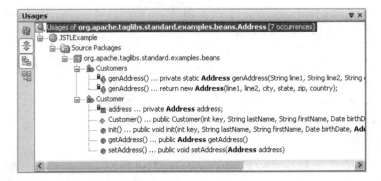

Figure 4-8   Usages window

Renaming All Occurrences of the Currently Selected Class, Method, or Field Name

If you want to rename a class, method, or field, you can use the Refactor | Rename command to update all occurrences of the identifier to the new name.

To rename a class, method, or field name:

1. In the Source Editor, move the insertion point to an occurrence in the code of the class, method, or field name that you want to rename.

2. Right-click and choose Refactor | Rename or press Alt-Shift-R.

3. If you want occurrences of the name in comments to also be changed, check the Apply Name on Comments checkbox in the Rename dialog box.

4. In the Rename dialog box, click Next.

5. In the Refactoring window (shown in Figure 4-9), which appears in the bottom of the IDE, verify the occurrences that are set to change. If there is an occurrence that you do not want to change, deselect that line's checkbox.

6. Click Do Refactoring to enact the changes.

You can initiate the renaming of a class or interface by renaming it inline in the Projects window. After you rename the node, you are prompted with the Rename dialog box to rename other occurrences. You can click Cancel if you do not want other occurrences to be renamed.

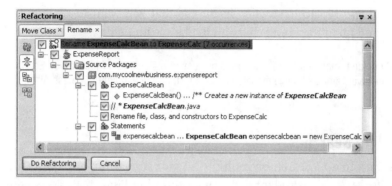

Figure 4-9   Refactoring preview window

Searching and Replacing Combinations of Characters in a File

If you merely want to find a combination of characters in your file, click in the file that you want to search, press Ctrl-F, and type the text that you want to find in the Find dialog box (as shown in Figure 4-10).

You can use a regular expression as your search criterion by selecting the Regular Expressions checkbox.

Unlike the Find Usages command, the Find command allows you to search for parts of words, do case-insensitive searches, and highlight matches in the current file.

Once you have dismissed the Find dialog box, you can jump between occurrences of the search string by pressing F3 (next occurrence) and Shift-F3 (previous occurrence).

To search for other occurrences of the currently selected text or the word surrounding the insertion point, press Ctrl-F3.

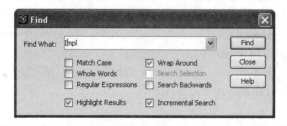

Figure 4-10   Find window for the Source Editor

To search and replace text, click in the file that you want to replace text, press Ctrl-H, and fill in the Find What and Replace With fields.

 By default, matches to a Find command remain highlighted in the Source Editor after you have dismissed the Find dialog box. To turn off the highlighting, press Alt-Shift-H.

Other File Searches

If you want to do a search on multiple files for something other than an occurrence of a specific Java identifier, you can use the Find in Projects command. The Find in Projects command enables you to search files within a given folder or project based on any combination of the following types of criteria:

- Matches to a substring or regular expression on text in the file
- Matches to a substring or regular expression on the filename
- Dates the files were modified
- File type
- Version control status (for files that are kept under version control and in a folder that is registered in the IDE's Versioning Manager)

To initiate such a file search, do one of the following:

- In the Projects window, right-click the node for the folder or project that you want to search in and choose Find (or press Ctrl-F).
- Choose Edit | Find in Projects to search for files in all open projects.
- Right-click a folder in the Files window and choose Find. If you choose Find this way, the project metadata, including the build script and the contents of the nbproject folder, are also searched.

After you enter the criteria in the Find in Projects dialog box (shown in Figure 4-11) and click Search, the results are displayed in the Search Results window with nodes for each matched file. For full-text searches, these nodes can be expanded to reveal the individual lines where matched text occurs. You can double-click a match to open that file in the Source Editor (and, in the case of full-text matches, jump to the line of the match).

Figure 4-11   Find in Projects dialog box

 The dialog box that appears when you press Ctrl-F or choose Edit | Find (or Edit | Find in Projects) depends on which IDE window has focus. If you have the Source Editor selected, the Find dialog box for an individual file appears. If you have a node selected in the Projects window (or one of the other tree-view windows), the dialog box for searching in multiple files is opened.

Moving a Class to a Different Package

If you want to place a class in a different package, you can use the IDE's refactoring features to update references to that class automatically throughout your project.

To move a class:

1. In the Projects window, drag the class from its current package to the package you want to place it in. (You can also use the Cut and Paste commands in the contextual menus or the corresponding keyboard shortcuts.)

2. In the Refactor Code for Moved Class dialog box (shown in Figure 4-12), click Next after verifying that the To Package and This Class fields reflect the destination package and the class that you are moving. (If you move multiple classes, a List of Classes text area is shown instead of the This Class field.)

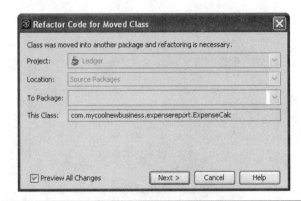

Figure 4-12   Refactor Code for Moved Classes dialog box

3. In the Refactoring window (shown in Figure 4-13), look at the preview of the code to be changed. If there is a modification that you do not want to be made, deselect the checkbox next to the line for that change.

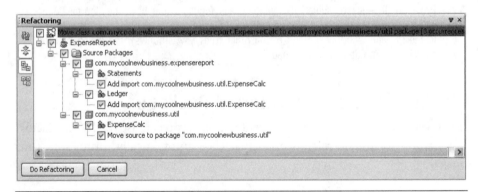

Figure 4-13   Refactoring window

4. Click Do Refactoring.

   If you find that the refactoring has had some consequences that you would like to reverse, you can choose Refactor | Undo.

You can also do an in-place rename of a package in the Projects window to initiate a Move Class refactoring. However, you cannot do an inline rename of a folder in the Files window.

Changing a Method's Signature

If you want to change a method's signature, you can use the IDE's Refactor | Change Method Parameters command to update other code in your project that uses that method. Specifically, you can

- Add parameters
- Change the order of parameters
- Change the access modifier for the method

You cannot use the Change Method Parameters command to remove a parameter from a method. If you remove a parameter from a method, you have to update any code that references that method manually.

To change a method's signature:

1. Right-click the method in the Source Editor or the Projects window and choose Refactor | Change Method Parameters.
2. Click Add if you want to add parameters to the method. Then edit the Name, Type, and (optionally) the Default Value cells for the parameter. You have to double-click a cell to make it editable.
3. To switch the order of parameters, select a parameter in the Parameters table and click Move Up or Move Down.
4. Select the preferred access modifier from the Visibility Modifier combo box.
5. Click Next.
6. In the Refactoring window, look at the preview of the code to be changed. If there is a modification that you do not want to be made, deselect the checkbox next to the line for that change.
7. Click Do Refactoring.

   If you find that the refactoring has had some consequences that you would like to reverse, you can choose Refactor | Undo.

Refactoring Commands

NetBeans IDE has special support for refactoring code. The term *refactoring* refers to renaming and rearranging code without changing what the code does. Reasons for refactoring include things such as the need to separate API from implementation, making code easier to read, and making code easier to reuse.

The IDE's refactoring support makes refactoring easier by enabling you to update all of the code in your project automatically to reflect changes that you make in other parts of your project.

For example, if you rename a class, references to that class in other classes are also updated.

You can access most refactoring commands from the Refactor menu on the main menu bar or by right-clicking in the Source Editor or on a class node in the Projects window and choosing from the Refactor submenu. The Find Usages command is in the Edit menu and the contextual (right-click) menu for the Source Editor and the Projects window.

Typically, the currently selected identifier is filled in as the code element to be refactored.

Table 4-8 provides a summary of the refactoring commands that are available. These commands are explained more thoroughly in task-specific topics throughout this chapter.

Table 4-8 Refactoring Commands

Command	Description
Rename	Renames all occurrences of the selected class, interface, method, or field name. See Renaming All Occurrences of the Currently Selected Class, Method, or Field Name on page 98.
Change Method Parameters	Enables you to change the parameters and the access modifier for the given method. See Changing a Method's Signature on page 103.
Encapsulate Fields	Generates accessor methods (getters and setters) for a field. See Generating Read/Write Properties on page 79.
Move Class	Moves a class to a different package and updates all references to that class with the new package name. See Moving a Class to a Different Package on page 101.
Find Usages	Displays all occurrences of the name of a given class, method, or field. See Finding Occurrences of the Currently Selected Class, Method, or Field Name on page 96.

Tracking Notes to Yourself in Your Code

The IDE has a task list feature that provides a way for you to write notes in your code and then view all of these notes in a single task (or "to do") list. You can use the task list as the center of operations when cleaning up loose ends in your code.

A line is displayed in the task list if it is "tagged" with (contains) any of the following text:

- @todo
- TODO
- FIXME
- XXX
- PENDING
- <<<<<<<

 When you type a tag in your code, it must be typed as a whole word for the IDE to recognize it. For example, if you do not put a space between the tag and the note, the note will not appear in the task list.

To view the task list, choose Window | To Do (or press Ctrl-6).

Once you have displayed the To Do window (shown in Figure 4-14), you can view tasks for the current file, for all open files, or for a specific folder by clicking the corresponding button at the top of the To Do window.

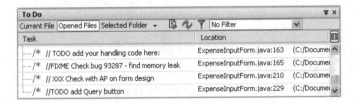

Figure 4-14   To Do window

You can sort task-list items by task, location, or priority by clicking the corresponding column titles. See Displaying Tasks by Priority on page 106 for information on displaying the Priority column.

You can jump from an entry in the task list straight to the line in the code where you wrote the note by double-clicking the entry.

Adding, Removing, and Changing Task-List Tags

To change the tags that are used for the task list:

1. Choose Tools | Options and select the Editing | To Do Settings node.
2. Click the ⬚ button in the Task Tags property.
3. In the To Do Settings dialog box, use the Add, Change, and Delete buttons to modify the contents of the Task List table.

Displaying Tasks by Priority

You can also display priorities for each task-list item. The available priorities are High, Medium-High, Medium, Medium-Low, and Low.

By default, the Priority column is not displayed. You can display the Priority column by clicking the ⊞ icon and selecting the Priority checkbox in the Change Visible Columns dialog box.

The priority values can be assigned by tag. By default, all tags are assigned Medium priority except the <<<<<<< tag, which is given High priority.

To change a priority value for a tag:

1. Choose Tools | Options and select the Editing | To Do Settings node.
2. Click the ⬚ button in the Task Tags property.
3. In the To Do Settings dialog box, select the new priority in the combo box in the Priority column for the tag that you want to change.

Filtering Task-List Entries

You can further limit the entries displayed in the task list by creating and using filters. When you use a filter, only entries that match criteria specified by the filter are displayed. Criteria include text that needs to appear in the note, the priority of the task, and/or the filename.

To create a filter:

1. Click the ▼ icon in the To Do window's toolbar.

2. In the Edit Filters dialog box, click the New button and then type a name for the filter in the Name field.

3. Fill in the details for the criterion.

4. Optionally, add additional criteria by clicking the More button and then filling in the details for the filters. You can select to have the filter match all or any of the criteria using the radio buttons at the top of the dialog box.

An entry for the newly defined filter appears in a combo box in the To Do Window toolbar.

Comparing Differences Between Two Files

You can generate a side-by-side comparison of two files with the differing lines highlighted. To compare two files, select the nodes for the two files in the Projects window and choose Tools | Diff.

The "diff" appears as a tab in the Source Editor.

 The Diff command appears in the Tools menu only when two (and no more than two) files are selected in the Projects, Files, or Favorites window.

Splitting the Source Editor

You can split the Source Editor to view two files simultaneously or to view different parts of the same file.

To split the Source Editor window:

1. Make sure at least two files are already open.

2. Click a tab on one file; hold down the mouse button; and drag the tab to the far left, far right, or bottom of the Source Editor window.

3. Release the mouse button when the red outline that appeared around the tab when you started dragging has changed to a rectangle indicating the placement of the split window.

To view different parts of the same file simultaneously:

1. Click the file's tab in the Source Editor and choose Clone Document to create a second tab for the same document.

2. Drag and drop one of the file tabs to create a split Source Editor area. (See the procedure above for info on dragging and dropping Source Editor tabs.)

Maximizing Space for the Source Editor

There are a number of things you can do to make more space for your code in the IDE, such as:

- Maximize a file in the Source Editor within the IDE by double-clicking that file's tab. When you do this, the file takes the entire space of the IDE except for the main menu and row of toolbars. You can make the other windows reappear as they were by double-clicking the tab again.

- Make other windows "sliding" so that they appear only when you click or mouse over a button representing that window on one of the edges of the IDE. You can make a window sliding by clicking its ◀▋ icon. You can return the window to its normal display by clicking the ▣ button within the sliding window. See Managing IDE Windows in Chapter 2 for information on working with windows in the IDE.

- Hide the IDE's toolbars. You can hide the main toolbars by choosing View | Toolbars and then individually choosing the toolbars that you want to hide. You can hide the Source Editor's toolbar by right-clicking in the Source Editor's left margin and choosing Show Toolbar.

Changing Source Editor Keyboard Shortcuts

You can change existing keyboard shortcuts or map other available commands to shortcuts. To change keyboard shortcuts for the Source Editor:

1. Choose Tools | Options and select the Editing | Editor Settings node.

2. Click the ⬚ button in the Global Key Bindings property to open the Global Key Bindings dialog box.

3. Select a key binding that you want to change, click Add, and type the short-cut that you want to use.

It is also possible to add keyboard shortcuts for specific file types. In the Options window, expand the Editor Settings node and select the node for the editor of the type of file you want to add a shortcut for. Click the button in the Key Bindings property to open the Key Bindings dialog box for that editor type.

The different editor types inherit shortcuts from the global level, and it is not possible to override these global shortcuts for a specific editor type.

You can modify noneditor keyboard shortcuts by choosing Tools | Keyboard Shortcuts and adding and/or deleting keyboard shortcuts there.

Some key combinations, such as those for clipboard and other common operations, are assigned as shortcuts in both the Source Editor and outside of the Source Editor. For example, Ctrl-F invokes a different Find dialog box, depending on whether you have a file selected in the Source Editor or a folder node selected in the Projects window.

If you change such a keyboard shortcut for the Source Editor, it will not affect the keyboard shortcut for other parts of the IDE, and vice versa.

Building Rich Clients

NetBeans IDE provides a number of tools for creating "rich" Java clients using Java Foundation Classes (JFC or "Swing") and AWT packages. These tools include:

- **Form Editor.** Provides both Design and Source views for you to create visual components. The Design view is an area where you can drag, drop, and rearrange the visual components that make up the user interface of the client you are building. The Source view contains the generated source code for the class you are designing and also allows you to enter your own code for the class.

- **Inspector window.** Provides a tree view of all of the components in the form, whether visual (such as menus, text fields, labels, and buttons) or nonvisual (such as button groups and data sources). You can drag and drop components in these windows between different containers, which is useful if the components that you drag from the Palette window to the Form Editor are not placed in the proper container. You can also add components directly through this window by right-clicking a container's node and choosing from the Add From Palette menu. This window appears in the same space as the Navigator window.

- **Palette window.** Provides a list of components that you can drag and drop onto your form.

- **Properties window.** Contains a list of editable properties for the selected component and access to special property editors for the more complex properties.

- **Connection Wizard.** Helps you create event listener and event handler code that links two components.

- **Form Tester.** Quickly displays a runtime view of the form under construction, allowing checks of resizing and other behavior.

- **Palette Manager.** Enables you to add custom components to the Palette window. Choose Tools | Palette Manager to open this window.

The Form Editor, Inspector window, Palette window, and Properties window are shown in Figure 4-15. You can access the Connection Wizard, Form Tester, and Palette Manager from buttons in the toolbar area of the Form Editor.

This section does not provide a complete guide to developing visual applications with Swing in NetBeans IDE; a whole book could be devoted to that. Instead, it

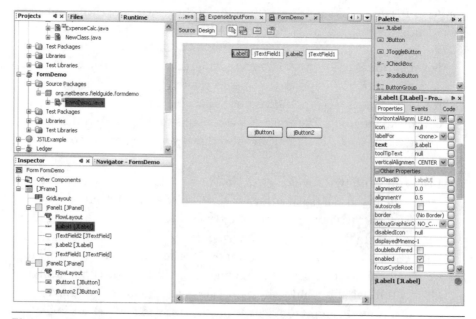

Figure 4-15 Form Editor windows, including the Inspector, Form Editor (Design View), Palette window, and Properties window

focuses on a few of the unique but somewhat tricky features of Swing and the IDE that assist in the designing of visual applications.

Layout Managers

One of the most important decisions you make when you start designing a form concerns which layout manager (or layout managers) to use in your form.

NetBeans IDE provides full support for the standard Swing layout managers:

- FlowLayout
- BorderLayout
- GridLayout
- GridBagLayout
- CardLayout
- BoxLayout (note that the "struts" and "glue" normally used with BoxLayout are not provided as out-of-the-box components)

In addition, support for forms without a layout manager (NullLayout) and forms with absolutely positioned components (AbsoluteLayout) is provided. Neither of these is recommended for production use, as their behavior across platforms or when resizing is unlikely to be acceptable.

Of these layouts, GridBagLayout is far and away the most powerful but suffers from bad press as being difficult to use. Fortunately, NetBeans IDE provides a clever tool—the customizer—to tame GridBagLayout to the point where you might well find it's the most commonly used layout in your forms.

 One of the ways in which AbsoluteLayout can be used is to lay out a form quickly, followed by changing the layout to GridBagLayout: The IDE converts the form, and then you can tweak the GridBagLayout to provide the final result. Unfortunately, this is not as useful as it might be; the conversion often introduces large offsets for the components, and massaging these into an acceptable state is often as much work as creating the layout from scratch.

Designing a Form with GridBagLayout

The IDE's GridBagLayout customizer (shown in Figure 4-16) provides extra support for fine-tuning the placement of components within the layout and adjustment of the constraints. You can drag components around the grid and modify constraints with buttons that are built into the same view.

To use the customizer:

1. Add the required components to your form by dragging and dropping those components from the Palette window to the Form Editor.

2. Set GridBagLayout as your layout manager by right-clicking the container's node (for example, that of a JFrame or JPanel component) in the Inspector window and choosing Set Layout | GridBagLayout.

3. Open the customizer by again right-clicking the container's node and choosing Customize Layout. The GridBagLayout Customizer window opens (see Figure 4-16).

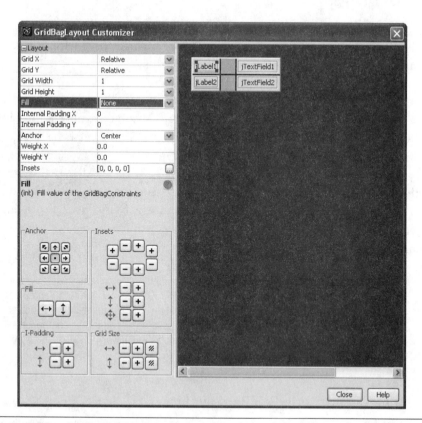

Figure 4-16   GridBagLayout Customizer window

4. Establish the relative positions you desire between the components by dragging them around the design area in the right pane.

5. Adjust the constraints for individual components. For each component, select the component in the right pane and modify the constraints in the left pane, either using the property sheet or the buttons in the bottom-left portion of the dialog box.

The following constraints can be individually adjusted for each component:

- **Grid X and Grid Y.** The grid position to be occupied by the component. Grid positions are numbered from top left, zero-based.
- **Grid Width and Grid Height.** Specifies how many grid positions are allocated for the component in each direction. Although "remainder" and "relative" can be specified, generally specifying an absolute position is easier to maintain.
- **Fill.** Specifies whether the component uses all of the vertical or horizontal space (or both) that is allocated to it.
- **Internal Padding X and Y.** Increases the size of the component, in pixels.
- **Anchor.** Places the component in one of nine positions within the space allocated to it (Center, North, North-West, and so on). Note that this setting has no effect if there is no free space remaining for the component.
- **Weight X and Weight Y.** Determines how much space a component should be given relative to other components in its row or column when the container window is resized. Components with larger weight values get more space allocated in their row or column when the window is resized. For example, if each of two components in a row has a "Weight X" of 1, they will equally share any increase in row width. One the other hand, if one has a "Weight X" of 1 and the other has 0.5, the first will get two-thirds of any increase and the second will get one-third. Note that specifying a weight has effect only if Fill is specified for the component in the appropriate direction.
- **Insets.** Determines the minimum amount of external space—in pixels—on each of the four sides of the component.

Limitations of GridBagLayout

If GridBagLayout is so powerful, why would one use anything else? Two reasons: limitations and convenience. A major limitation of GridBagLayout is that it has no mechanism to force two columns or rows to have the same size. GridLayout can be used to overcome this—see the example below—although only if the rows or columns are adjacent. If your form has this problem, consider using the jGoodies Forms layout (http://www.jgoodies.com/freeware/forms/).

Convenience also plays a part: Often, the container you're designing just naturally fits with, say, BorderLayout. Or perhaps the ease of use of FlowLayout works well with your container.

> The IDE makes it easy to use different layouts for different containers. A container nested in a form can be designed independently by right-clicking the container node in the Inspector window and choosing Design This Container. To return to working on the whole form, right-click the container node again and choose Design Top Container. This can also be helpful with highly nested forms to enable drag-and-drop placement of components within a specific container. Note that adding a component to a container can also be accomplished by right-clicking the container node and choosing Add from Palette.

An Example Using GridBagLayout

A relatively simple form that provides a bit of complexity in its layout is shown in Figure 4-17. Aspects that require special attention:

- The Options and Available Options columns should have the same width, with the Remove and Add buttons centered under them.
- The Sort Descending and Case Sensitive checkboxes should be centered under the Options column.
- The OK/Cancel/Help button bar should stay bottom-right under the Available Options column if the form is resized.

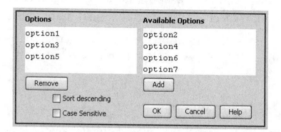

Figure 4-17   GridBagLayout example

The Inspector window for this form is shown in Figure 4-18. Notice that the panel bothOptionsColumnsPanel has GridLayout specified, to ensure that our first constraint is satisfied.

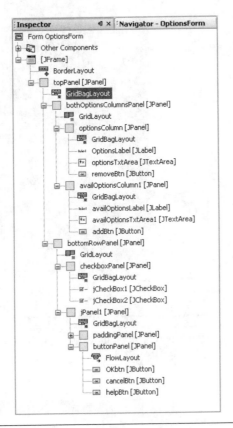

Figure 4-18   Inspector window

The panels optionsColumn and availOptionsColumn are similarly laid out with GridBagLayout, with the two JTextAreas having Fill and Weights of 1 in both directions: for an example, see the Customizer detail in Figure 4-19.

The final bit of tailoring is to add a padding panel—containing no components—to force the button bar down to the bottom of jPanel7. Note that in the customizer view of jPanel7 in Figure 4-20, the empty panel has been given a weight of 1 in both directions: in this case, only the Weight Y value is actually required.

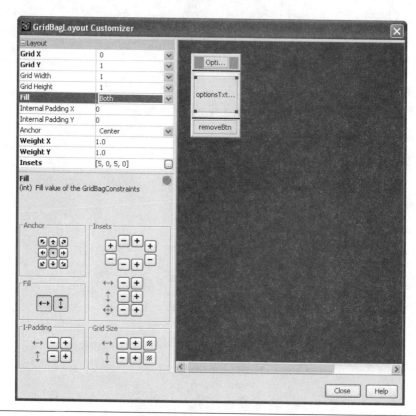

Figure 4-19 GridBagLayout Customizer window with the example components as they appear when the customizer is opened

Figure 4-20 Layout section of GridBagLayout Customizer window showing padding panel

Specifying Component Behavior and Appearance

You can use the Properties window to set the behavior and appearance of components that you have added to a form. The Properties window displays the properties of the component that is selected in the Inspector or the Form Editor. The properties come in three categories:

- Properties—a configurable list of characteristics for the component. Technically speaking, these are the JavaBeans properties for the component.
- Events—a list of event listeners that you can attach to a component. You can specify event listeners here (or remove them here) or use the Connection Wizard. See Generating Event Listening and Handling Methods later in this chapter.
- Code—some NetBeans IDE-specific properties that you can use to customize the way the code is generated. See Customizing Generated Code later in this chapter.

To edit component properties:

1. Select the property category by clicking the appropriate button at the top of the Properties window (Properties, Events, or Code).
2. Edit the component's properties in the Properties window by selecting the property and entering the desired value.
3. If a property has a [...] button, you can click it to open a special property editor that enables you to modify the property and the initialization code generated for it.
4. In the property editor, use the Select Mode combo box to choose each custom editor for the property and make the necessary changes.

For some components, the key property is listed in bold in the Properties window. For example, the model property for the JTable and JList components is marked in bold.

Generating Event Listening and Handling Methods

The IDE relieves you of the task of providing the infrastructure required around event handling by generating the code to link the occurrence of the event with the invocation of a private method in the form class. For example, a JButton named myBtn might have the code:

```
myBtn.addActionListener(new java.awt.event.ActionListener() {
    public void actionPerformed(java.awt.event.ActionEvent evt) {
        myBtnActionPerformed(evt);
    }
```

added to its initialization, where the method `myBtnActionPerformed` is generated as:

```
private void myBtnActionPerformed(java.awt.event.ActionEvent evt) {
    // TODO add your handling code here:
}
```

Comments—generated or otherwise—within your Java code that start with "TODO" have special significance. To see a list of your "TODO" lines, display the "TODO" window via Window ToDo or press Ctrl-6. From the displayed window, you can navigate to the source line with the TODO with a double-click in the TODO window. See Tracking Notes to Yourself in Your Code earlier in this chapter for more information.

Generation of this event infrastructure code can be done in a couple of different ways:

■ By right-clicking the component and choosing the event to be handled from the Events menu.

The IDE generates the event handler and positions the cursor to the appropriate TODO line in the generated private method for completion of the event handling code.

■ By using the Connection Wizard to generate code for the case when an event on a component should result in the modification of another component.

To use the Connection Wizard:

1. Enter "connection mode" by clicking the ⊞ icon in the Form Editor's toolbar.

2. Open the Connection Wizard by clicking successively on the two components—first the component that will fire the event and then the component upon which an operation is to be performed.

3. In the Select Source Event page of the wizard (shown in Figure 4-21), select the event to be fired.

4. In the Specify Target Operation page (shown in Figure 4-22), specify the operation to be performed on the target component. You can specify a property to set, call a method, or write your own custom code.

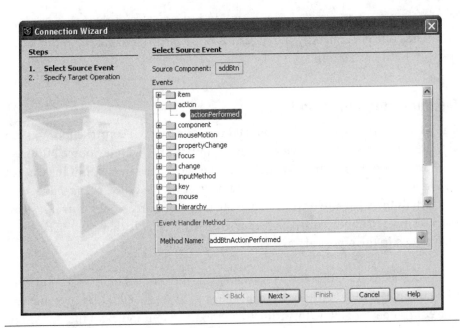

Figure 4-21   Connection Wizard, Select Source Event page

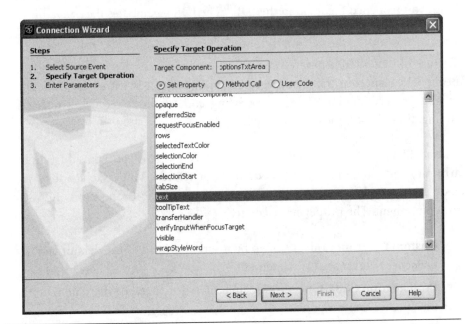

Figure 4-22   Connection Wizard, Specify Target Operation page

The Connection Wizard approach is simply a "point and click" approach to the task. The code generated by the wizard is not guarded and can be modified in the editor after generation.

Customizing Generated Code

The NetBeans IDE dynamically generates the code for GUI construction. You can view this code in the Source view of the Form Editor (click the Source button in the Form Editor's toolbar). In addition to the code generated within the class in its *class-name*.java file, the IDE maintains an XML file called *class-name*.form that details the structure of the form. Note that the source-code control systems (such as CVS) supported by NetBeans ensure by default that the .form file is maintained in the repository as well as the .java file.

The generated code within the .java source file is delimited by special comments (for example, //GEN-BEGIN:initComponents ... //GEN-END:initComponents). The editor does not allow this code to be modified and indicates the unmodifiable code with a pale blue background. Although you could modify this code outside the IDE, it is not recommended, because those modifications would be lost if you reopened the form in the IDE. (The IDE regenerates the .java file of a form created in the IDE from the .form files each time you open the file in the IDE.)

The use of delimited generated code prompted vigorous discussion in the NetBeans IDE team, but the advantages are significant: It is extremely difficult to reliably "reverse-engineer" arbitrary Swing code without requiring restrictive coding discipline on the developer's part.

Instead of this, NetBeans IDE provides "hooks" where you can add (almost) arbitrary code to be part of the code to be generated. This code is added via a code-aware window accessed from the Code tab of the Properties window for the component. The properties used are:

- **Custom Creation Code.** Code to be inserted instead of the default new *ComponentClassName*(); statement.
- **Pre-Creation Code.** One or more lines of code to precede the statement that instantiates the component.
- **Post-Creation Code.** One or more lines of code to follow the statement that instantiates the component.

- **Pre-Init Code.** One or more lines of code to precede the first statement that initializes the properties of the component.
- **Post-Init Code.** One or more lines of code to follow the last statement that initializes the properties of the component.

In addition, the initial values of the various properties of components can be specified in various ways:

- A static value.
- A property from a component written to the JavaBeans architecture.
- A property of another component on the form.
- A call to a method of the form or one of its components. You can choose from a list of methods that return the appropriate data type.
- Code you define, which will be included in the generated code.

CHAPTER 5

Debugging Java Applications

NETBEANS IDE PROVIDES A RICH ENVIRONMENT for troubleshooting and optimizing your applications. Built-in debugging support allows you to step through your code incrementally and monitor aspects of the running application, such as values of variables, the current sequence of method calls, the status of different threads, and the creation of objects.

When using the IDE's debugger, there is no reason for you to litter your code with `System.out.println` statements to diagnose any problems that occur in your application. Instead, you can use the debugger to designate points of interest in your code with breakpoints (which are stored in the IDE, not in your code), pause your program at those breakpoints, and use the various debugging windows to evaluate the state of the running program.

In addition, you can change code while debugging and dynamically reload the class in the debugger without having to restart the debugging session.

Following are some of the things that you can do within the IDE's debugger:

- Step through application code line by line.
- Step through JDK source code.
- Execute specific chunks of code (using breakpoints as delimiters).
- Suspend execution when a condition that you have specified is met (such as when an iterator reaches a certain value).
- Suspend execution at an exception, either at the line of code that causes the exception or in the exception itself.
- Track the value of a variable or expression.
- Track the object referenced by a variable (fixed watch).
- Fix code on the fly and continue the debugging session with the Apply Code Changes command.
- Suspend threads individually or collectively.
- Step back to the beginning of a previously called method (pop a call) in the current call stack.
- Run multiple debugging sessions at the same time. For example, you might need this capability to debug a client-server application.

Starting a Debugging Session

The simplest way to start using the debugger is to choose Run | Step Into. The program counter (marked by green background highlighting and the ⇨ icon, as shown in Figure 5-1) stops one line into the main method of your main project.

```
import java.awt.Toolkit;
import java.awt.event.ActionListener;
import java.awt.event.WindowListener;
import javax.swing.JFrame;

/**
 * Main window of the Anagram Game application.
 */
public class Anagrams extends JFrame {

    public static void main(String[] args) {
        new Anagrams().setVisible(true);
    }

    private int wordIdx = 0;

    /** Creates new form Anagrams */
    public Anagrams() {
        initComponents();
```

Figure 5-1   A suspended program with the green program counter showing the next line to be executed

You can then step through your code incrementally with any of the Step commands to observe the program flow and monitor the evolving values of variables in the Local Variables window. See Stepping Through Code later in this chapter for a description of all of the Step commands and the ensuing topics for information on how to take advantage of the debugger's capabilities.

You can also use the Run to Cursor command to start a debugging session. In the Source Editor, click in the line where you want execution to suspend initially and choose Run | Run to Cursor. This command works for starting a debugging session only if you select a line of code in the project's main class or a class directly called by the main class in the main project.

More likely, you will want to start stepping through code at some point after the start of the main method. In this case, you can specify some point in the program where you want to suspend the debugged execution initially and then start the debugger. To do this:

1. Set a line breakpoint in your main project by opening a class in the Source Editor and clicking in the left margin next to the line where you want to set the breakpoint (or by pressing Ctrl-F8).

   You know that the breakpoint has been set when the pink ▣ glyph appears in the margin and the line has pink background highlighting (as shown in Figure 5-2).

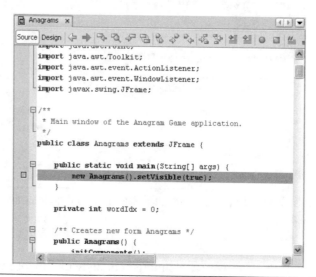

Figure 5-2   Code in the Source Editor with a debugger breakpoint set

2. Press F5 to start debugging the main project.

When the execution of the program stops at the breakpoint (which you can see when the pink breakpoint highlight is replaced by the green highlight of the program counter), you can step through the code line by line while viewing the status of variables, threads, and other information.

See the ensuing topics for details on stepping and viewing program information.

If you have set up a free-form project, you need to do some extra configuration to get the debugging commands to work. See Chapter 12 for more details.

Debugger Windows

When you start debugging a program, the Debugger Console appears as a tab in the lower-left corner of the IDE (as shown in Figure 5-3). The Debugger Console logs the execution status of the debugged program (such as whether the code is stopped at a breakpoint). In addition, a tab opens in the Output window to log any application output (as well the output from the Ant build script the IDE uses when running the command).

In the lower-right corner, several windows (Watches, Local Variables, and Call Stack) open as tabs and provide current information on the debugging session, such as the current values of variables and a list of current method calls. You can also open individual debugging windows by choosing them from the Windows | Debugging menu.

Most of the windows display values according to the debugger's current *context*. In general, the current context corresponds to one method call in one thread in one session. You can change the context (for example, designate a different current thread in the Threads window) without affecting the way the debugged program runs.

See Table 5-1 for a list of all of the windows available and how to open them.

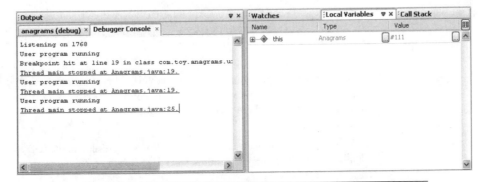

Figure 5-3 Windows that appear when you start debugging in the IDE, including the Debugger Console, and windows for Watches, Local Variables, and the Call Stack

Table 5-1   Debugger Windows

Debugger Window	Open With	Description
Local Variables	Alt-Shift-1 (or Window | Debugging | Local Variables)	Displays all fields and local variables in the debugger's current context and their current values. Fields are listed under the `this` node.
Watches	Alt-Shift-2 (or Window | Debugging | Watches)	Displays the names of fields, local variables, or expressions that you have placed a watch on. Though all of your watches are displayed no matter the current context, the value displayed is the value for that context (not for the context that the watch was set in). For example, if you have a watch on the `this` keyword, the `this` referred to in the Watches window will always correspond to the object referred to from the current method call.
Call Stack	Alt-Shift-3 (or Window | Debugging | Call Stack)	Displays all method calls in the current chain of calls. The Call Stack window enables you to jump directly to code of a method call, back up the program's execution to a previous method call, or select a context for viewing local variable values.
Classes	Alt-Shift-4 (or Window | Debugging | Classes)	Provides a tree view of classes for the currently debugged application grouped by classloader.
Breakpoints	Alt-Shift-5 (or Window | Debugging | Breakpoints)	Displays all breakpoints that you have set in all running debugging sessions.
Threads	Alt-Shift-6 (or Window | Debugging | Threads)	Displays the threads in the current session. In this window, you can switch the context by designating another thread as the current thread.
Sessions	Alt-Shift-7 (or Window | Debugging | Sessions)	Displays a node for each debugging session in the IDE. From this window, you can switch the current session.
Sources	Alt-Shift-8 (or Window | Debugging | Sources)	Displays sources that are available for debugging and enables you to specify which ones to use. For example, you can use this window to enable debugging with JDK sources.

Attaching the Debugger to a Running Application

If you need to debug an application that is running on another machine or is running in a different virtual machine, you can attach the IDE's debugger to that application:

1. Start in debug mode the application that you are going to debug. This entails adding some special arguments to the script that launches the application.

   For Windows users using a Sun JDK, the argument list might look like the following (all in one line and no space after -Xrunjdwp:):

   ```
   java -Xdebug -Xnoagent -Djava.compiler=NONE
   -Xrunjdwp:transport=dt_shmem,server=y,address=MyAppName,suspend=n
   -classpath C:\my_apps\classes mypackage.MyApp
   ```

   On other operating systems (or on a Windows machine when you are debugging an application running on a different machine), the argument list might look something like the following:

   ```
   java -Xdebug -Xnoagent -Djava.compiler=NONE
   -Xrunjdwp:transport=dt_socket,server=y,address=8888,suspend=n
   -classpath HOME/my_apps/classes mypackage.MyApp
   ```

   See Table 5-2 for a key to these options. For more complete documentation of the options, visit http://java.sun.com/products/jpda/doc/conninv.html.

2. In the IDE, open the project that contains the source code for the application to be debugged.

3. Choose Run | Attach Debugger.

4. In the Attach dialog box, select the connector from the Connector combo box.

   Choose SharedMemoryAttach if you want to attach to an application that has been started with the dt_shem transport. Choose SocketAttach if you want to attach to an application that has been started with the dt_socket transport.

   See the Connector row of Table 5-3 for information on the different types of connectors.

5. Fill in the rest of the fields. The fields that appear after Connector depend upon the kind of connector that you have selected. See Table 5-3 for a key to the different fields.

Table 5-2 Debugger Launch Parameters

Launch Parameter or Subparameter	Description
-Xdebug	Enables the application to be debugged.
-Xnoagent	Disables the sun.tools.debug agent so that the JPDA debugger can properly attach its own agent.
-Djava.compiler=NONE	Disables the JIT (Just-In-Time) compiler.
-Xrunjdwp	Loads the reference implementation of the Java Debug Wire Protocol, which enables remote debugging.
transport	Name of the transport to be used when debugging the application. The value can be dt_shmem (for a shared memory connection) or dt_socket (for a socket connection). Shared memory connections are available only on Windows machines.
server	If this value equals n, the application attempts to attach to the debugger at the address specified in the address subparameter. If this value equals y, the application listens for a connection at this address.
address	For socket connections, specifies a port number used for communication between the debugger and the application. For shared memory connections, specifies a name that refers to the shared memory to be used. This name can consist of any combination of characters that are valid in filenames on a Windows machine except the backslash. You use this name in the Name field of the Attach dialog box when you attach the debugger to the running application.
suspend	If the value is n, the application starts immediately. If the value is y, the application waits until a debugger has attached to it before executing.

Table 5-3 Attach Dialog Box Fields

Field	Description
Connector	Specifies the type of JPDA connector to use. On Windows machines, you can choose between shared memory connectors and socket connectors. On other systems, you can only use a socket connector. For both shared memory connectors and socket connectors, there are Attach and Listen variants. You can use an Attach connector to attach to a running application. You can use a Listen connector if you want the running application to initiate the connection to the debugger. If you use the Listen connector, multiple applications running on different JVMs can connect to the debugger.

(continued)

Field	Description
Transport	Specifies the JPDA transport protocol to use. This field is automatically filled in according to what you have selected in the Connector field.
Host	(Only for socket attach connections.) The host name of the computer where the debugged application is running.
Port	(Only for socket connections.) The port number that the application attaches to or listens on. You can assign a port number in the address subparameter of the Xrunjdwp parameter that you pass to the JVM of the application that is to be debugged. If you do not use this suboption, a port number is assigned automatically, and you can determine the assigned port number by looking at the output of the process.
Timeout	The number of seconds that the debugger waits for a connection to be established.
Name	(Only for shared memory connections.) Specifies the shared memory to be used for the debugging session. This value must correspond to the value of the address subparameter of the Xrunjdwp parameter that you pass to the JVM of the application that is to be debugged.
Local Address	(Only for socket listen connections.) The host name of the computer that you are running on.

Starting the Debugger Outside of the Project's Main Class

If you have multiple executable classes in your project, there might be times when you want to start the debugger from a class different from the one that is specified as the project's main class.

To start the debugger on a class other than the project's main class, right-click the file's node in the Projects window or Files window and choose Debug File.

You can start the debugger on a file only if it has a main method.

Stepping Through Code

Once execution of your program is paused, you have several ways of resuming execution of the code. You can step through code line by line (Step In) or in greater increments. See Table 5-4 for the commands available for stepping or continuing execution and the following subtopics for a task-based look at the commands.

Table 5-4   Debugger Step Commands

Step Command	Description
Step Into (F7)	Executes the current line. If the line is a call to a method or constructor, and there is source available for the called code, the program counter moves to the declaration of the method or constructor. Otherwise, the program counter moves to the next line in the file.
Step Over (F8)	Executes the current line and moves the program counter to the next line in the file. If the executed line is a call to a method or constructor, the code in the method or constructor is also executed.
Step Out Of (Alt-Shift-F7)	Executes the rest of the code in the current method or constructor and moves the program counter to the line after the caller of the method or constructor. This command is useful if you have stepped into a method that you do not need to analyze.
Run to Cursor (F4)	Executes all of the lines in the program between the current line and the insertion point in the Source Editor.
Pause	Stops all threads in the current session.
Continue (Ctrl-F5)	Resumes execution of the program until the next breakpoint.

Executing Code Line by Line

You can have the debugger step a line at a time by choosing Run | Step Into (F7). If you use the Step Into command on a method call, the debugger enters the method and pauses at the first line, unless the method is part of a library that you have not specified for use in the debugger. See Stepping into the JDK and Other Libraries later in this chapter for details on making sources available for use in the debugger.

Executing a Method without Stepping into It

You can execute a method without having the debugger pause within the method by choosing Run | Step Over (F8). After you use the Step Over command, the debugger pauses again at the line after the method call.

Resuming Execution Through the End of a Method

If you have stepped into a method that you do not need to continue analyzing, you can have the debugger complete execution of the method and then pause again at the line after the method call.

To complete execution of a method in this way, choose Run | Step Out Of (Alt-Shift-F7).

Continuing to the Next Breakpoint

If you do not need to observe every line of code while you are debugging, you can continue execution until the next breakpoint or until execution is otherwise suspended.

To continue execution of a program that has been suspended at a breakpoint, choose Run | Continue or press Ctrl-F5.

Continuing to the Cursor Position

When execution is suspended, you can continue to a specific line without setting a breakpoint by placing the cursor in that line and choosing Run | Run to Cursor (F4).

Stepping into the JDK and Other Libraries

When you are debugging, you can step into the code for the JDK and any other libraries if you have the source code that is associated with them registered in the IDE's Library Manager. See Making External Sources and Javadoc Available in the IDE in Chapter 3 for information on associating source code with a library.

By default, the IDE does not step into JDK sources when you are debugging. If you use the Step In command on a JDK method call, the IDE executes the method and returns the program counter to the line after the method call (as though you used the Step Over command).

To enable stepping into JDK sources for a debugged application:

1. Start the debugger for the application.
2. Open the Sources window (shown in Figure 5-4) by choosing Window | Debugging | Sources or by pressing Alt-Shift-8.
3. Select the Use for Debugging checkbox for the JDK.

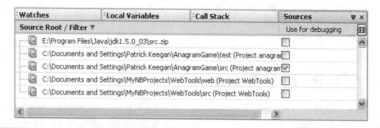

Figure 5-4   Sources window

Limiting the Classes That You Can Step into for a Library

If you are using a library for debugging, you can set a filter to exclude some of the sources from being used.

To exclude classes from being used in the debugger:

1. Start the debugger for the application.
2. Open the Sources window by choosing Window | Debugging | Sources or by pressing Alt-Shift-8.
3. Right-click the line for the library that you want to create an exclusion filter for and choose Add Class Exclusion Filter.
4. Type a filter in the Add Class Exclusion Filter dialog box.

The filter can be

- A fully qualified class name.
- A package name or class name with an asterisk (*) at the end to create a wildcard. For example, you could type the following to exclude all classes in the javax.swing package: javax.swing.*
- An expression with a wildcard at the beginning. For example, to exclude all classes that have Test at the end of their names, you could use: *Test

You can create multiple class exclusion filters.

To disable the filter, deselect the Use in Debugging checkbox next to the filter in the Sources window.

To delete a class exclusion filter, right-click the filter and choose Delete.

Setting Breakpoints

A *breakpoint* is a marker that you can set to specify where execution should pause when you are running your application in the IDE's debugger. Breakpoints are stored in the IDE (not in your application's code) and persist between debugging sessions and IDE sessions.

When execution pauses on a breakpoint, the line where execution has paused is highlighted in green in the Source Editor, and a message is printed in the Debugger Console with information on the breakpoint that has been reached.

In their simplest form, breakpoints provide a way for you to pause the running program at a specific point so that you can

- Monitor the values of variables at that point in the program's execution.
- Take control of program execution by stepping through code line by line or method by method.

However, you can also use breakpoints as a diagnostic tool to do things such as:

- Detect when the value of a field or local variable is changed (which, for example, could help you determine what part of code assigned an inappropriate value to a field).
- Detect when an object is created (which might, for example, be useful when trying to track down a memory leak).

You can set multiple breakpoints, and you can set different types of breakpoints. The simplest kind of breakpoint is a line breakpoint, where execution of the program stops at a specific line. You can also set breakpoints on other situations, such as the calling of a method, the throwing of an exception, or the changing of a variable's value. In addition, you can set conditions in some types of breakpoints so that they suspend execution of the program only under specific circumstances. See Table 5-5 for a summary of the types of breakpoints.

Setting a Line Breakpoint

To set a line breakpoint, click the left margin of the line where you want to set the breakpoint or click in the line and press Ctrl-F8.

Table 5-5 Breakpoint Categories

Breakpoint Type	Description
Line	Set on a line of code. When the debugger reaches that line, it stops before executing the line. The breakpoint is marked by pink background highlighting and the ▣ icon. You can also specify conditions for line breakpoints.
Class	Execution is suspended when the class is referenced from another class and before any lines of the class with the breakpoint are executed.
Exception	Execution is suspended when an exception occurs. You can specify whether execution stops on caught exceptions, uncaught exceptions, or both.
Method	Execution is suspended when the method is called.
Variable	Execution is suspended when the variable is accessed. You can also configure the breakpoint to have execution suspended only when the variable is modified.
Thread	Execution is suspended whenever a thread is started or terminated. You can also set the breakpoint on the thread's death (or both the start and death of the thread).

To delete the breakpoint, click the left margin of the line or click in the line and press Ctrl-F8.

If you want to customize a line breakpoint, you can do so through the Breakpoints window. Choose Window | Debugging | Breakpoints or press Alt-Shift-5. In the Breakpoints window, right-click the breakpoint and choose Customize.

Setting a Breakpoint on a Class Call

You can set a breakpoint on a class so that the debugger pauses when code from the class is about to be accessed and/or when the class is unloaded from memory.

To set a breakpoint on a class:

1. Choose Run | New Breakpoint (Ctrl-Shift-F8).

2. In the New Breakpoint dialog box, select Class from the Breakpoint Type combo box.

3. Enter the class and package names. These fields should be filled in automatically with the class currently displayed in the Source Editor.

You can specify multiple classes for the breakpoint to apply to, either by using wildcards in the Package Name and Class Name fields or by selecting the Exclusion Filter checkbox.

Use the asterisk to create wildcards in the Package Name and Class Name fields if you want the breakpoint to apply to multiple classes or all classes in a package. For example, if you enter just an asterisk (*) in the Class Name field, the breakpoint will apply to all classes in the package specified in the Package Name field.

Use the Exclusion Filter checkbox if you want the breakpoint to apply to all classes (including JDK classes) except for the ones that match the classes or packages specified in the Package Name and Class Name fields. You can set multiple breakpoints with the Exclusion Filter on. For example, you might set an exclusion filter on `com.mydomain.mypackage.mylib.*` because you want the class breakpoint to apply to all of your classes except those in the package `mylib`. However, if you do not want the debugger to pause at the loading of each JDK class that is called, you could also set a class breakpoint with an exclusion filter on `java.*`.

Setting a Breakpoint on a Method or Constructor Call

You can set a breakpoint so that the debugger pauses when a method or constructor is called before any lines of the method or constructor are executed.

To set a breakpoint on a method or constructor:

1. Choose Run | New Breakpoint (Ctrl-Shift-8).
2. In the New Breakpoint dialog box, select Method from the Breakpoint Type combo box.
3. Enter the class, package, and method names. These fields are filled in automatically according to the class open in the Source Editor and the location of the insertion point.

You can make the breakpoint apply to all methods and constructors in the class by checking the All Methods for Given Classes checkbox.

Setting a Breakpoint on an Exception

You can set a breakpoint so that the debugger pauses when an exception is thrown in your program.

To set a breakpoint on an exception:

1. Choose Run | New Breakpoint (Ctrl-Shift-F8).

2. In the New Breakpoint dialog box, select Exception from the Breakpoint Type combo box.

3. In the Exception Class Name field, select the type of exception that you would like to set the breakpoint on.

4. In the Stop On combo box, select whether you want the breakpoint to apply to caught exceptions, uncaught exceptions, or both.

Setting a Breakpoint on a Field or Local Variable

You can set a breakpoint so that the debugger pauses when a field or variable is accessed (or only when the field or variable is modified).

To set a breakpoint on a field or variable:

1. Choose Run | New Breakpoint (Ctrl-Shift-F8).

2. In the New Breakpoint dialog box, select Variable from the Breakpoint Type combo box.

3. Fill in the Package Name, Class Name, and Field Name fields.

4. Select an option from the Stop On combo box.

   If you select Variable Access, execution is suspended every time that field or variable is accessed in the code.

   If you select Variable Modification, execution is suspended only if the field or variable is modified.

 Most of the fields of the New Breakpoint dialog box are correctly filled in for you if you have the variable selected when you press Ctrl-Shift-F8. You might have to select (highlight) the whole variable name for this to work. Otherwise, information for the method that contains the variable might be filled in instead.

Setting a Breakpoint on the Start or Death of a Thread

You can monitor the creation or death of threads in your program by setting a breakpoint to have execution suspended every time a new thread is created or ended.

To set a breakpoint on threads:

1. Choose Run | New Breakpoint (Ctrl-Shift-F8).

2. In the New Breakpoint dialog box, select Thread from the Breakpoint Type combo box.

3. In the Set Breakpoint On field, select Thread Start, Thread Death, or Thread Start or Death.

Managing Breakpoints

You can use the Breakpoints window, shown in Figure 5-5, to manage breakpoints in one place. You can put breakpoints in groups, temporarily disable breakpoints, and provide customizations to the breakpoints from this window. To open the Breakpoints window, choose Window | Debugging | Breakpoints or press Alt-Shift-5.

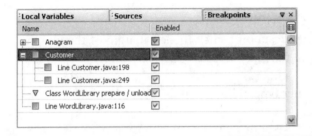

Figure 5-5   Breakpoints window

Grouping Related Breakpoints

In some cases, you might have several related breakpoints that you would like to be able to enable, disable, or delete together. Or maybe you merely want to consolidate some breakpoints under one node to make the Breakpoints window less cluttered.

To group some breakpoints:

1. Open the Breakpoints window by choosing Window | Debugging | Breakpoints (Alt-Shift-5).

2. Shift-click or Ctrl-click to select the breakpoints that you want to group. Then right-click the selection and choose Set Group Name.

3. The breakpoints are grouped under an expandable node.

Enabling and Disabling Breakpoints

You might find it useful to keep breakpoints set throughout your application, but you might not want to have all of the breakpoints active at all times. If this is the case, you can disable a breakpoint or breakpoint group and preserve it for later use.

To disable a breakpoint or breakpoint group:

1. Open the Breakpoints window by choosing Window | Debugging | Breakpoints (Alt-Shift-5).
2. In the Breakpoints window, right-click the breakpoint or breakpoint group and choose Disable.

Deleting a Breakpoint

To delete a line breakpoint, click the left margin of the line that has the breakpoint or click in the line and press Ctrl-F8.

To delete another type of breakpoint:

1. Open the Breakpoints window by choosing Window | Debugging | Breakpoints (Alt-Shift-5).
2. In the Breakpoints window, right-click the breakpoint and choose Delete.

Customizing Breakpoint Behavior

There are a number of things that you can do to customize when a breakpoint is hit and what happens in the IDE when a breakpoint is hit. The following subtopics cover some of those things.

Logging Breakpoints without Suspending Execution

If you would like to monitor when a breakpoint is hit without suspending execution each time the breakpoint is hit, you can configure the breakpoint so that it does not cause suspension of execution. When such a breakpoint is hit in the code, a message is printed in the Debugger Console window.

To turn off suspension of execution when a breakpoint is hit:

1. Open the Breakpoints window by choosing Window | Debugging | Breakpoints (Alt-Shift-5).

2. In the Breakpoints window, double-click the breakpoint to open the Customize Breakpoint window. (For line breakpoints, right-click the breakpoint and choose Customize.)

3. In the Action combo box, select No Thread (Continue).

Customizing Console Messages When Breakpoints Are Hit

You can customize the text that is printed to the console when a breakpoint is hit in your code.

To customize the console message that is printed when a breakpoint is reached:

1. Open the Breakpoints window by choosing Window | Debugging | Breakpoints (Alt-Shift-5).

2. In the Breakpoints window, double-click the breakpoint to open the Customize Breakpoint window. (For line breakpoints, right-click the breakpoint and choose Customize.)

3. In the Print Text combo box, modify the text that you want printed.

To make the printed text more meaningful, you can use some substitution codes to have things like the thread name and the line number printed. See Table 5-6 for a list of the substitution codes available.

Table 5-6   Substitution Codes for Breakpoint Console Text

Substitution Code	Prints
{className}	The name of the class where the breakpoint is hit. This code does not work for thread breakpoints.
{lineNumber}	The line number at which execution is suspended. This code does not work for thread breakpoints.
{methodName}	The method in which execution is suspended. This code does not work for thread breakpoints.

(continued)

Table 5-6 Substitution Codes for Breakpoint Console Text (*Continued*)

Substitution Code	Prints
{threadName}	The thread in which the breakpoint is hit.
{variableValue}	The value of the variable (for breakpoints set on variables) or the value of the exception (for exception breakpoints).
{variableType}	The variable type (for breakpoints set on variables) or the exception type (for exception breakpoints).

Making Breakpoints Conditional

You can set up a breakpoint to suspend execution of the code only if a certain condition is met. For example, if you have a long For loop, and you want to see what happens just before the loop finishes, you can make the breakpoint contingent on the iterator's reaching a certain value.

Here are some examples of conditions you can place upon a breakpoint:

- i==4 (which means that the execution will stop on the breakpoint only if the variable i equals 4 in the current scope)
- *ObjectVariable*!=null (which means that execution will not stop at the breakpoint until *ObjectVariable* is assigned a value)
- *MethodName* (where *Method* has a Boolean return type and execution will stop at the breakpoint only if Method returns true)
- *CollectionX*.contains(*ObjectX*) (which means that execution will stop at the breakpoint only if *ObjectX* is in the collection)

To make a breakpoint conditional:

1. Open the Breakpoints window by pressing Alt-Shift-5.
2. In the Breakpoints window, right-click the breakpoint that you want to place a condition on and choose Customize.
3. In the Customize Breakpoint dialog box, fill in the Condition field with the condition that needs to be satisfied for execution to be suspended at the breakpoint.

Conditional breakpoints are marked with the ⬛ icon.

Monitoring Variables and Expressions

As you step through a program, you can monitor the running values of fields and local variables in the following ways:

- By holding the cursor over an identifier in the Source Editor to display a tool-tip containing the value of the identifier in the current debugging context.
- By monitoring the values of variables and fields displayed in the Local Variables window.
- By setting a watch for an identifier or other expression and monitoring its value in the Watches window.

The Local Variables window (shown in Figure 5-6) displays all variables that are currently in scope in the current execution context of the program, and provides and lists their types and values. If the value of the variable is an object reference, the value is given with the pound sign (#) and a number that serves as an identifier of the object's instance. You can jump to the source code for a variable by double-clicking the variable name.

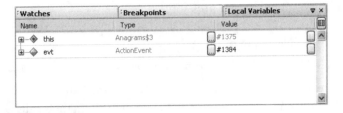

Figure 5-6   Local Variables window

You can also create a more custom view of variables and expressions by setting watches and viewing them in the Watches window.

The Watches window (Alt-Shift-2), shown in Figure 5-7, is distinct from the Local Variables window in the following ways:

- The Watches window shows values for variables or expressions that you specify, which keeps the window uncluttered.
- The Watches window displays all watches that you have set, whether or not the variables are in context. If the variable exists separately in different contexts,

the value given in the watches window applies to the value in the current context (not necessarily the context in which the watch was set).

▪ Watches persist across debugging sessions.

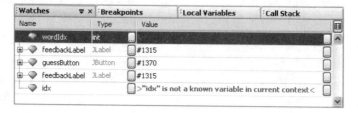

Figure 5-7   Watches window

Setting a Watch on a Variable, Field, or Other Expression

To set a watch on an identifier such as a variable or field, right-click the variable or field in the Source Editor and choose New Watch. The identifier is then added to the Watches window.

To create a watch for another expression:

1. Choose Run | New Watch.
2. In the New Watch dialog box, type an expression that you want evaluated.

   The expression must be written in Java syntax and can include local variables, fields of the current object, static fields, and method calls.

   You can even create an instance of an object and call one of its methods. When doing so, be sure to refer to the class by its fully qualified name.

Monitoring the Object Assigned to a Variable

You can create a so-called *fixed watch* to monitor an object that is assigned to a variable (rather than the value of the variable itself).

To create a fixed watch:

1. After starting a debugging session, open the Local Variables window (Alt-Shift-1).

2. Right-click the variable that you would like to set the fixed watch for and choose Create Fixed Watch.

A fixed watch is added to the Watches window with an ◆ icon. Because a fixed watch applies to a specific object instance created during the debugging session, the fixed watch is removed when the debugging session is finished.

Displaying the Value of a Class's toString() Method

You can add a column to the Local Variables and Watches windows to display the results of an object's toString() method. Doing so provides a way to get more useful information (such as the values of currently assigned fields) on an object than the numeric identifier of the object's instance that the Value column provides.

To display the toString() column in one of those windows:

1. Open the Local Variables window (Alt-Shift-1) or the Watches window (Alt-Shift-2).
2. Click the ▦ button in the upper-right corner of the window.
3. In the Change Visible Columns dialog box, select the toString() checkbox.

 If you do not see the toString() column appear initially, try narrowing the width of the Value column to provide room for the toString() column to appear.

Changing Values of Variables or Expressions

As you debug a program, you can change the value of a variable or expression that is displayed in the Local Variables or Watches window. For example, you might increase the value of an iterator to get to the end of a loop faster.

To change the value of a variable:

1. Open the Watches window or the Local Variables window.
2. In the Value field of the variable or expression, type the new value and press Enter.

Displaying Variables from Previous Method Calls

The Call Stack window displays all of the calls within the current chain of method calls. If you would like to view the status of variables at another call in the chain, you can open the Call Stack window (Alt-Shift-3), right-click the method's node, and choose Make Current.

Making a different method current does not change the location of the program counter. If you continue execution with one of the step commands or the Continue command, the program will resume from where execution was suspended.

Backing Up from a Method to Its Call

Under some circumstances, it might be useful for you to step back in your code. For example, if you hit a breakpoint and would like to see how the code leading up to that breakpoint works, you can remove *(pop)* the current call from the call stack to re-execute the method.

You can open the Call Stack window to view all of the method calls within the current chain of method calls in the current thread. The current call is marked with the ■ icon. Other calls in the stack are marked with the □ icon.

To back up to a previous method call:

1. Open the Call Stack window (Alt-Shift-3).
2. Right-click the line in the Call Stack window that represents the place in the code that you want to return to and choose Pop to Here.

   The program counter returns to the line where the call was made. You can then re-execute the method.

 When you pop a call, the effects of the previously executed code are not undone, so re-executing the code might cause the program to behave differently than it would during normal execution.

Monitoring and Controlling Execution of Threads

The IDE's Threads window (Alt-Shift-7), shown in Figure 5-8, enables you to view the status of threads in the currently debugged program. It also enables you to change the thread that is being monitored in other debugger windows (such as

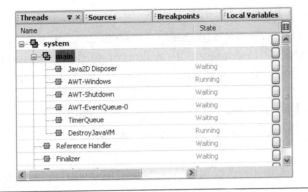

Figure 5-8   Threads window

Call Stack and Local Variables) and to suspend individual threads. See Table 5-7 for a guide to the icons used in the Threads window.

Table 5-7   Key to Icons in the Threads Window

	Currently monitored thread
	Currently monitored thread group
	Running thread
	Suspended thread
	Thread group

Changing the current thread does not affect the way the program executes.

Switching the Currently Monitored Thread

The contents of the Call Stack and Local Variables windows are dependent on the thread being currently monitored in the debugger (otherwise known as the *current thread*). To switch the currently monitored thread:

1. Open the Threads window by pressing Alt-Shift-7.
2. Right-click the thread that you want to monitor and choose Make Current.

Suspending a Single Thread

By default, when your program hits a breakpoint, all threads are suspended. However, you can also configure a breakpoint so that only its thread is suspended when the breakpoint is hit:

1. Open the Breakpoints window by pressing Alt-Shift-5.

2. In the Breakpoints window, right-click the breakpoint and choose Customize.

3. In the Customize Breakpoint dialog box, select Current from the Suspend combo box.

Isolating Debugging to a Single Thread

By default, all threads in the application are executed in the debugger. If you would like to isolate the debugging so that only one thread is run in the debugger:

1. Make sure that the thread that you want debugged is designated as the current thread in the Threads window (Alt-Shift-7). The current thread is marked with the ▣ icon.

2. Open the Sessions window by pressing Alt-Shift-6.

3. In the Sessions window, right-click the session's node and choose Scope | Debug Current Thread.

Fixing Code During a Debugging Session

Using the IDE's Apply Code Changes feature (called Fix in NetBeans IDE 4.0), it is possible to fine-tune code in the middle of a debugging session and continue debugging without starting a new debugging session. This can save you a lot of time that would otherwise be spent waiting for sources to be rebuilt and restarting your debugging session.

The Apply Code Changes feature is useful for situations such as when you need to:

▪ Fine-tune the appearance of a visual component that you have created.

▪ Change the logic within a method.

Applying code changes does not work if you do any of the following during the debugging session:

- Add or remove methods or fields.
- Change the access modifiers of a class, field, or method.
- Refactor the class hierarchy.
- Change code that has not yet been loaded into the virtual machine.

To use the Apply Code Changes command while debugging:

1. When execution is suspended during a debugging session, make whatever code changes are necessary in the Source Editor.
2. Choose Run | Apply Code Changes to recompile the file and make the recompiled class available to the debugger.
3. Load the fixed code into the debugger.

   If you are changing the current method, this is done automatically. The method is automatically "popped" from the call stack, meaning that the program counter returns to the line where the method is called. Then you can run the changed code by stepping back into the method (F7) or stepping over the method (F8).

   For a UI element, such as a JDialog component, you can close the component (or the component's container) and then reopen it to load the fixed code in the debugger.
4. Repeat steps 1 to 3 as necessary.

Viewing Multiple Debugger Windows Simultaneously

By default, the debugger's windows appear in a tabbed area in the lower-right corner of the IDE in which only one of the tabs is viewable at a time. If you want to view multiple debugger windows simultaneously, you can use drag-and-drop to split a tab into its own window or to move the tab into a different window (such as the window occupied by the Debugger Console). You can also drag the splitter between windows to change the size of each window.

To create a separate window area for a debugger tab, drag the window's tab to one side of the current window until a red outline for the location of the new window appears. Then release the mouse button. See Figures 5-9, 5-10, and 5-11 for snapshots of the process.

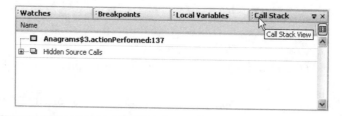

Figure 5-9   Call Stack window before moving it by dragging its tab to the left and dropping it in the lower left corner of the screen

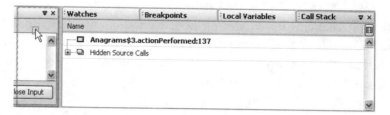

Figure 5-10   Call Stack window and the outlined area to the left where it is to be dropped

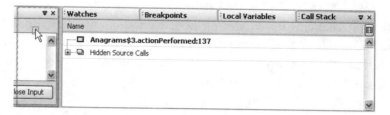

Figure 5-11   Call Stack after it has been moved to the new window area

## CHAPTER 6

Developing Web Applications

- Representation of Web Applications in the IDE
- Adding Files and Libraries to Your Web Application
- Editing and Refactoring Web Application Files
- Deploying a Web Application
- Testing and Debugging Your Web Application
- Creating and Deploying Applets
- Changing the IDE's Default Web Browser
- Monitoring HTTP Transactions

NETBEANS IDE IS AN IDEAL ENVIRONMENT FOR DEVELOPING web applications. The IDE eliminates a lot of the nuisances you normally would encounter, particularly in setting up the application and in the steps between coding, deploying, debugging, and redeploying your application. And because Ant is the basis for this automation, there are no proprietary mysteries you need to unravel if you want to make the project work without the IDE as an intermediary.

Following are some of the things the IDE does to make web application development easier:

- Provides a built-in Tomcat web server on which to deploy, test, and debug your applications.
- Sets up the file and folder structure of a web application for you.
- Generates and maintains the content of deployment descriptors, including the registering of any servlets that you add to your project.
- Generates and maintains an Ant script with targets (commands) for compiling, cleaning, testing, WAR file creation, and deployment to a server. This script saves you from having to move files manually to the web server.
- Ensures that the configuration files that appear in the WEB-INF folder of your application are not deleted when you run the Clean command to remove results of previous builds.
- Provides syntax highlighting; code completion; and other aids for editing servlet, JSP, HTML, and tag library files.
- Provides the Compile JSP command, which enables you to detect syntax errors in JSP files before deploying to your server, whether the errors occur at compile time or during the translation of the JSP file into a servlet.
- Provides comprehensive debugging support, which includes stepping into JSP files and tracking HTTP requests.

This chapter focuses on issues specific to web applications—creating and editing web components, debugging HTTP transactions, and so on—but does not include information on project creation. See Chapter 3 for information on creating projects.

Most of the topics in this chapter assume that you are using the Tomcat web server, but it is also possible to use the Sun Java System Application Server

(SJSAS), which supports full J2EE applications and includes full support for web services. Most of the tasks detailed here that involve the Tomcat server are very similar to the equivalent tasks you would perform if deploying to SJSAS. See Chapter 10 for more information on working with the Sun Java System Application Server and Chapter 9 for information on developing, exposing, and consuming web services.

Representation of Web Applications in the IDE

Web applications are based on a somewhat intricate architecture where the development-time layout of files differs from that of a built application. The IDE helps you manage this process by:

- Providing a development-time-oriented view of your project in the Projects window. This view gives you easy access to your sources and information about your classpath but hides build results and project metadata. Perhaps more importantly, working in the Projects window ensures that none of the files you create will be inadvertently deleted when you run the Clean command on your project (as could happen, for example, if you worked directly in the WEB-INF folder of a built application).

- Providing a file-oriented view of your project in the Files window. This window is particularly useful for accessing and customizing your build script and for browsing your project outputs, such as the project's WAR file and its contents.

- Creating and maintaining an Ant script, which is used when you run typical commands such as Build Project and Run Project. Among other things, the Ant script automates the placement of your files in the built application, the packaging of those files into a WAR file, and deployment to the specified server.

Project View of Web Applications

The Projects window provides a "logical" representation of the application's source structure, with nodes for the following:

- Web Pages (for HTML, JSP, and image files that users of the application will have direct access to through their web browsers)

- Source Packages (for Java source packages, which in turn contain servlets and other Java classes)

- Test Packages (for unit tests)

- Configuration Files (for your deployment descriptor and other files)

- Web Services (where you can create and register web services; see Chapter 9 for more on development of web services)

- Libraries (where you can add libraries or include the results of other IDE projects)

- Test Libraries (where you can add any libraries necessary for running unit tests on your application)

File View of Web Applications

If you open the Files window, you will see the physical organization of the files on disk (as shown in Figure 6-1). The IDE also adds the nbproject (to hold project metadata) and test (for unit tests) folders, but these are not included in the final built application.

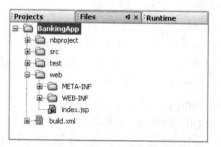

Figure 6-1   Files window with web application folder structure

When you build the application, either through the IDE or by directly running an Ant target, a build folder is created to hold the compiled classes, and the dist folder is created to hold the generated WAR file, as shown in Figure 6-2.

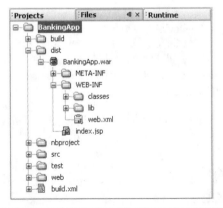

Figure 6-2   Files window showing the structure of the built WAR file

Web Application Structure

Apache Jakarta provides guidelines on how to structure your web applications to ensure that they work properly with the Tomcat server. When you create a project in the IDE and select the Jakarta source structure, this structure is respected. (Similarly, you can set up a project to use the Java BluePrints structure, which is preferred if you will be deploying to the Sun Java System Application Server.)

The following is a quick rundown on the important structural elements of the built application according to the Jakarta guidelines:

- The root folder (known as the document base), which contains all of the other files in folders in the application.
- Files that are directly available to the users of the application through their web browsers, such as HTML files, images, and JSP files.
- The WEB-INF folder, which contains the deployment descriptor file (web.xml) and the classes, lib, tags, and other folders and files. The contents of WEB-INF comprise the bulk of the application and are not directly available to users.
- The classes folder contains compiled class and servlet files with their package hierarchy reflected by subfolders.

You can find additional information on Tomcat source structure at http://jakarta.apache. org/tomcat/tomcat-5.0-doc/appdev/source.html.

You can also use the Java BluePrints structure for web applications. This structure is designed primarily with enterprise applications in mind, so it is useful if you plan to extend your web applications later to include Enterprise JavaBeans components. For web applications, the main practical difference between the Java BluePrints and Apache Jakarta guidelines is in file layout. For example, under the Java BluePrints guidelines, the src folder contains a java folder, which holds the source packages, and a conf folder, which contains the manifest.

You can find more information about Java BluePrints at http://java.sun.com/blueprints/code/projectconventions.html.

See Table 6-1 for information on how the various source elements of a web application map to their representation in the IDE and where they end up in the deployed application.

Table 6-1 Matrix of Web Application Elements (Using the Apache Jakarta Structure) and Their Representation in the IDE

Content	Representation in the Projects Window	Representation in the Files Window	Location Within the Built WAR File (Located in the dist Folder)
web pages	Web Pages node	web folder	root of the file
Java source files, servlets, and so on	Source Packages node	src folder	WEB-INF/classes folder
unit tests	Test Packages node	test folder	N/A
deployment descriptor (web.xml)	Configuration Files node	web/WEB-INF folder	WEB-INF folder
Tomcat context configuration file (context.xml)	Configuration Files node	web/META-INF folder	META-INF folder
libraries	Libraries node	web/WEB-INF/lib folder	WEB-INF/lib folder
Test classpath entries	Test Libraries node	test folder	N/A
project metadata including build script	Project Properties dialog box, which you can open by right-clicking the project's node and choosing Properties.	build.xml file, nbproject folder	N/A

Adding Files and Libraries to Your Web Application

Once you have created a web project through the New Project wizard, you can start populating it with web pages and code.

The most straightforward way to create files is by opening the Projects window, right-clicking the project's node or the specific folder where you want to place the file, and choosing New and then a template from the submenu (see Figure 6-3). A short wizard appears for the template, enabling you to set the name and other characteristics of the file. In general, the wizard guides you to help make sure that the files are placed in an appropriate directory to fit the structure of a well-designed web application.

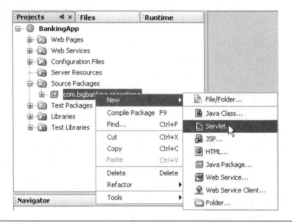

Figure 6-3   Creating a new servlet from a package's contextual menu

The New submenu of a node's contextual menu directly displays a selection of commonly used templates. If you want to see the full selection, choose New | File/Folder.

The templates are grouped into several categories, such as Java Classes, Web, and Database. In addition to servlet and JSP file templates, the Web category contains templates for filters, web application listeners, tag files, and tag handlers, which contain useful sample code for those specific types of files.

Conceptually, files in a web application break down into a few different types of files, the function of which determines where you place the file in the application. The main types of files that you need to add to the project are

- Web pages and other public files, meaning files that users of the application can access directly through their web browsers. Typically, these include JSP files, HTML files, and image files.

- Private files, meaning files that are not directly viewable to the end users and that typically do the bulk of the processing in the application. These include Java classes, JSP files, servlets, and tag libraries, and end up within the web/ WEB-INF/classes folder of the compiled web application.

- External resources, files created outside of the project that the files in the project depend on. These can include tag libraries, JAR files that are output from other IDE projects, and other JAR files, and are kept within the WEB-INF/lib folder of the compiled web application.

In addition, there are configuration files such as the deployment descriptor (web.xml) and files specific to the server you are deploying to, but the IDE generates and maintains these files for you. For example, if you create a servlet in the IDE, the servlet is registered in the web.xml file automatically.

 Tag libraries can be added to your web application as libraries or as source. See Adding Tags and Tag Libraries later in this chapter for more information on working with tag libraries.

Creating Web Pages and Other Public Files

Generally, you add web pages and other public files directly within the Web Pages node of the Projects window or in a folder of your creation within that node. When the application is built, these files are placed by the project's Ant script in the application's web folder.

To add a publicly viewable HTML file, right-click the Web Pages node and choose New | HTML.

To add a publicly viewable JSP file, right-click the Web Pages node and choose New | JSP. The ensuing wizard enables you to specify whether the JSP file uses standard syntax (and has the .jsp extension) or uses XML syntax (has the .jspx extension). You can also have the file created as a fragment (using the .jspf extension), which you would later reference from other pages with include statements.

Creating Classes, Servlets, and Other Private Files

As with general Java projects, classes are organized within packages under the Source Packages node. For most projects, this node corresponds with a folder on your disk called `src`. When the application is built, these files are placed by the Ant script in the application's WEB-INF/classes directory.

To add a class to your project, right-click the Source Packages node or the node of a specific package and choose New | Java Class. If you have not created a package for the class you are adding, you can do so in the wizard as you are creating the class.

To add a servlet to your project, right-click the Source Packages node or the node of a specific package and choose New | Servlet. The wizard for creating the servlet also guides you through registering the servlet in the application's deployment descriptor (`web.xml` file).

If you would like to add a file based on a more specific template, right-click a package node and choose New | File/Folder to get a broader list of templates, including some for JavaBeans components, `.properties` files, XML files, and specialized web components. Note that many of the web templates have useful skeleton code and suggestions within the comments to get you started developing these kinds of objects.

See Table 6-2 for a list of templates that you can find in the Web category of the New File wizard.

Table 6-2 Web Templates

Template	Description
JSP	Enables you to create a JSP file (standard syntax), JSP document (XML syntax), or a JSP fragment (which would be statically referenced from another file).
Servlet	Creates a Java class that extends the `HttpServlet` class. Also enables you to register the servlet in the project's deployment descriptor (`web.xml`) file.
Filter	Creates a Java class that implements the `javax.servlet.Filter` interface. Filters enable you to modify HTTP requests to a servlet and responses from the servlet. In the wizard, you can create either a basic filter or one that wraps the `ServletRequest` and `ServletResponse` objects.
	In the template's wizard, you can register the filter in the project's deployment descriptor (`web.xml`) file.

(continued)

Table 6-2   Web Templates (*Continued*)

Template	Description
Web Application Listener	Creates a Java class that implements one or more of the listener interfaces available for servlets, such as ServletContextListener and HttpSessionListener. Depending on the interfaces you select in the wizard, the created class will listen for events, such as when servlet contexts are initialized or destroyed, the servlet session is created or destroyed, or attributes are added to or removed from a context or session. In the template's wizard, you can register the listener in the project's deployment descriptor (web.xml) file.
Tag Library Descriptor	Creates a descriptor for a custom tag library. You can then register tag files and tag handlers in this file manually or when you use the New File wizard to create new tag files and tag handlers.
Tag File	Creates an empty .tag file with comments suggesting JSP syntax elements that you can use to create a custom tag.
Tag Handler	Creates a Java class for custom JSP tags. The template includes code comments with sample code and suggestions for how you might go about creating the custom tags.
HTML	Creates an HTML file with the basic tags entered.
Web Service	Creates a simple web service. See Chapter 9 for more information on extending web applications with web services.
Message Handler	Creates a SOAP-based message handler for web services. See Adding Message Handlers to a Web Service in Chapter 9.
Web Service Client	Creates a web service client based on JSR 109. See Chapter 9 for more information on consuming web services with web applications.

Adding External Resources to Your Project

If your web application needs to be packaged with any libraries, you can add them through the Libraries node. If your project has been set up to work with the Tomcat server, the JSP and servlet libraries are included automatically and listed under a subnode for the Tomcat server.

You can add external resources to your project in one of the following three forms:

▪ An individual folder or JAR file.

▪ A cluster of resources (library). This cluster might include multiple JAR files, sources for the JAR files (which are necessary for code completion or if you want to step through the library's code with the debugger), and Javadoc documentation. You can create such a cluster in the Library Manager (Tools menu).

- The output of another IDE project.

To add an individual folder or JAR file to your project, right-click the Libraries node of your project, choose Add JAR/Folder, and navigate to the folder or JAR file in the file chooser.

To add a cluster of related resources to your project, right-click the Libraries node, choose Add Library, and select the library from the list in the Add Library dialog box. If the library you are looking for is not there, you can add it to the list by choosing Manage Libraries.

 Besides providing a way to cluster resources, the Library Manager makes it easy to access commonly used resources. Even if you do not need to cluster resources, you still might want to add individual resources to the Library Manager to save yourself from having to dig through file choosers to add resources to other projects.

To add the results of another IDE project, right-click the Libraries node of the current project, choose Add Project, and navigate to the project's folder on your disk. In the file chooser, NetBeans IDE project folders are marked with the icon.

 If you want to add a JAR file or the output of a project to the WAR file without making it part of the project's compilation classpath, you can do so through the Packaging node in the Project Properties dialog box. See Customizing Contents of the WAR File later in this chapter.

Adding Tags and Tag Libraries

Tags and tag libraries can be added to a web project in any of the following forms:

- Packaged in a JAR file containing a tag library descriptor file (TLD) and the associated tags, in the form of tag files (using JSP syntax) and/or tag handlers (written in Java). Such tag libraries appear in a web application's WEB-INF/ lib folder or in the server's shared libraries folder. You can add a tag library to a web project through the web project's Libraries node (see Adding External Resources to Your Project on page 160).

If you are developing a tag library from scratch, you can create a Java Library project for that library and then add the library to a web project by right-clicking the web project's Libraries node and choosing Add Project. See Chapter 3 for information on creating Java Library projects.

▪ As tag files (using either standard or document syntax) included in the web application's WEB-INF/tags folder. You can add new tag files to your project by right-clicking the project's node and choosing New | File/Folder and then selecting the Tag File template from the Web category in the wizard.

▪ As a TLD file located in the WEB-INF/tlds folder and tag handlers (written as Java files) within the Source Packages node. You can add new TLD files and tag handlers to your project by right-clicking the project's node and choosing New | File/Folder and then selecting the templates from the Web category in the wizard.

Editing and Refactoring Web Application Files

The IDE's Source Editor provides a lot of features that make the typing and changing of code for various web application components easier. This section goes over a few of the features that are particularly useful for web applications. See Chapter 4 for more information on IDE editing and refactoring features.

Completing Tags

The IDE enables you to have tags and tag attributes completed automatically in JSP, HTML, and XML files. The tag completion feature not only reduces the number of keystrokes that you type, but also provides popup documentation for the possible ways to complete the tag or attribute that you are typing, as shown in Figure 6-4.

Open the tag completion popup by typing the beginning of a tag and pressing Ctrl-spacebar or waiting a second for code completion to kick in automatically. If there is only one way to complete the word you are typing, the end of the word is filled in automatically. If there are multiple ways to complete the tag, a popup list of those possibilities is displayed. You can keep typing to narrow the list or select the text you want, using the mouse or arrow keys.

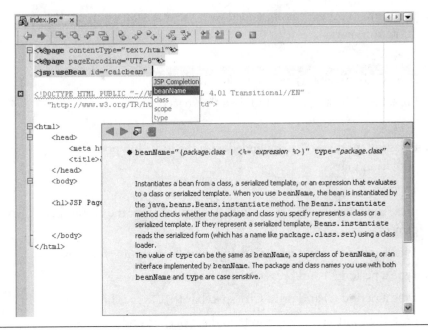

Figure 6-4   The code completion feature in a JSP file

For example, if you want to add the following statement in a JSP file

```
<jsp:useBean id="hello" scope="page" class="org.mydomain.mypackage.MyClass" />
```

you can enter it in the following steps (don't worry—the number of steps illustrated here may seem daunting, but it is only because they are presented in such minute detail):

1. Type `<jsp:u`
2. Press Ctrl-spacebar (`seBean` is appended).
3. Type `i`
4. Press Ctrl-spacebar (`d=""` is appended with the insertion point left between the quotation marks).
5. Type `hello`
6. Press the right-arrow key and then the spacebar.
7. Type `s`

8. Press Enter (`cope=""` is appended with the insertion point left between the quotation marks).

9. Type p

10. Press Ctrl-spacebar (`age` is appended).

11. Press the right-arrow key and then the spacebar.

12. Type c

13. Press Enter (`lass=""` is appended with the insertion point left between the quotation marks).

14. Type o

15. Press Ctrl-spacebar (`rg` is appended, assuming that the class is part of your project).

16. Type a period (.) and press Ctrl-spacebar (`mydomain` is filled in).

17. Type a period (.) and press Ctrl-spacebar (`mypackage` is filled in).

18. Type a period (.) and press Ctrl-spacebar (`MyClass` is filled in).

19. Press the right-arrow key and then the spacebar, and type `/>`.

See Generating Code Snippets in Chapter 4 for information on completing Java expressions and configuring code completion.

Expanding Abbreviations for JSP Files

For commonly used JSP code snippets, you can take advantage of abbreviations in the Source Editor to reduce the number of keystrokes. Abbreviations are expanded when you type the abbreviation and then press the spacebar.

See Table 6-3 for a list of abbreviations for JSP files. You can also expand abbreviations for other types of files. See Chapter 4, Table 4-1, for a list of abbreviations for Java classes.

If an abbreviation is the same as text that you want to type (for example, you do not want it to be expanded into something else), press Shift-spacebar to keep it from expanding.

You can modify the list of abbreviations in the Abbreviations dialog box for a type of file. See Adding, Changing, and Removing Abbreviations in Chapter 4.

Table 6-3 JSP Abbreviations in the Source Editor

Abbreviation	Expands To
ag	application.getValue("
ap	application.putValue("
ar	application.removeValue("
cfgi	config.getInitParameter("
oup	out.print("
oupl	out.println("
pcg	pageContext.getAttribute("
pcgn	pageContext.getAttributeNamesInScope(
pcgs	pageContext.getAttributesScope("
pcr	pageContext.removeAttribute("
pcs	pageContext.setAttribute("
rg	request.getParameter("
sg	session.getValue("
sp	session.putValue("
sr	session.removeValue("
jspf	<jsp:forward page="
jg	<jsp:getProperty name="
jspg	<jsp:getProperty name="
jspi	<jsp:include page="
jspp	<jsp:plugin type="
jsps	<jsp:setProperty name="
jspu	<jsp:useBean id="
pg	<%@ page
pga	<%@ page autoFlush="
pgb	<%@ page buffer="
pgc	<%@ page contentType="
pgerr	<%@ page errorPage="
pgex	<%@ page extends="
pgie	<%@ page isErrorPage="
pgim	<%@ page import="
pgin	<%@ page info="
pgit	<%@ page isThreadSafe="
pgl	<%@ page language="
pgs	<%@ page session="
tglb	<%@ taglib uri="

Editing the Deployment Descriptor Manually

Though the IDE guides you through the adding of entries for the deployment descriptor (web.xml file) as you add servlets, filters, and listeners to your project, you might have occasion to edit the file by hand.

To open the deployment descriptor in the Source Editor, open the Projects window, expand the Configuration Files node (or the Web Pages | Web-INF node), and double-click the web.xml file. The file opens as a multitab document in the Source Editor with the General tab open (as shown in Figure 6-5). You can edit different parts of the web.xml file with the visual editors for different elements of the file (General, Servlets, Filters, and Pages), or you can click the XML tab to edit the file's XML source directly (see Figure 6-6).

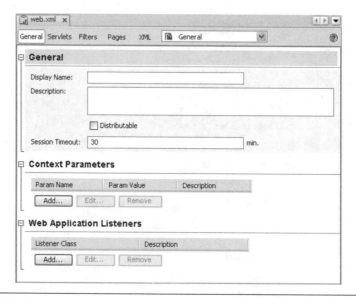

Figure 6-5   Deployment descriptor visual editor

Refactoring Web Components

NetBeans IDE's refactoring support extends to web applications and enterprise applications. For example, you can do the following:

- Rename classes, methods, and fields of servlets, tag handlers, and other web components. See Renaming All Occurrences of the Currently Selected Class, Method, or Field Name in Chapter 4.

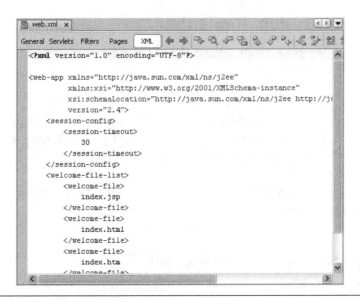

Figure 6-6   Deployment descriptor XML editor

- Move classes to a different package or project (as a result, the class is packaged in a different WAR file). See Moving a Class to a Different Package in Chapter 4.

- Change method parameters, including parameter names, parameter types, and method visibility. You can also add method parameters. See Changing a Method's Signature in Chapter 4.

- Changing visibility of fields and adding getter and setter accessor methods. See Generating Read/Write Properties in Chapter 4.

When you rename a web component class (such as a servlet or tag handler), any corresponding name entries in the application's deployment descriptor (web.xml file) and/or tag library descriptor (TLD) are updated as well. When you move a class and the deployment descriptor is affected, you are prompted with a Confirm Changes dialog box to make sure that you want to process changes to the deployment descriptor.

 Be careful not to rename or change the parameters of a servlet method that must be implemented with a given name according to the Servlet or Enterprise JavaBeans specifications.

Deploying a Web Application

By default, a web application is deployed to the server you have specified when you run that project.

For applications that you deploy to the Tomcat server, the application is deployed *in place,* meaning that the IDE creates an XML file that is placed in the server's `conf/Catalina/localhost/` directory and points Tomcat to the IDE project's `build` directory where the application files reside.

When you build a web project in the IDE, a WAR file is also created, which you can manually deploy to a server.

Customizing Contents of the WAR File

By default, a web project's generated WAR file includes

- All files displayed within the project's Web Pages node, including the `web.xml` and `context.xml` files
- Compiled class files of the source files within the Java Sources node, plus any other files placed there without the `.java` and `.form` file extensions
- Any libraries that you have added to the project's Libraries node

You can also add JAR files to the WAR file and filter out contents that would normally appear.

To customize a WAR file's contents:

1. Right-click the project's node in the Projects window and choose Properties.
2. Select the Build | Packaging node.
3. If you want to filter out contents from the generated WAR file, modify the regular expression in the Exclude from WAR File field.
4. If you want to add folders or files, do so through the Add JAR/Folder, Add Library, or Add Project button.

   The Add JAR/Folder button enables you to add individual JAR files or folders, whether or not they come from IDE projects.

   The Add Library button enables you to add any JAR files or clusters of JAR files that you have designated in the IDE's Library Manager.

The Add Project button enables you to add the JAR file that is output from another IDE project. When you add an IDE project to the WAR file, that project's JAR file is rebuilt every time you build the web application project.

Undeploying a Web Application

When you stop a web application that you have run through the IDE, the application remains deployed through a reference to that application in the form of an XML file in Tomcat's `conf/Catalina/localhost` directory.

To undeploy such an application from Tomcat:

1. Open the Runtime window.
2. Expand the Servers node; then expand the node for the Tomcat server and the server's Web Applications node.
3. Right-click the node for the running web application and choose Undeploy.

Redeploying a Web Application

To remove your application from the server and then redeploy it, right-click the project's node and choose Redeploy Project.

Creating a WAR File

When you run the Build Project command on a web project in the IDE, a WAR file is created automatically and placed in the `dist` folder of the project. You can access this file and browse its contents in the Files window.

Deploying to a Different Tomcat Server

The IDE comes bundled with the Tomcat server, which facilitates web application development and testing. If you have a different Tomcat installation that you want to test on and/or deploy to, you can register that installation with the IDE. You can easily switch your application to work with the different server installations. This is particularly useful if you want to develop and test on one installation and then deploy to a production environment.

To set up the IDE to recognize a different Tomcat installation:

1. Choose Tools | Server Manager.
2. Click the Add Server button.
3. On the Choose Server page of the wizard that opens, select a server from the Server combo box, enter an IDE display name for that server in the Name field, and click Next.
4. On the Tomcat Server Instance Properties page, specify the Tomcat installation directory (and base directory, if it is a shared installation), and fill in an administrative username and password.

   You can also determine whether to enable the IDE's HTTP Monitor. If the HTTP Monitor is enabled, you can monitor your application's server requests, cookies, and so on, which makes it easier to debug your application. However, this option slows the server, so you will probably want this option disabled if you are using this server as your production server. See Monitoring HTTP Transactions later in this chapter for information on using the HTTP Monitor.
5. Verify that the server is not using a port number used by another server. In the IDE, you can view the server's port number by mousing over the server's node and viewing the node's tooltip.

   If another server instance is using the same port, you need to stop one of the servers and change the port it is using. Stop the server by right-clicking the server's node, choosing Start/Stop Server, and clicking Stop Server. Then right-click the server node, choose Properties, and change the Server Port property. Restart the server by right-clicking the node, choosing Start/Stop Server, and clicking Start Server.
6. If you have any existing web applications within the IDE that you want to run on the newly added server, modify the properties for each project to use the server. You can do so by right-clicking the project's node in the Projects window, choosing Properties, selecting the Run node, and choosing the server from the Server combo box.

 If you later want to change the server's configuration, you can access the server's properties by opening the Runtime window, expanding the Servers node, right-clicking the specific server's node, and choosing Properties.

Testing and Debugging Your Web Application

NetBeans IDE provides a rich environment for troubleshooting and optimizing your web applications. Some of the features to ease testing of web applications include

- The Compile JSP command, which enables you to check individual JSP files for errors before deploying to the server.
- Debugger integration with JSP files, which means that you can set breakpoints in JSP files and step through a JSP in the debugger (as opposed to having to step through the generated servlet code).
- Ability to step through tag files.
- Ability to evaluate Expression Language (EL) expressions in JSP files during a debugging session (by mousing over the expression or setting a watch).
- The HTTP Monitor, which keeps track of HTTP communication between servlets and the server. This feature is covered in detail in Monitoring HTTP Transactions later in this chapter.

See Chapter 5 for more information on the IDE's general debugging features that these features extend.

Checking for JSP Errors

JSP files are not compiled like typical Java files before they are deployed. Instead, they are compiled by the server after they have been deployed (where in fact they are first translated to servlets, which are then compiled). This makes it more cumbersome to correct errors that normally are detected when compiling, because it forces you to deploy the application, discover the error, undeploy, correct the error, and redeploy.

However, NetBeans IDE enables you to compile JSP files to check for errors before you package and deploy the application. You can either compile individual JSP files manually or specify that they be compiled when you build the project.

To compile a JSP file manually, select the file in the Projects window or in the Source Editor, and select Build | Compile File or press F9.

To have all JSP files compiled when you run the Build Project command, right-click the project's node, choose Properties, select the Compiling node, and select the Test Compile All JSP Files During Builds checkbox.

The compilation results are reported in the Output window, where you can discover any errors, whether they occur in the translation to the servlet or in the compilation of the servlet.

The compiled files themselves are placed in the project's `build/generated` folder, which you can view from the Files window. These files are not used when you are building and packaging the application for deployment.

Viewing a JSP File's Servlet

The generation of a servlet from a JSP file happens dynamically on the server where the web application is deployed. You can view this generated servlet once you have run the project or the specific JSP associated with it by right-clicking the file and choosing View Servlet.

 If you would like to see the servlet code that is generated when you run the Compile JSP command, open the Files window; open the `build/generated/src` folder; and navigate to the file, which is named according to the JSP filename but with a `_jsp` suffix and `.java` extension.

Viewing a File in a Web Browser

You can open components of a web application in a web browser from the IDE.

To view a specific JSP page in a web browser, you need to run that file individually by right-clicking the file in the Source Editor and choosing Run File (or pressing Shift-F6).

To open an HTML file in the web browser, right-click the HTML page's node in the Projects window and choose View.

 The View command for HTML files is not available from the Source Editor. If you want to view the current HTML file in the Source Editor without your fingers leaving the keyboard, press Ctrl-Shift-1 to jump to the file's node in the Projects window, press Shift-F10 to open the node's contextual menu, press the down-arrow key to select View, and press Enter.

Passing Request Parameters to a Web Application

You can manually test the way the web application will respond to certain input by running the application with certain request parameters specified ahead of time.

To pass request parameters to a JSP page:

1. Right-click the JSP file's node and choose Properties.
2. In the Request Parameters property, enter the parameters in URL query string format (where the expression begins with a URL; continues with a question mark [?] to mark the beginning of the query; and completes with the parameters as name/value pairs, where the pairs are separated by ampersands [&]).

To pass request parameters to a servlet:

1. Right-click the servlet's node in the Projects window and choose Tools | Set Servlet Execution URI.
2. In the dialog box, append a question mark plus the name/value pairs, with each pair separated by an ampersand.

Debugging JSP and Tag Files

One of the IDE's features that has long made NetBeans IDE a favorite with web developers is the ability of the debugger to step into JSP files. You can set breakpoints in JSP files and step through the JSP line by line while monitoring the values of variables and other aspects of the running program.

NetBeans IDE 4.1 adds the ability to step into tag files.

To set a breakpoint in a JSP or tag file, select the line where you would like to pause execution and press Ctrl-F8. See Chapter 5 for more information on debugging.

Creating and Deploying Applets

NetBeans IDE 4.1 does not have a specific project type for applets, so the development cycle for applets is a little different from that for other types of projects.

You cannot designate an applet as a main project, which means that several project-specific commands (such as Run Project) do not apply to applets.

However, you can still create, test, and deploy applets fairly easily. The general outline of applet development is as follows:

1. Create a Java Library project to hold the applet.
2. Create an applet from one of the templates in the New File wizard and fill in code for the applet.
3. Test the applet in the JDK's applet viewer by right-clicking the applet's node in the Projects window and choosing Run File.
4. Create a JAR file for the applet by right-clicking the applet's project node and choosing Build Project.
5. If you want to add the applet to a web application, add the applet's project (or just the applet's JAR file) through the web project's Project Properties dialog box (Build | Packaging Panel).

Creating an Applet

To create an applet:

1. Choose New Project, select the General category, select the Java Library template, and click Next.
2. Enter a name and location for the project, and click Finish to exit the wizard.
3. In the Projects window, expand the node for the project you have just created. Then right-click the Source Packages node and choose New | File/Folder.
4. In the New File wizard, select one of the available applet templates. There are four available:

   ▪ Java Classes category, JApplet template. This template extends `javax.swing.JApplet` and is recommended over the Applet template, which is based on the less flexible `java.applet.Applet` class.

   ▪ Java GUI Forms category, JApplet template. This template extends `javax.swing.JApplet` and enables you to use the IDE's Form Editor to design your applet visually. This template is recommended over the JApplet template in the AWT Forms subcategory.

   ▪ Java Classes category, Applet template. This template extends `java.applet.Applet`.

- Java GUI Forms | AWT Forms category, Applet template. This template extends `java.applet.Applet` and enables you to use the IDE's Form Editor to design your applet visually.

5. Click Next, specify a name and a package for the applet, and then click Finish.

You can then code the applet, either by hand or with the assistance of the Form Editor.

Running and Debugging an Applet in the Applet Viewer

As you are developing the applet, you can use the JDK's applet viewer to test the applet's functionality. When you use the Run File and Debug File commands, the applet is automatically displayed in the applet viewer.

To run an applet, right-click the applet's node in the Projects window and choose Run File.

To start debugging an applet:

1. Set a breakpoint in the code by selecting the line where you first want execution to pause and press Ctrl-F8.
2. Right-click the applet's node in the Projects window and choose Debug File.

Running an Applet in a Web Browser

If you want to see how your applet behaves in an actual web browser, you can open an HTML launcher for the applet.

To run an applet in a web browser:

1. Open the Files window and expand the project's `build` directory.
2. Right-click the HTML launcher file (it should have the same name as the applet class but with an HTML extension) and choose View.

The applet opens in the default web browser specified in the IDE. See Changing the IDE's Default Web Browser later in this chapter if you would like to change the IDE's default web browser.

If you want to customize the HTML launcher file, you can copy the generated launcher file into the folder that contains the applet source file. This prevents the launcher file from being overwritten every time you run the applet.

When you run the applet or build the applet's project, the HTML file is copied into the folder with the compiled applet class. If you do not want this file to be included in the JAR that is created when you build the project, you can modify the filter for the JAR file's contents. In the Projects window, right-click the project's node and choose Properties. In the dialog box, select the Packaging node and modify the regular expression in the Exclude From JAR File field. For example, you could add a comma plus an expression like `**/Myapplet.html` to make sure that your launcher file (no matter which directory it is in) is excluded from the built JAR file.

Packaging an Applet into a JAR File

If you want to put an applet into a JAR file, you can do so by right-clicking the applet's project node in the Projects window and choosing Build Project.

The applet is compiled, and the compiled class files are placed in a JAR file in the `dist` folder, which you can view with the Files window.

Packaging an Applet into a WAR File

To add an applet to a web application:

1. Put the applet into a JAR file. See Packaging an Applet into a JAR File above for information on how to do this in the IDE.
2. Right-click the web application's project node in the Projects window and choose Properties.
3. In the Project Properties dialog box, select the Build | Packaging node.
4. Click the Add Project button, navigate to the applet's project folder, and click Add Project JAR Files.

Setting Applet Permissions

When you create and run an applet through the IDE, an `applet.policy` file is created with all permissions granted and is placed in the root folder of the project (which you can view through the Files window). You can modify this file by double-clicking its node to open it in the Source Editor.

You can also specify a different policy file for the applet. To specify a different policy file:

1. Right-click the web application's project node in the Projects window and choose Properties.
2. In the Project Properties dialog box, select the Run node.
3. In the VM Options field, modify the value of the `-Djava.security.policy` option to point to the policy file.

Changing the IDE's Default Web Browser

To change the IDE's default web browser, choose Tools | Setup Wizard and select a browser from the Web Browser combo box.

If the IDE cannot find a given web browser on your system, you might need to specify the executable for that web browser.

To point the IDE to a web browser that is listed in the Setup Wizard:

1. Choose Tools | Options and expand the IDE Configuration | Server and External Tools Settings | Web Browsers node.
2. Select the subnode for the browser that you want and modify the Browser Executable property.

To add to the IDE's list of web browsers:

1. Choose Tools | Options and expand the IDE Configuration | Server and External Tools Settings | Web Browsers node.
2. Right-click the Web Browsers node, choose New | External Browser, type the browser's name, and click Finish.
3. Select the subnode for the added browser and modify the Browser Executable property to point to that browser's executable.

Monitoring HTTP Transactions

NetBeans IDE provides a built-in HTTP Monitor to help isolate problems with data flow from JSP and servlet execution on a web server. There is no need to add logic to your web application to trace HTTP requests and associated state information. The NetBeans IDE built-in HTTP Monitor can do this for you.

When the IDE is configured with a web container, or a web application is deployed with a NetBeans HTTP Monitor servlet filter and filter mapping, the HTTP Monitor will automatically record all HTTP requests made to the web container. For each HTTP request that is processed by the web container, the HTTP Monitor not only records the request, but also records state information maintained in the web container.

By using the HTTP Monitor, you can analyze HTTP requests and store HTTP GET and HTTP POST requests for future analysis sessions. You can also edit these stored requests and replay them. This is a powerful feature to help isolate data flow and state information passed within an HTTP request to a web container. HTTP requests are stored until you exit the IDE. You can also save them so that they are available in subsequent IDE sessions.

Following are some of the things that you can do with the IDE's HTTP Monitor:

- Analyze HTTP request records
- Save HTTP request records
- Edit HTTP request records
- Refresh HTTP request records
- Sort HTTP request records
- Delete HTTP request records
- Replay HTTP request records

In the following sections, you will learn how to set up the HTTP Monitor, analyze the data the HTTP Monitor collects, and replay recorded HTTP requests.

Setting Up the HTTP Monitor

When you run a web application, and the HTTP Monitor is enabled, the HTTP Monitor should appear in the bottom of the IDE. The HTTP Monitor generally is automatically enabled for Tomcat but not for Sun Java System Application Server. If the HTTP Monitor is not displayed in the bottom of the IDE when you run an application, you can enable it by performing the following tasks.

1. Expand the Runtime window's Servers node to show your registered web server. Then right-click the server's node and choose Properties.

2. Place a checkbox in the Enable HTTP Monitor property.

3. If the registered web server is currently running, stop and restart it by right-clicking your registered web server under the Runtime window's Servers node and selecting Start / Stop Server.

Figure 6-7 shows the Enable HTTP Monitor property in the Sun Java System Application Server 8 Properties dialog box.

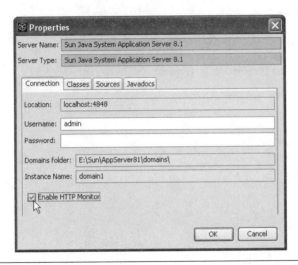

Figure 6-7   Properties dialog box for the Sun Java System Application Server

Setting Up the HTTP Monitor for Servers Started Outside of the IDE

You can also use the HTTP Monitor on web servers started outside of the IDE. To do so, execute the following tasks:

1. Go to the directory where the IDE is installed, and copy the `modules/org-netbeans-modules-schema2beans.jar` and `modules/org-netbeans-modules-web-httpmonitor.jar` files to your web module's `WEB-INF/lib` directory.

2. Add a filter declaration that is appropriate for your servlet's version to the top of your web module's `WEB-INF/web.xml` file.

Filters and filter mapping entries must be specified at the beginning of a deployment descriptor. See the examples below for filters for the servlets corresponding to the 2.3 and 2.4 versions of the Servlet specification.

A Servlet 2.4 filter declaration might look like the following:

```
<filter>
  <filter-name>HTTPMonitorFilter</filter-name>
  <filter-class>
    org.netbeans.modules.web.monitor.server.MonitorFilter
  </filter-class>
  <init-param>
    <param-name>
      netbeans.monitor.ide
    </param-name>
    <param-value>
      name-of-host-running NetBeans IDE:http-server-port
    </param-value>
  </init-param>
</filter>
<filter-mapping>
  <filter-name>
    HTTPMonitorFilter
  </filter-name>
  <url-pattern>
    /*
  </url-pattern>
  <dispatcher>
    REQUEST
  </dispatcher>
  <dispatcher>
    FORWARD
  </dispatcher>
  <dispatcher>
    INCLUDE
  </dispatcher>
  <dispatcher>
    ERROR
  </dispatcher>
</filter-mapping>
```

A Servlet 2.3 filter declaration might look like the following:

```
<filter>
  <filter-name>HTTPMonitorFilter</filter-name>
  <filter-class>
```

```
      org.netbeans.modules.web.monitor.server.MonitorFilter
  </filter-class>
  <init-param>
    <param-name>
      netbeans.monitor.ide
    </param-name>
    <param-value>
      name-of-host-running NetBeans IDE:http-server-port
    </param-value>
  </init-param>
</filter>
<filter-mapping>
  <filter-name>
    HTTPMonitorFilter
  </filter-name>
  <url-pattern>
    /*
  </url-pattern>
</filter-mapping>
```

A web application can be monitored with the IDE HTTP Monitor from multiple NetBeans IDEs by adding more `init-param` entries to the servlet filter declaration in the web deployment descriptor. For instance, you would add an `init-param` entry such as the one shown below:

```
<init-param>
  <param-name>
    netbeans.monitor.ide
  </param-name>
  <param-value>
    name-of-2nd-host-running NetBeans IDE:http-server-port
  </param-value>
</init-param>
```

When you deploy the web module you have been monitoring with the HTTP Monitor to a production server, remember to remove the Servlet filter and filter mapping declarations from the web module's deployment descriptor. Otherwise, the web module will be open for HTTP monitoring from those NetBeans IDEs specified in the `init-param` section(s) of the servlet filter in the web module's deployment descriptor.

Analyzing the Collected Data

After you have set up the HTTP Monitor, you can use the HTTP Monitor to debug your web application by observing data flow from your JSP page and servlet execution on the web server. The HTTP Monitor records data about each incoming request. The HTTP Monitor is automatically displayed in the bottom of the IDE. A snapshot of the HTTP Monitor is shown in Figure 6-8.

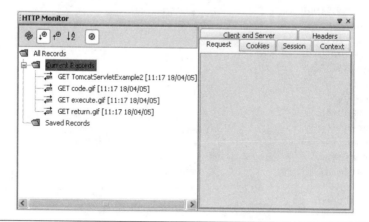

Figure 6-8   HTTP Monitor

The HTTP Monitor consists of two panels. On the left is a tree view of HTTP request records. Every HTTP request made to the HTTP server is recorded in the HTTP Monitor. Requests resulting from internal dispatches are reflected by nested nodes under those web containers that support it. In addition, forwarded or included requests are nested under the node corresponding to the main request.

Displayed on the right panel of the HTTP Monitor is additional data for a selected HTTP request record on the left panel. When you select an HTTP request record on the left, session data corresponding to the selected record is displayed in the right panel. The additional session information available in the right panel includes detailed request information; cookie name/value pairs; session data; servlet context; context attributes; initialization parameters; and client-server information, such as client protocol, client IP address, server platform, and server hostname, along with additional HTTP request header information. The right panel allows you to view specific data in each of these categories by selecting a tab corresponding to the information you would like to see. Figure 6-9 shows the additional session information for a selected HTTP request record.

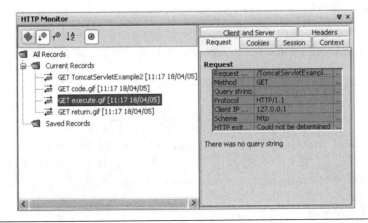

Figure 6-9   HTTP Monitor with a record selected and its request data displayed

In the tree view (left panel of the HTTP Monitor), there are two categories of
records that can be viewed: Current Records and Saved Records. The Current
Records category represents HTTP request records collected since the IDE has
been started. Current records persist across restarts of the web server but do not
persist across restarts of the IDE. For current records to persist across IDE
restarts, they must be saved. Individual current records may be saved by selecting a HTTP request record, right-clicking the selected current record, and
choosing Save from the contextual menu. You can select multiple HTTP request
records by pressing the Shift key or Ctrl key. Figure 6-10 illustrates the selecting
and saving of multiple HTTP requests.

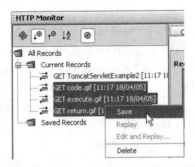

Figure 6-10   Saving multiple records in the HTTP Monitor

Notice that when you save HTTP requests, the selected records are moved to the Saved Records category. The selected records are not copied. You should keep this in mind should you want to replay a sequence of HTTP requests.

The tree view (left panel of the HTTP Monitor) also provides several options for viewing the HTTP requests in the upper-left portion of the panel, in the form of five buttons. For example, you can reload all the HTTP request records, sort the HTTP request records by timestamp in descending or ascending order, sort the records alphabetically, and show or hide the timestamp for each HTTP request record. Table 6-4 summarizes the action of each button.

Table 6-4 HTTP Monitor Toolbar Buttons

Request Record View Button	Action
reload	Reloads all the HTTP request records currently stored
descending sort	Sorts HTTP request records by timestamp in descending order
ascending sort	Sorts HTTP request records by timestamp in ascending order
alphabetically sort	Sorts the HTTP request records alphabetically
time stamp	Hides or displays the timestamps in the list of HTTP requests

In addition to being saved, HTTP records may be deleted. The IDE provides much flexibility for deleting HTTP records. For example, individual and multiple current records or all current records may be deleted. Individual saved records, multiple saved records, or all saved records can also be deleted.

To remove a record, right-click the record to be deleted and choose the Delete option from the contextual menu. To remove multiple records, select additional records, using the Shift or Ctrl key; then right-click the selected records and choose the Delete option from the contextual menu. To remove all current records, right-click the current records folder and choose the Delete option. To remove all Saved Records, right-click the Saved Records folder and choose the Delete option from the contextual menu.

Replaying HTTP Requests

The most powerful feature of the HTTP Monitor is the editing and replaying of HTTP requests. By editing and replaying HTTP requests, you can quickly and easily trace and diagnose problems with the flow of data from JSP pages and servlet execution on the web server. When you replay an HTTP request, the response appears in your web browser. Thus you can track the result of a given HTTP request by having it replayed in your web browser.

 The IDE opens your default web browser when you replay HTTP requests. If the IDE cannot find the operating system's default web browser, you can configure the web browser manually. See Changing the IDE's Default Web Browser earlier in this chapter.

Both current records and saved records may be replayed. To replay an HTTP request, select the HTTP request to replay in the left panel (tree view) and choose the Replay option from the contextual menu. Figure 6-11 shows a Current Record being selected for replay.

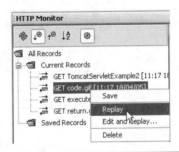

Figure 6-11   Selecting a record to be replayed in the HTTP Monitor

Notice that the selected record is replayed in your browser after you have chosen Replay from the contextual menu.

In addition to replaying HTTP requests, you can edit an HTTP request before replaying it. To edit an HTTP request before replaying it, select an HTTP request in the left panel (tree view)—either a Current Record or Saved Record—right-click the record, and choose the Edit and Replay option from the contextual menu. After you choose the Edit and Replay option, a dialog box is displayed, where you can make various modifications.

The supported modifications in the edit and replay of an HTTP request include options to edit a parameter to query, modify request URI parameters, modify cookies, modify server execution properties, and modify HTTP request parameters.

On the Query tab (see Figure 6-12), you can add a query parameter or delete a query parameter and modify URI request parameters. On the Request tab, you can modify the request URI by selecting the ellipsis (...) button next to the request parameter value. You can change the request method from a GET to a POST or PUT by selecting from the combo box to the right of the Request Method type in the left column. If you click the ellipsis button in the request protocol's far-right column, the Request Edit Property dialog box appears, which enables you to modify the request protocol. On the Cookies tab, you can add, modify, or delete cookies associated with the HTTP request. On the Server tab, you can modify server execution values, such as the hostname and port where the HTTP request should be executed. You can add, modify, and delete HTTP headers in the Headers tab.

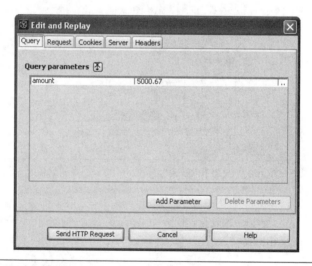

Figure 6-12   HTTP Monitor Edit and Replay dialog box

After making your desired edits to the HTTP request, you can replay the modified request by clicking the Send HTTP Request button. The resulting HTTP request and response are sent to your web browser, where the results are displayed.

Introduction to J2EE
Development in NetBeans IDE

7

- Configuring the IDE for J2EE Development
- Getting the Most from the Java BluePrints
  Solutions Catalog

THE JAVA 2 PLATFORM, ENTERPRISE EDITION (J2EE) DEFINES the standard for developing multi-tier enterprise applications. The J2EE platform simplifies enterprise applications by basing them on standardized, modular components; by providing a complete set of services to those components; and by handling many details of application behavior automatically, without complex programming. The J2EE platform is targeted for developers who want to write distributed transactional applications for the enterprise and leverage the speed, security, and reliability of server-side technology.

NetBeans IDE 4.1 introduces comprehensive support for the J2EE developer. There are advanced wizards to create entire J2EE applications and individual components, such as web applications, servlets, JavaServer Faces applications, Enterprise JavaBeans modules (EJB modules), Enterprise JavaBeans components (enterprise beans), and web services. In addition, the IDE provides a complete runtime environment based on the Sun Java System Application Server 8.1. This application server is the reference implementation of the J2EE 1.4 platform.

Sun Java System Application Server 8.1, which is available separately or as part of a technology bundle with NetBeans IDE 4.1, is a J2EE 1.4-compliant application server that is free for development, deployment, and redistribution. It offers the ideal companion to the IDE for all the developers who need an integrated environment where complete J2EE applications can be developed, built, assembled, deployed, and debugged.

Configuring the IDE for J2EE Development

To explore all the capabilities of NetBeans IDE related to development of J2EE applications and web services development, you need to make sure your environment is correctly configured. If you have downloaded the bundle containing both NetBeans IDE and Sun Java System Application Server, you have a preconfigured development environment, and you can skip the following steps. If you have downloaded a stand-alone NetBeans IDE, you will also need to install Sun Java System Application Server 8.1, available from http://java.sun.com/j2ee/1.4/ download.html. This application server is the core of the J2EE 1.4 SDK and is free for development, deployment, and redistribution.

Before you can deploy an enterprise application, web application, JSP, servlet, or EJB module, the server to which you are going to deploy needs to be registered with the IDE. By default, only the bundled Tomcat web server is registered with the IDE.

To register a Sun Java System Application Server instance:

1. In the IDE, choose Tools | Server Manager.
2. In the Server Manager, click the Add Server button. The Add Server Instance wizard (shown in Figure 7-1) appears and displays the types of servers that are compatible with the IDE.

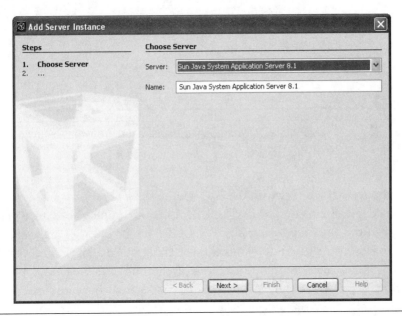

Figure 7-1   Add Server Instance wizard, Choose Server page

3. On the Choose Server page of the wizard, select the type of server you want to register (Sun Java System Application Server 8.1) and click Next.
4. On the Enter Application Server Location page, specify the local installation of the server.
5. On the Enter Registration Properties of an Application Server Instance page (shown in Figure 7-2), specify server-specific information in the panels that follow and click Finish. (Remember that the Admin username is admin and the default password is adminadmin, unless you picked a different one at installation time.)

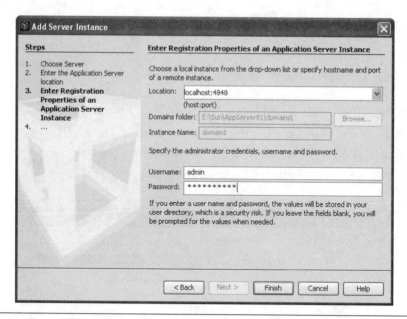

Figure 7-2   Add Server Instance wizard, Enter Registration Properties of an Application Server Instance page

When you register a server with the IDE, you make its libraries available for production, deployment, or both. If you deploy your applications to a remote instance of the Sun Java System Application Server, its libraries are available at runtime. However, during development, you might need a local instance of this server. You can have multiple instances of the Sun Java System Application Server registered with the IDE. Once you have registered your local instance, you can open the wizard again to register remote instances (by selecting a remote machine name and its port number in the Location field of the Enter Registration Properties of an Application Server Instance page of the wizard).

When a server is registered with the IDE, you can see its node in the Runtime window under the Servers node. When you create a project in the New Project wizard, you select the server to which you want to deploy your application. After you create the application, you can change the server by right-clicking the project, choosing Properties, clicking the Run node, and selecting a different server.

Now you are ready to create web services, enterprise beans, and J2EE applications.

Getting the Most from the Java BluePrints Solutions Catalog

NetBeans IDE provides a unique capability for learning and understanding best practices for Java application development with its integration of the Java Blue-Prints Solutions Catalog. The Java BluePrints Solutions Catalog has long been accepted as the source of Java application best practices and Java suggested guidelines. The Java BluePrints Solutions Catalog also illustrates these best practices and guidelines through various example applications. It provides a huge repository of example applications from which you can literally cut and paste source code, or tailor code for your own specific application.

In NetBeans IDE, you can directly access the catalog and install example Java BluePrints Solutions directly into the IDE as a new project. This feature provides you a unique opportunity to learn and understand quickly various Java Blue-Prints best practices and recommended guidelines.

 The version of the Java BluePrints Solutions Catalog available in NetBeans IDE 4.1 is an early access version. Shortly after NetBeans IDE 4.1 is released, a final version of the catalog is due and should be available for the IDE through the IDE's Update Center (choose Tools | Update Center).

In the NetBeans IDE 4.1 release, the following Java BluePrints Solutions are available, grouped into the Web Tier and Web Services categories:

- Web Tier
  - Handling Command Submissions
  - Tabbed View
  - Server-Side Validation
  - Client-Side Validation
- Web Services
  - Accessing Web Services From J2EE Components
  - Accessing Web Services From a Stand-Alone Java Client
  - Designing Document Oriented Services
  - Using Schema-Defined Types to Represent XML Documents in a Service Interface
  - Using Strings to Represent XML Documents in a Service Interface
  - ServiceLocator Pattern for J2EE Components Acting As Clients of Web Services

Accessing the Java BluePrints Solutions Catalog

When you install NetBeans IDE, the Java BluePrints Solutions Catalog is available without any additional installation steps. You can access the catalog by choosing Help | BluePrints Solutions Catalog. The catalog is displayed in the IDE's main document area (where the Source Editor also appears) as shown in Figure 7-3.

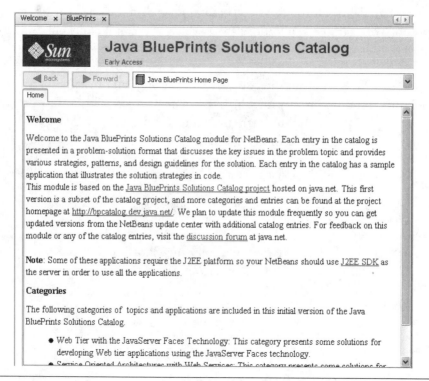

Figure 7-3   Java BluePrints Solutions Catalog in the NetBeans IDE main window

Navigating the Java BluePrints Solutions Catalog

Because the Java BluePrints Solutions Catalog displayed in the NetBeans IDE main window follows the browser paradigm, it is easy to navigate. You will notice a drop-down list from which you can select different Java BluePrints Solutions (see Figure 7-4).

The solutions are grouped into categories, within which you can navigate by clicking the Back or Forward button. You can also use the drop-down list to

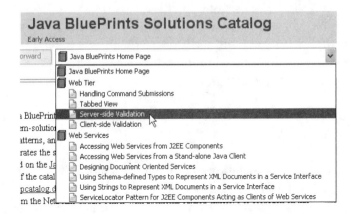

Figure 7-4   Java BluePrints Solutions Catalog with the combo box listing the different solutions available

select a specific solution within a category. When a specific Java BluePrints Solution is selected, there are two or three tabs to choose among, as shown in Figure 7-5.

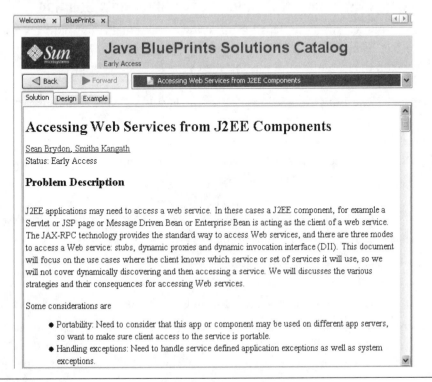

Figure 7-5   A selected blueprint with the Solution tab selected

The Solution tab displays a description of the issue the Java BluePrints Solution is trying to solve. The Design tab describes the design of the solution so you can understand the implementation decisions made and the design best practices used in the solution. All of the solutions in the Java BluePrints Solutions Catalog have both the Solution and Design tabs.

To view the solution or design for a given Java BluePrints Solution, simply select the appropriate tab.

For some Java BluePrints Solutions, there is a third tab, called the Example tab, that allows you to install an example implementation of the Java BluePrints Solution in NetBeans IDE as a NetBeans project. This is a very useful capability, because it allows you to see a running, working example implementation of the Java BluePrints Solution by being able to run or even debug the solution. In addition, it is very easy to pull source code from a working implementation into your own specific application or project.

Creating a NetBeans Project for a Java BluePrints Solution

This section describes the steps for installing a Java BluePrints Solutions example in NetBeans IDE as a NetBeans project. In addition, the section describes how to run the example once it is installed as a NetBeans project.

To install a Java BluePrints Solution from the Java BluePrints Solutions Catalog:

1. Choose Help | BluePrints Solutions Catalog.
2. Once the catalog is displayed, select the solution you want to work with from the drop-down list in the display.
3. In the solution you have selected, click the Example tab (if there is an Example tab for that solution). If the Example tab exists and you click it, you will see a screen that looks similar to Figure 7-6.

   If the Example button is not there, this particular example cannot be installed in the IDE.
4. On the Example screen for the solution, click the Install Example button.

   This will begin the installation and setup of a new NetBeans IDE project for the selected Java BluePrints Solution. The IDE's New Project wizard is launched with the Java BluePrints Solution you have chosen to install selected as the project. For example, the J2EE Client of Document Oriented Services project template would be chosen (as shown in Figure 7-7) if you clicked Install Example in the screen for the Accessing Web Services From J2EE Components solution.

Figure 7-6 A solution with its Example tab selected

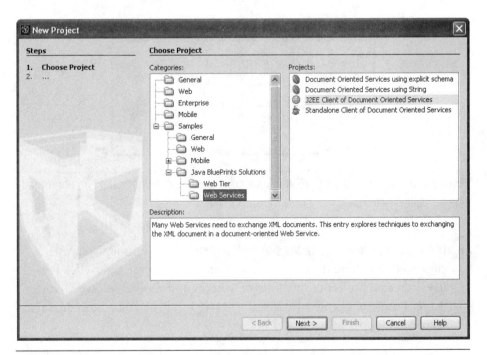

Figure 7-7 New Project wizard with a Java BluePrints Solution selected

5. Click the Next button to continue the installation and setup of the Java BluePrints Solution.

6. The next screen of the wizard asks you to supply a project name (or to accept the default name) and a project location (or to accept the default) and asks whether to set this as the main project in NetBeans IDE.

   In almost all cases, you should accept the defaults shown in the wizard. Only if you want to change the name or location given to the project or to set it as the main project should you change the default settings displayed in this wizard.

7. Click the Finish button to complete the installation and setup of the Java BluePrints Solution as a NetBeans IDE project.

   After completing the wizard, you might see the warning dialog box shown in Figure 7-8. This generally occurs if you do not have the Sun Java System Application Server registered with the IDE. It is possible to set the project to work with a different server (such as Tomcat), but some of the features in the server might not work if the server is not fully J2EE compliant.

Figure 7-8   Warning dialog box that appears if the IDE does not detect an appropriate server for the project

8. If you see the warning dialog box, follow the instructions it gives. After clicking OK to close the dialog box and open the project, right-click the newly created project in the Projects window and choose Resolve Missing Server Problem. The Resolve Missing Server Problem dialog box (shown in Figure 7-9) appears.

Figure 7-9   Resolve Missing Server Problem dialog box

9. In the Resolve Missing Server Problem dialog box, select a target server. If you have a Sun Java System Application Server installed with NetBeans IDE, you will see options for both the Sun Java System Application Server and for Tomcat. Choose the desired server for your project and click OK.

If you would like to use the Sun Java System Application Server with the Java Blue-Prints Solution you are installing, but the server does not appear in the list of servers in the Resolve Missing Server Problem dialog box, click Cancel to exit the dialog box.

If necessary, download and install the application server. Then register the application server in the IDE's Server Manager (available through the Tools menu). After that, you can go back to the Resolve Missing Server Problem dialog box and select the Sun Java System Application Server as the target server.

Once you have the Java BluePrints Solution created as a NetBeans IDE project, you can perform operations such as building, deploying, and debugging.

You can also install the available Java BluePrints Solutions as IDE projects straight from the New Project wizard. In the New Project wizard, you can expand the Sample folder category to show BluePrints Solutions folder. The BluePrints Solutions folder contains the same Java BluePrints Solutions as the ones in the catalog that have an Example tab.

Running a Java BluePrints Solutions Project

To run a NetBeans IDE project that has been created from the Java BluePrints Solutions Catalog, you perform the same operations as you would when running other J2EE applications in the IDE—that is, you open the Projects window, right-click the newly created project for your Java BluePrints Solution, and choose Run Project. NetBeans IDE will build the newly created Java BluePrints Solutions project, deploy it to the target server, and load the application's home page in your default web browser automatically.

Once you have the Java BluePrints Solution created as a project in NetBeans IDE, you can perform a large number of operations. For example, you can deploy the application to your target server, as you have already seen; you can run the application in a debugger; you can use the HTTP Monitor to analyze the HTTP requests that are passed between your browser and the deployed application; and you can make changes to the source files by editing the project source.

In fact, using the Java BluePrints Solutions Catalog and one of its applications is an excellent way to learn some of the J2EE technologies and best practices on how to use the technologies. In addition, these solutions are an excellent source from which you can cut and paste code for an application you are developing.

## CHAPTER 8

Extending Web Applications with Business Logic: Introducing Enterprise Beans

- EJB Project Type Wizards
- Adding Enterprise Beans, Files, and Libraries to Your EJB Module
- Adding Business Logic to an Enterprise Bean
- Adding a Simple Business Method
- Enterprise Bean Deployment Descriptors

FOR MANY NETBEANS IDE USERS, as well as web application developers, Enterprise JavaBeans technology might be new or apparently complex. However, starting with Version 4.1, NetBeans IDE exposes wizards and other features to create enterprise beans easily and add business methods to them. Once these business methods are implemented (in Java code), they can be called either from other enterprise beans or from a web application's servlets or utility classes.

The benefits of encapsulating application code within EJB business methods are numerous:

- Enterprise beans support *transactions,* the mechanisms that manage the concurrent access of shared objects. Transaction settings are declarative, via the deployment descriptor files.
- Enterprise beans can be used by many clients, across machines or not (remote and/or local access).
- Enterprise beans' business methods can be secured declaratively, without source code modification.
- Enterprise beans access external resources like databases, message queues, mail sessions, and web services declaratively via Java Naming and Directory Interface (JNDI) naming. The JNDI naming service enables components to locate other components and resources. To locate a Java Database Connectivity (JDBC) resource, for example, an enterprise bean invokes the JNDI lookup method. The JNDI naming service maintains a set of bindings that relates names to objects. The lookup method passes a JNDI name parameter and returns the related object.

See Table 8-1 for a list of all of the enterprise bean types.

Table 8-1 Types of Enterprise Beans

Enterprise Bean Type	Description
Session	Performs a task for a client or implements a web service. A session bean can be stateful for conversation handling between the client (the user of the business logic) and the server, or stateless.
Entity	Represents a business entity object that exists in persistent storage, typically SQL databases (and possibly others).
Message-Driven	Acts as a listener for the Java Message Service API, processing messages asynchronously.

EJB Project Type Wizards

The first thing to do in developing enterprise beans is to create an EJB Module project that can contain one or more enterprise beans. To give an analogy from the web application concept: Whereas a web application is a deployable J2EE component containing a collection of servlets, web pages, and JSP files, an EJB module is a deployable J2EE component that contains a collection of enterprise beans.

To create an EJB Module project:

1. Choose the EJB Module project type, which is in the Enterprise project category (as shown in Figure 8-1).

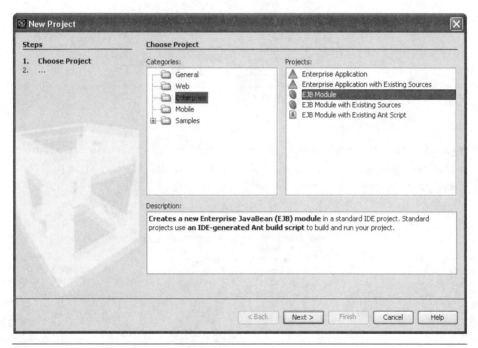

Figure 8-1   New Project wizard with EJB Module project type selected

2. On the Name and Location page of the wizard, specify the location of the project, its name, and whether you want to add this J2EE component to an existing J2EE application (EAR project).

   You can add the module to a J2EE Application project later—when you create the J2EE project, for example.

Once you complete the wizard, your project is created and visible in the Projects window, as shown in Figure 8-2. For now, it contains no enterprise beans. Adding Enterprise Beans, Files, and Libraries to Your EJB Module later in this chapter explains how to populate the module.

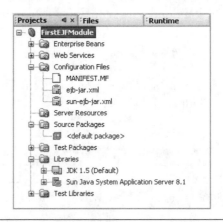

Figure 8-2   Projects window with EJB Module project showing

You can select the Files window (shown in Figure 8-3) to see which directories and files have been created on disk. See the sidebar EJB Module Structure for a description of the conventions used for this structure.

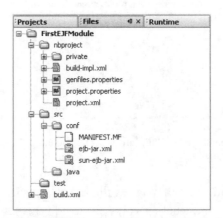

Figure 8-3   Files window with EJB Module project showing

EJB Module Structure

The J2EE BluePrints provide guidelines on how to structure your J2EE applications and EJB modules to ensure that they work properly with different application servers. When you create a project in the IDE, this J2EE BluePrints convention structure is respected.

Following is a quick description of the structural elements of the built EJB module:

- The `src/java` folder, which contains all the Java source files in the application.
- The `src/conf` folder, which contains the J2EE deployment descriptors and the application server's specific deployment descriptors.
- The `setup` directory, which contains server-specific resource files. This folder does not appear until you have added any of these resources (through the Server Resources node in the Projects window or via the server's administration features).

You can find additional information on these conventions at:

https://conventions.dev.java.net

See Table 8-2 for information on how the various source elements of an EJB module map to their representation in the IDE and where they end up in the deployed component.

Table 8-2   Matrix of EJB Module Elements and Their Representation in the IDE

Content	Representation in the Projects Window	Representation in the Files Window	Location within the Built EJB JAR File (Located in the `dist` Folder)
Enterprise beans	Enterprise Beans node	`src/java` folder	Root of the file
Java source files, helper classes, enterprise bean Java files, etc.	Source Packages node	`src/java` folder	Package structure for the JAR file
Unit tests	Test Packages node	`test` folder	N/A
Deployment descriptor (`ejb-jar.xml`, `webservices.xml`)	Configuration Files node	`src/conf` folder	`META-INF` folder

(continued)

Table 8-2   Matrix of EJB Module Elements and Their Representation in the IDE (*Contd.*)

Content	Representation in the Projects Window	Representation in the Files Window	Location within the Built EJB JAR File (Located in the dist Folder)
Application server's deployment descriptors	Configuration Files node	src/conf folder	META-INF folder
Application server-specific resources or scripts (such as SQL)	Configuration Files node (visible when some J2EE resources exist there)	setup folder	N/A. The resources in this folder are registered automatically at deployment time for the Sun Application Server target.
Web services	Web Services node	src area (Java code)	
Libraries	Libraries node	Location of the libraries folder	JAR libraries included in the EJB module JAR file, at the top location.
Test classpath entries	Test Libraries node	test folder	N/A
Project metadata, including build script	Project Properties dialog box, which you can open by right-clicking the project's node and choosing Properties.	build.xml file, nbproject folder	N/A
EJB module build area (*.class files)	Not shown	build and build/generated	Main content for the EJB module archive JAR file.

Adding Enterprise Beans, Files, and Libraries to Your EJB Module

Once you have created an EJB Module project through the New Project wizard, you can start populating it with new enterprise beans and helper Java classes.

The most straightforward way to create files is to open the Projects window, right-click the node where you want to place the file, and choose New and then a template from the submenu. A short wizard appears for the template, enabling you to set the name and other characteristics of the file. Choose the Session Bean template, as shown in Figure 8-4.

Figure 8-4   Adding a file to an EJB module

The wizard will create a session bean and add it to the EJB module. You can specify the bean name and package (make sure you select or create a Java package there instead of leaving it blank). You can specify whether this session bean will have a local and/or a remote interface (local is the default) and whether the bean is stateful or stateless. For now, accept the default values to create a local stateless session bean, as shown in Figure 8-5.

Notice the new logical representation of the enterprise bean in the Projects window under the Enterprise Beans node (shown in Figure 8-6). This enterprise bean is a set of Java files (four for a simple session bean):

- The local interface (*BeanName*`local.java`)
- The local home interface (*BeanName*`LocalHome.java`)
- The bean implementation itself (*BeanName*`Bean.java`)
- The business interface (*BeanName*`LocalBusiness.java`)

The Projects window's logical view hides the complexity of this enterprise bean by showing only a single node that exposes some important methods for the bean, like the local methods.

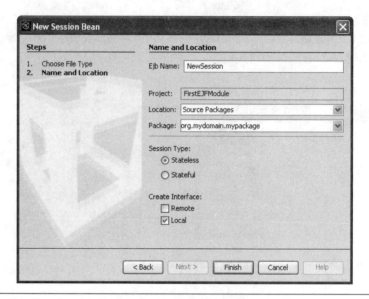

Figure 8-5   New Session Bean page of the New File wizard

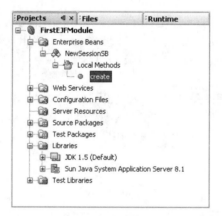

Figure 8-6   Projects window showing a new enterprise bean

 "Where are my Java files?" When you work with an enterprise bean's node in the Projects window, you do not see all of the Java files and deployment descriptors that are part of the bean. NetBeans IDE keeps all of these files synchronized automatically when you work with the bean's node. If you want to see the individual Java files, you can browse them within the Source Packages node.

Adding Business Logic to an Enterprise Bean

In this section, you learn about the different method types you can add to an enterprise bean. Remember that NetBeans IDE offers the necessary wizards that greatly simplify the work of coding business logic within enterprise beans.

A J2EE application gets its work done through methods that the client calls on the bean. The following method types are either automatically generated via the wizard with default implementation or can be added via popup menu actions in the Projects window or the Source Editor window for an enterprise bean implementation class. The IDE takes care of necessary extra generation (such as updating the local or remote interfaces with the correct signature entry).

- **Business methods.** A client calls business methods on a bean through the bean's remote interface (or local interface, as applicable).

  You have to add business methods to the bean yourself; the IDE doesn't generate any default business-method declarations. However, when you specify a business method, the IDE places matching method declarations in the bean class and in the remote, local, or remote and local interfaces.

Business methods are the most important methods for an enterprise bean. These are the ones called by other enterprise beans or web tier components, like JSP files or servlets. A special NetBeans wizard is available to simplify the coding of calling an EJB business method. From a servlet or enterprise bean file in the Source Editor, right-click to activate the popup menu, and choose Enterprise Resources | Call Enterprise Bean.

- **Life-cycle methods.** The container calls several methods to manage the life cycle of an enterprise bean. Depending on the type of bean, the container works through the methods in slightly different ways. You have the option of specifying parameters for some of these methods.

  The IDE automatically generates the appropriate life-cycle method declarations for each type of bean and places them in the bean class.

- **Finder methods.** The client goes through the home interface to find an entity bean instance by its primary key. You can also add other finder methods.

  NetBeans automatically generates a findByPrimaryKey method declaration in the local home interface of every entity bean (and in the bean's home interface, if it has one). The IDE also places a corresponding ejbFindByPrimaryKey method declaration in the bean class of every entity bean that manages its own persistence (that is, a *bean-managed persistent entity bean,* or BMP entity bean). If you add another finder method, the IDE automatically places the corresponding method declarations in the local home (and home) interface and, for BMP entity beans, in the bean class.

An entity bean that delegates its persistence to the container is called a *container-managed persistent entity bean,* or CMP entity bean. Finder methods that are added to CMP entity beans include EJB Query Language (EJB QL) statements, which are converted automatically to the kind of SQL code the server needs.

The server integration plug-in module is what does this EJB QL conversion. NetBeans IDE 4.1 comes with a server integration plug-in for the Sun Java System Application Server. If you deploy to a different application server, you would need a corresponding plug-in module for that server to get the same functionality in the IDE as you get when deploying to the Sun Java System Application Server. Choose Tools | Update Center to check the IDE's update center for plug-in modules for other servers.

- **Create methods.** The container initializes the enterprise bean instance, using the create method's arguments.

- **Home methods.** An entity bean can use a home method for a lightweight operation that doesn't require access to any particular instance of the bean. (By contrast, a business method does require access to a particular instance.) It is up to you to add the home method explicitly; the IDE generates the corresponding method declaration in the bean class and the bean's local home or home interface. An entity bean can have any number of home methods.

- **Select methods.** A CMP entity bean can use a select method. Like a finder method, a select method can query the database and return a local or remote interface or a collection. In addition, a select method can query a related entity bean within the same EJB module and return values from its persistent fields. Select methods aren't exposed in remote-type interfaces and can't be invoked by a client.

- onMessage **methods.** A client sends a message through a Java Message Service (JMS) destination to call an onMessage method on a message-driven bean.

Adding a Simple Business Method

To add a business method:

1. Choose the Add | Business Method popup menu item from an enterprise bean's node (as shown in Figure 8-7) or choose EJB Methods | Add Business

Method from within the Source Editor for a bean implementation class (as shown in Figure 8-8).

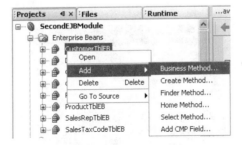

Figure 8-7   Projects window and adding a method to an enterprise bean

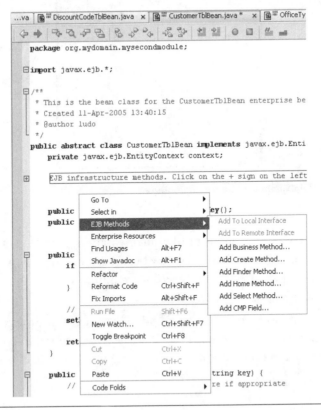

Figure 8-8   Source Editor and adding a method to an enterprise bean

2. In the Add Business Method dialog box (shown in Figure 8-9), enter a method name, a list of parameters and their type, as well as possible exceptions that will be thrown by this business method.

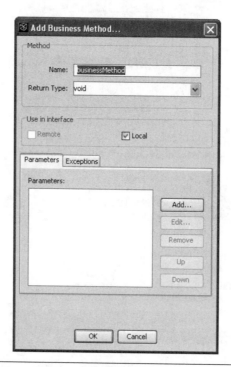

Figure 8-9   Add Business Method dialog box

Notice the change inside the bean implementation Java file (as shown in Figure 8-10). It now contains the new business method body, and now you can use the capabilities of the IDE's Source Editor to finish the implementation of the method.

3. When you are done coding the method, right-click your project's node in the Projects window and choose Build Project to trigger the compilation of the Java files and the creation of the EJB Archive (JAR) file in the dist directory.

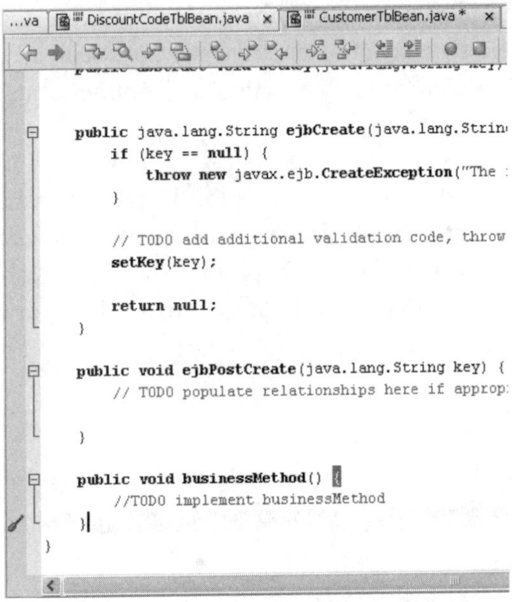

Figure 8-10 Source Editor with new business method added

Enterprise Bean Deployment Descriptors

One of the goals of the NetBeans IDE is to keep you from having to deal with deployment descriptors as much as possible. This is achieved via the zero-configuration concept implemented in the IDE. When you use the provided commands—such as Call Enterprise Bean, Use Database, Call Message, or Call Web Service Operation—the IDE performs the following tasks:

- Generates the Java code snippet for the JDNI lookup code in the caller Java file.
- Makes sure to update the J2EE deployment descriptor file by adding the corresponding EJB-REF or RESOURCE-REF elements.
- Modifies the J2EE project to add the necessary project dependencies if the call goes to a class or resource in another IDE project. The resulting packaging has to use the J2EE Application Project type to make sure all the J2EE modules are correctly assembled into a J2EE Application Archive (EAR) file before deployment.

Of course, you are still allowed to edit the deployment descriptors. Here also, the NetBeans IDE offers significant ease-of-use features, such as two editing modes (direct XML editing with code completion and online validation features, and visual editing).

The visual editor for a deployment descriptor file (shown in Figure 8-11) is activated by double-clicking the deployment descriptor's file node in the Projects window. A set of views is available. For a J2EE EJB module, for example, General and XML views are available. Also, a combo box to the right of the buttons for the views allows you to jump directly to a particular section in the deployment descriptor file.

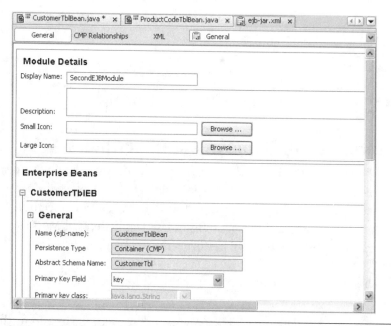

Figure 8-11   Visual deployment descriptor editor

If you want to edit the file's XML code directly, you can switch to the XML view of the file by clicking the XML button located at the top of the visual editor.

The XML editor (shown in Figure 8-12) also has a code completion feature to make hand coding faster and more accurate. See Generating Code Snippets in Chapter 4 for a general discussion of how code completion works.

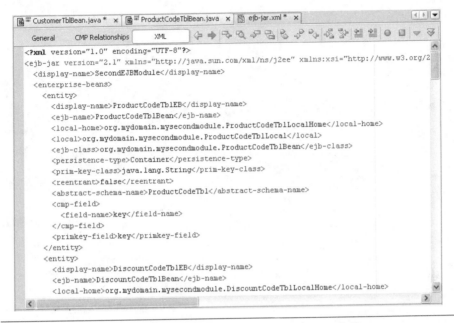

Figure 8-12 XML deployment descriptor editor with code completion

Also note the toolbar on this editor. The last icon (<image>) activates the XML validation action so that you can verify the conformance of the deployment descriptor
file with the DTD or schema. See Figure 8-13 for an example of the output after
running the XML Validation command.

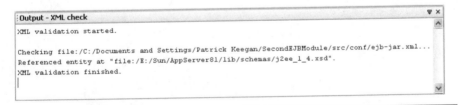

Figure 8-13 Output of XML validation

## CHAPTER 9

Extending J2EE Applications with Web Services

- Consuming Existing Web Services
- Implementing a Web Service in a Web Application
- Implementing Web Services within an EJB Module
- Testing Web Services
- Adding Message Handlers to a Web Service

IN THE FOLLOWING SECTIONS, YOU WILL LEARN HOW EASY IT IS to create and add web services to J2EE applications (both web applications and EJB modules) and how to publish them so that they can be used by other applications and tested from within the IDE.

What Is a Web Service?

The W3C organization defines web services as follows: "A Web service is a software system identified by a URI whose public interfaces and bindings are defined and described using XML. Its definition can be discovered by other software systems. These systems may then interact with the Web service in a manner prescribed by its definition, using XML-based messages conveyed by Internet protocols."

The implementation for a web service can be done in any language, and a web service can be accessed by many different platforms, because the messages are XML-based. The J2EE 1.4 platform has a specification (JSR 109) for web services creation for web applications (J2EE web tier-based) and EJB Modules. NetBeans IDE 4.1 supports the creation of such web services in J2EE applications, as well as the consumption of published web services within J2EE applications.

Web services allow applications to expose business operations to other applications, regardless of their implementation. This is possible via the use of the following standards:

- **XML, the common markup language for communication.** Service providers, which make services available, and service requestors, which use services, communicate via XML messages.
- **SOAP, the common message format for exchanging information.** These XML messages follow a well-defined format. Simple Object Access Protocol (SOAP) provides a common message format for web services.
- **WSDL, the common service specification format.** In addition to common message format and markup language, there must be a common format that all service providers can use to specify service details, such as the service type, the service parameters, and how to access the service. Web Services Description Language (WSDL) provides web services such common specification formats.

Consuming Existing Web Services

For a web service to be usable by other applications, a WSDL file must be published for the web service. It is this WSDL file that the application uses to construct the necessary artifacts. The NetBeans Web Service Client wizard automates the creation process and updates the deployment descriptor files with the appropriate `<service-ref>` elements.

To create a WSDL file:

1. Open the Web Service Client wizard by right-clicking the node of a web application project and choosing New | Web Service Client.

2. In the wizard (shown in Figure 9-1), pick a WSDL file from the URL of the running service or from a local directory on your system.

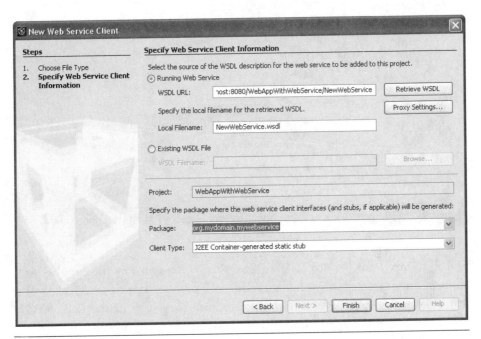

Figure 9-1   New File wizard, create web service client

Make sure you pick a package name for the generated interfaces that your user code will use to access and interact with this web service. Then choose a client type from the Client Type combo box. Two types of web service clients can be generated:

- **J2EE Container-generated static stub.** Defines the packaging of web services into standard J2EE modules, including a new deployment descriptor, and defines web services that are implemented as session beans or servlets. This is the recommended and portable (via the J2EE 1.4 specification) way.

- **IDE-generated static stub.** Defines the mapping of WSDL to Java classes and vice versa. It also defines a client API to invoke a remote web service and a runtime environment on the server to host a web service.

3. Click the Finish button.

4. In the Projects window, you should see a new logical node under the Web Services References node (see Figure 9-2). Explore the children of this node; for each web service operation defined in the WSDL file, the IDE shows a node that has the operation's name and a popup menu that allows you to test this operation directly within the IDE without writing a single line of code.

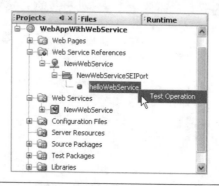

Figure 9-2   Projects window with populated Web Service References node

The necessary Web Service References entry in the web.xml file for this web application is updated, so you can use this web service from either a servlet or a utility Java class within your web application. The entry in the web.xml file should look something like the following code block:

```
<service-ref>
    <service-ref-name>service/SforceService</service-ref-name>
    <service-interface>org.mydomain.mywebservice.NewWebService
    </service-interface>
    <wsdl-file>WEB-INF/wsdl/enterprise.wsdl</wsdl-file>
    <jaxrpc-mapping-file>WEB-INF/wsdl/enterprise-mapping.xml
    </jaxrpc-mapping-file>
    <port-component-ref>
      <service-endpoint-interface>
          org.mydomain.mywebservice
      </service-endpoint-interface>
    </port-component-ref>
  </service-ref>
```

Publishing of the WSDL file is often done via a Universal Discovery, Description, and Integration (UDDI) registry. NetBeans IDE 4.1 does not provide a user interface for publishing web services to a UDDI registry. However this does not prevent you from using WSDL files that come from a UDDI registry or other source.

Although most of the time, the IDE selects the correct `wscompile` tool options for generating client code from the WSDL file, you can refine these options.

To modify the `wscompile` tool options for a project:

1. Right-click the project's main node and choose Properties to open the Project Properties dialog box.
2. Select the Web Services | Web Services Clients node (see Figure 9-3).

   For example, you can use checkboxes to set or disable the `wsi` or `strict` flags and other `wscompile` tool flags.

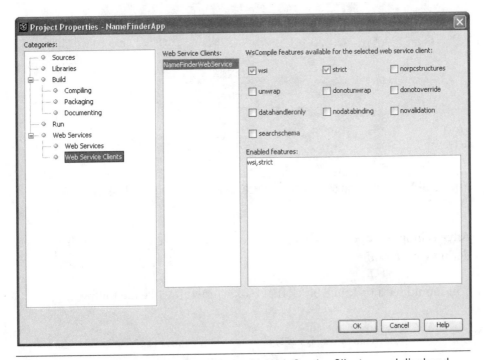

Figure 9-3   Project Properties dialog box with Web Service Clients panel displayed

Now you will want to call an operation for a web service within your Java code. To call an operation:

1. Right-click the location in your Java source code where you want to insert some code, and choose Web Service Client Resources | Call Web Service Operation (see Figure 9-4).

2. Select an operation from the Select Operation to Invoke dialog box.

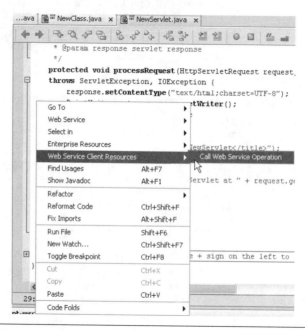

Figure 9-4   Generating code in the Source Editor for calling a web service operation

After calling the operation, you can see the new code that the IDE has added within your Java file.

You should see a try/catch block that looks something like the following:

```
try {
    getNewWebServiceSEIPort().helloWebService(

    /*TODO enter operation arguments */);
} catch(java.rmi.RemoteException ex) {
    // TODO handle remote exception
}
```

And you should see some private methods that do the web service reference lookup from the initial context and the RPC Port accessor for the selected operation, as follows:

```
private org.mydomain.mywebservices.NewWebServiceSEI
    getNewWebServiceSEIPort() {
 org.mydomain.mywebservices.NewWebServiceSEI
    newWebServiceSEIPort = null;
 try {
        javax.naming.InitialContext ic =
            new javax.naming.InitialContext();
        newWebService = (org.mydomain.mywebservices.NewWebService)
        ic.lookup("java:comp/env/service/NameFinderWebService");
    } catch(javax.naming.NamingException ex) {
        // TODO handle JNDI naming exception
    }
    return nameFinderWebService;
}

private org.mydomain.mywebservices.NewWebServiceSEI
  getNewWebServiceSEIPort() {
    org.mydomain.mywebservices.NewWebServiceSEI
        newWebServiceSEIPort = null;
 try {
        newWebServiceSEIPort =
            getNewWebService().getNewWebServiceSEIPort()
    } catch(javax.xml.rpc.ServiceException ex) {
        // TODO handle service exception
    }
    return newWebServiceSEIPort;
}
```

 Notice the // TODO statements in the added code. NetBeans J2EE wizards always add some TODO statements so that you can quickly find in the Java source code the areas you need to fill in, such as business logic that you need to complete. You can view all outstanding TODO statements in a single list by choosing Window | To Do.

Implementing a Web Service in a Web Application

In the IDE, you can create a web service by implementing an existing WSDL file, exposing existing code, or creating one from scratch. The IDE generates deployment information in the deployment descriptors, the necessary Java code that describes this web service (the default implementation; the Service Endpoint Interface, also called *SEI*; and a compilation target in the Ant build script).

A simple way to create a web service is to start from scratch.

Creating a Web Service

To create a new web service:

1. Right-click a web application's project node and choose New | Web Service.
2. In the New Web Service wizard (see Figure 9-5), specify a name and a Java package, select the From Scratch radio button, and click Finish.

   It is strongly recommended that you do *not* use the default package (which would occur if you left the Package field blank).

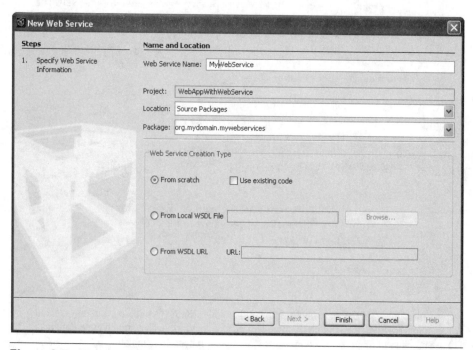

Figure 9-5 New Web Service wizard

A new web service with no operations is added to your project. You can see a logical node representing this new component in the Web Services node in the Projects window. A new servlet entry is added to the web.xml file, and a webservice-description entry is added in the webservices.xml description file (a sibling of the web.xml file). Most of the time, you don't need to worry at all about these entries, as they are automatically updated by the IDE when necessary.

As a developer, you will use the Projects window most (as opposed to the Files window). It synthesizes the implementation details of a web service (such as its implementation class and its SEI) and allows you to:

- Explore the existing operations
- Add new operations for the web service
- Register the web service to the runtime registry that will allow you to test it from within the IDE
- Configure any web service message handler classes that might be associated with it

Adding an Operation

Choose Add Operation (either by right-clicking the web service's node in the Projects window, as shown in Figure 9-6, or by right-clicking within the web service in the Source Editor). In the Add Operation dialog box (shown in Figure 9-7), you can configure the list of parameters for this operation, as well as the return type and any exceptions.

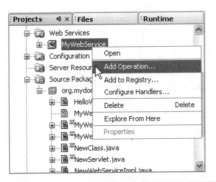

Figure 9-6　Adding an operation to a web service

The operation is added to the Java class implementing the web service (see Figure 9-8). The IDE automatically synchronizes the SEI, so you need to concentrate only on developing the operation method body.

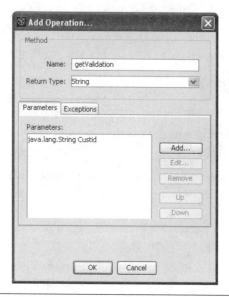

Figure 9-7 Add Operation dialog box

```
/**
 * Web service operation
 */
public String getValidation(java.lang.String Custid) {
    // TODO implement operation
    return null;
}
```

Figure 9-8 Adding an operation to a web service

Compiling the Web Service

Now that the web service has been added to your J2EE web application project, you just need to call the Build Project or Deploy Project command (available by right-clicking the project's node) to trigger an Ant build process that will invoke the wscompile tool with the correct parameters. The web application will be packaged as a WAR file and deployed to the target server for this project. The Ant output might look like the following (keeping in mind that by default the lines do not wrap the way they do in this excerpt):

```
init:
deps-module-jar:
deps-ear-jar:
deps-jar:
```

```
library-inclusion-in-archive:
library-inclusion-in-manifest:
Copying 2 files to C:\Documents and Settings\ludo\WebAppWithWebService\build\web
wscompile-init:
NewWebService_wscompile:
command line: wscompile C:\j2sdk1.4.2_06\jre\bin\java.exe -classpath
"C:\j2sdk1.4.2_06\lib\tools.jar;C:\Sun\AppServer81\lib\j2ee.jar;C:\Sun\AppServer81
\lib\saaj-api.jar;C:\Sun\AppServer81\lib\saaj-
impl.jar;C:\Sun\AppServer81\lib\jaxrpc-api.jar;C:\Sun\AppServer81\lib\jaxrpc-
impl.jar;C:\Documents and
Settings\ludo\WebAppWithWebService\build\web\WEB-INF\classes"
com.sun.xml.rpc.tools.wscompile.Main -d "C:\Documents and
Settings\ludo\WebAppWithWebService\build\generated\wssrc" -
features:documentliteral -gen:server -keep -mapping "C:\Documents and
Settings\ludo\WebAppWithWebService\build\web\WEB-INF\wsdl\NewWebService-
mapping.xml" -nd "C:\Documents and
Settings\ludo\WebAppWithWebService\build\web\WEB-INF\wsdl" -verbose -
Xprintstacktrace "C:\Documents and
Settings\ludo\WebAppWithWebService\src\java\com\acme\NewWebService-config.xml"
[creating model: NewWebService]
[creating service: NewWebService]
[creating port: org.mydomain.mywebservice NewWebServiceSEI]
[creating operation: getValidation]
[CustomClassGenerator: generating JavaClass for: getValidation]
[CustomClassGenerator: generating JavaClass for: getValidationResponse]
[LiteralObjectSerializerGenerator: writing  serializer/deserializer for:
getValidation]
[LiteralObjectSerializerGenerator: writing  serializer/deserializer for:
getValidationResponse]
[SerializerRegistryGenerator: creating serializer registry:
org.mydomain.mywebservice.NewWebService_SerializerRegistry]
compile:
compile-jsps:
Building jar: C:\Documents and
Settings\ludo\WebAppWithWebService\dist\WebAppWithWebService.war
do-dist:
dist:
run-deploy:
Starting server Sun Java System Application Server 8
C:\Sun\AppServer81\bin\asadmin.bat start-domain --domaindir
C:\Sun\AppServer81\domains\ domain1

Distributing C:\Documents and
Settings\ludo\WebAppWithWebService\dist\WebAppWithWebService.war to
[localhost:4848_server]
deployment started : 0%
Deployment of application WebAppWithWebService completed successfully
Enable of WebAppWithWebServicein target server completed successfully
```

```
run-display-browser:
Browsing: http://localhost:1228/WebAppWithWebService/
run:
BUILD SUCCESSFUL (total time: 12 seconds)
```

You can use a web browser (as shown in Figure 9-9) to query the deployed and running web application for the published WSDL file for this web service. In this case, the file is http://localhost:1228/WebAppWithWebService/NewWebService?WSDL.

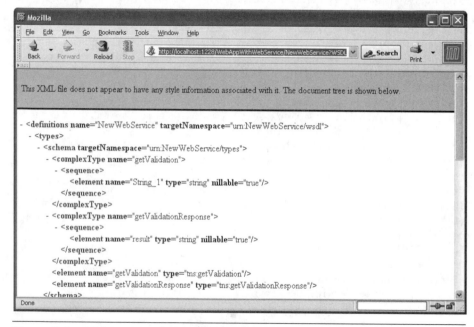

Figure 9-9   Web browser displaying the WDSL file for the web service

Your web service is now published and available to anyone so that other applications (J2EE applications, .NET applications, or J2ME applications) can interoperate with its operations.

Creating Web Services from WSDL

You can also create a web service from a WSDL document. A typical scenario when this is necessary is when business partners formulate the way they will communicate in web services. The "contract" between them would be the WSDL, in which they would agree on the data and messages that will be exchanged, as well as on how these messages will be sent and received. Then this WSDL is used to implement the web service.

The elements of a WSDL document can be categorized into *abstract* and *concrete* parts. The *types, message,* and *portType* elements describe the data that form the messages sent and received by web services and clients, as well as the operations that will use these messages. These sections constitute the abstract portion of the WSDL. The *binding* and *service* elements describe the protocols and transport mechanisms used to send and receive the messages, as well as the actual address of the endpoint. This is considered to be the concrete portion of the WSDL.

When you are creating a web service from a WSDL in NetBeans IDE, a new WSDL is created and packaged with the web service. The abstract portion of the original WSDL is copied to the new one. The concrete portion of the original WSDL is normalized for SOAP binding. Because the JAX-RPC runtime that is used in NetBeans IDE only supports SOAP over HTTP binding, the WSDL is searched for the first occurrence of this binding. If found, it is copied into the new WSDL. If not, a SOAP/HTTP binding is created for the first portType defined in the original WSDL. Thus, the web service created from WSDL in Net-Beans IDE will always have exactly one SOAP binding and one service port corresponding to that binding. The service element that is added will be named according to the web service name specified in the wizard, replacing the service element in the original WSDL.

To create a web service from a WSDL file, click the From Local WSDL File radio button or the From WSDL URL radio button in the wizard, depending on the source of the WSDL document. When the web service is created, classes for the service endpoint interface and implementation bean will be created. These classes will contain all the operations described in the WSDL. The implementation bean class will be displayed in the Source Editor, and you may then enter code to implement these operations. If the WSDL file describes operations that use complex types, classes for these types (known as *value types*) are also generated so that you may use them in your implementation code.

Because the WSDL document governs the interface to the web service, you may not add new operations to web services that are created from the WSDL, because these operations will not be reflected back in the WSDL.

Note that WSDLs that import other WSDLs are not supported by this facility.

Web Service Types

By default, NetBeans creates *document/literal* web services. This refers to the way the SOAP message is sent over the wire and is expressed in the SOAP binding part of the WSDL. The document/literal nomenclature comes from the way SOAP messages are described in the SOAP binding of a WSDL document—namely, its `style` and `use` attributes.

The `style` attribute refers to the formatting of the SOAP message. This basically refers to what the SOAP body will contain when it is sent over the wire.

There are two ways to format a SOAP message: RPC and document. When the style is RPC, the contents of the SOAP body are dictated by the rules of the SOAP specification—that is, the first child element is named after the operation, and its children are interpreted as the parameters of the method call. The endpoint will interpret this as an XML representation of a method call—that is, a remote procedure call. On the other hand, if the style attribute is `document`, the SOAP body consists of arbitrary XML, not constrained by any rules and able to contain whatever is agreed upon by the sender and receiver.

The `use` attribute describes how data is converted between XML and software objects—that is, how it is serialized to XML.

If the `use` attribute is `encoded`, the rules to encode/decode the data are dictated by some rules for encoding, the most common of which is the SOAP encoding specified in the SOAP specification. Section 5 of the SOAP specification defines how data should be serialized to XML. In this case, web services or clients see data in terms of objects.

If the `use` attribute is `literal`, the rules for encoding the data are dictated by an XML schema. There are no encoding rules, and the web service or client sees the data in terms of XML. Here, the developer does the work of parsing the XML to search for needed data.

Thus, document/literal web services typically are used to exchange business documents, whereas RPC/encoded web services typically are used to invoke remote objects. For this reason, document/literal is preferred over RPC/encoded because in document/literal, you have full control of the messages that are being exchanged. The WS-I Basic Profile, which is a specification for web services interoperability, does not support RPC/encoded web services. Following are the advantages of document/literal over RPC/encoded web services:

- Document/literal formatting is more interoperable than RPC/encoded formatting because RPC formatting tends to bind the messages to programming language structures.
- Document/literal web services scale better than RPC/encoded because of the overhead involved in marshalling and unmarshalling RPC data.
- Document-centric web services lend themselves to validation of the documents being exchanged. This is cumbersome to do with RPC-style services.

Implementing Web Services within an EJB Module

To implement a web service in an EJB module, you will use a similar web service wizard described for the web application. Most of the artifacts that are created and the deployment descriptor entries that are added for the module are similar to those in a web application. You will follow the same procedure for adding SOAP message handlers and configuring them in web services.

One significant difference is the implementation bean of a web service in an EJB module. JSR 109 requires that web services be implemented in the EJB module as stateless session beans. Thus, the implementation of the web service operations in an EJB module is contained in the session bean class. The module's deployment descriptor will have a stateless session bean entry, but this will declare an endpoint interface instead of a local or remote interface. Also, a web service in an EJB module does not have a home interface.

Once you have created a web service within an EJB module, you will see the web service logical node in the Projects window (shown in Figure 9-10). The source code you will manipulate is the stateless session bean implementation class. The developer experience is similar to the development of a web service with a web application.

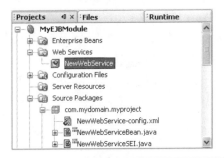

Figure 9-10   Web service within an EJB module

In the Source Packages node, you can see the service bean class as well as the SEI and the service XML config file.

Testing Web Services

NetBeans IDE has a built-in test environment for publishing web services, either for those created by you and deployed within a web application or a J2EE application or those published externally. All you need is access to the WSDL file for this web service. You can use the Web Services Registry tool from the Web Services node in the IDE's Runtime window (shown in Figure 9-11) to register the web services in the IDE.

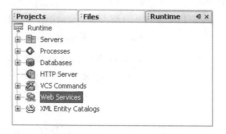

Figure 9-11   Web Services registry in the Runtime window

To add a web service to the registry:

1. Right-click the Web Services node in the Runtime window and choose Add Web Service to activate the wizard.

2. In the wizard (see Figure 9-12), enter the WSDL file (either as a URL or local file) and click the Add button.

   Once you specify the file and click the Add button, the service's operations are available as nodes in the registry, and you can use the Test Operation command.

To test the web service operation:

1. In the Runtime window, expand the Web Services node and navigate to the node for the operation you want to test (this node should have no sub-nodes); right-click that node and choose Test Operation (see Figure 9-13).

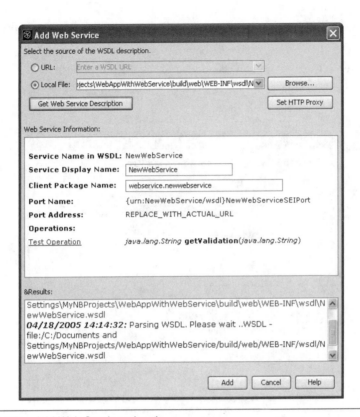

Figure 9-12   Add Web Service wizard

Figure 9-13   Choosing the Test Operation command on a web service in the Runtime window

2. In the wizard that appears (see Figure 9-14), enter any input parameters for this operation and click Submit.

The web service operation is called, and the output parameters are displayed in the Results area.

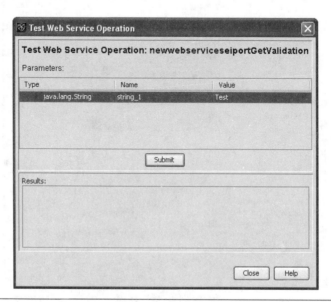

Figure 9-14   The Test Web Service Operation dialog box

Adding Message Handlers to a Web Service

NetBeans IDE makes it easy to develop J2EE web services and clients because it shields application developers from the underlying SOAP messages. Instead of writing code to build and parse SOAP messages, application developers merely implement the service methods and invoke them from remote clients.

However, there might be times when you want to add functionality to web service applications without having to change the web service or client code. For example, you might want to encrypt remote calls at the SOAP message level. SOAP message handlers provide the mechanism for adding this functionality without having to change the business logic. Handlers accomplish this by intercepting the SOAP message as it makes its way between the client and service.

A SOAP message handler is a stateless instance that accesses SOAP messages representing RPC requests, responses, or faults. Tied to service endpoints, handlers enable you to process SOAP messages and to extend the functionality of the service. For a given service endpoint, one or more handlers may reside on the server and client.

A SOAP request is handled as follows:

- The client handler is invoked before the SOAP request is sent to the server.
- The service handler is invoked before the SOAP request is dispatched to the service endpoint.

A SOAP response is processed in this order:

1. The service handler is invoked before the SOAP response is sent back to the client.
2. The client handler is invoked before the SOAP response is transformed into a Java method return and passed back to the client program.

To create a message handler in a web application in the IDE:

1. Right-click the web application's node in the Projects window and choose New | Message Handler.
2. On the New Message Handler page of the New File wizard (shown in Figure 9-15), enter a name and package for the handler and click Finish.

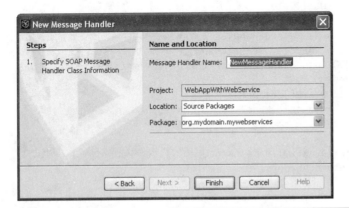

Figure 9-15   New Message Handler page of the New File wizard

The new Java file created contains the core code for the message handler, as shown in the code sample below.

One interesting method here is handleRequest(MessageContext context), which is called before the SOAP message is dispatched to the endpoint. The generated handler class provides a default implementation of this method (as an example), which prints out the contents of the SOAP body plus some date information. Note that the MessageContext parameter provides a context for obtaining the transmitted SOAP message. You may then use the SAAJ API (SOAP with Attachments API for Java) to access and manipulate the SOAP message.

Another method, handleResponse(MessageContext context), is called before the response message is sent back to the caller. This method, together with handleFault, provides only the default implementation; it is left to you to provide your own implementation.

```
package org.mydomain.mywebservice ;

import javax.xml.rpc.handler.MessageContext;
import javax.xml.rpc.handler.HandlerInfo;
import javax.xml.rpc.handler.soap.SOAPMessageContext;
import javax.xml.namespace.QName;
import javax.xml.soap.SOAPElement;
import javax.xml.soap.SOAPMessage;
import javax.xml.soap.SOAPPart;
import javax.xml.soap.SOAPEnvelope;
import javax.xml.soap.SOAPHeader;
import javax.xml.soap.SOAPBody;
import java.util.Date;

public class NewMessageHandler extends
javax.xml.rpc.handler.GenericHandler {
    // TODO Change and enhance the handle methods to suit individual
    // needs.
    private QName[] headers;
    public void init(HandlerInfo config) {
        headers = config.getHeaders();
    }
    public javax.xml.namespace.QName[] getHeaders() {
        return headers;
    }
    // Currently prints out the contents of the SOAP body plus some date
    // information.
    public boolean handleRequest(MessageContext context) {
```

```
try{
    SOAPMessageContext smc = (SOAPMessageContext) context;
    SOAPMessage msg = smc.getMessage();
    SOAPPart sp = msg.getSOAPPart();
    SOAPEnvelope se = sp.getEnvelope();
    SOAPHeader shd = se.getHeader();

    SOAPBody sb = se.getBody();
    java.util.Iterator childElems = sb.getChildElements();
    SOAPElement child;
    StringBuffer message = new StringBuffer();
    while (childElems.hasNext()) {
        child = (SOAPElement) childElems.next();
        message.append(new Date().toString() + "--");
        formLogMessage(child, message);
    }

    System.out.println("Log message: " + message.toString());
} catch(Exception e){
    e.printStackTrace();
}
return true;
}

public boolean handleResponse(MessageContext context) {
    return true;
}

public boolean handleFault(MessageContext context) {
    return true;
}

public void destroy() {
}

private void formLogMessage(SOAPElement child, StringBuffer message) {
    message.append(child.getElementName().getLocalName());
    message.append(child.getValue() != null ? ":" + child.getValue()
        + " " : " ");

    try{
        java.util.Iterator childElems = child.getChildElements();
        while (childElems.hasNext()) {
            Object c = childElems.next();
            if(c instanceof SOAPElement)
                formLogMessage((SOAPElement)c, message);
        }
    }catch(Exception e){
```

```
                    e.printStackTrace();
        }
    }
}
```

Once this message handler is created, you need to associate it with your web service.

To associate a message handler with a web service:

1. Right-click the web service in the Projects window and choose Configure Handlers.

2. In the Configure SOAP Message Handlers dialog box (shown in Figure 9-16), click Add, and navigate to and select the message handler.

   The IDE automatically updates the `webservices.xml` file under the `WEB-INF` directory of your web application by adding the `<handler>` element.

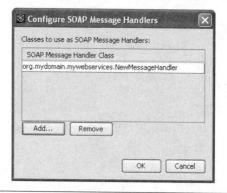

Figure 9-16 Configure SOAP Message Handlers dialog box

Following is an example of a `webservices.xml` file that the IDE has updated for you. (In general, you do not have to worry about this file at all. The IDE keeps it up to date for you.)

```xml
<?xml version='1.0' encoding='UTF-8' ?>
<webservices xmlns='http://java.sun.com/xml/ns/j2ee' version='1.1'>
    <webservice-description>
        <webservice-description-name>
            NewWebService
        </webservice-description-name>
```

```
<wsdl-file>WEB-INF/wsdl/NewWebService.wsdl</wsdl-file>
<jaxrpc-mapping-file>
      WEB-INF/wsdl/NewWebService-mapping.xml
</jaxrpc-mapping-file>
<port-component xmlns:wsdl-port_ns='urn:NewWebService/wsdl'>
      <port-component-name>NewWebService</port-component-name>
      <wsdl-port>wsdl-port_ns:NewWebServiceSEIPort</wsdl-port>

      <service-endpoint-interface>
          org.mydomain.mywebservice .NewWebServiceSEI
        </service-endpoint-interface>
      <service-impl-bean>
            <servlet-link>WSServlet_NewWebService</servlet-link>
      </service-impl-bean>
      <handler>
        <handler-name></handler-name>

        <handler-class>
              org.mydomain.mywebservice.NewMessageHandler
          </handler-class>
      </handler>
    </port-component>
  </webservice-description>
</webservices>
```

To see the effect of the message handler on the web service, perform the following steps:

1. Run the web application by right-clicking its node in the Projects window and choosing Run Project.

2. Add the web service to the IDE registry by right-clicking the web service's node in the Projects window and choosing Add to Registry.

3. Switch to the Runtime window of the IDE; then navigate through the hierarchy of web service nodes, right-click an operation node, and choose Test Operation (as shown in Figure 9-13).

4. In the Test Web Service Operation dialog box (shown in Figure 9-14), enter the input parameters and click the Submit button.

You can see the handler trace in the application server log file by opening the Runtime window, expanding the Servers node, right-clicking the Sun Java System Application Server node, and choosing View Server Log. A trace that looks something like the following should be displayed:

```
[#|2005-02-20T16:59:01.293-0800|DPL5306:Servlet Web service Endpoint
[NewWebService] listening at address [http://129.145.133.80:1228/
WebAppWithWebService/NewWebService]|#]
[#|2005-02-20T16:59:02.084-
0800|javax.enterprise.system.tools.deployment|DPL5306:Servlet Web service
Endpoint [NewWebService] listening at address [http://
129.145.133.80:1228/WebAppWithWebService/NewWebService]|#]
[#|2005-02-20T16:59:14.292-0800||javax.enterprise.system.stream.out|Log
message: Sun Feb 20 16:59:14 PST 2005--getValidation String_1:klkl |#]
[#|2005-02-20T17:05:40.297-0800|javax.enterprise.system.stream.out|
Log message: Sun Feb 20 17:05:40 PST 2005--getValidation String_1:fdfd
|#]
```

## CHAPTER 10

Developing Full-Scale J2EE Applications

- Creating Entity Beans with the Top-Down Approach
- Creating Entity Beans with the Bottom-Up Approach
- Assembling J2EE Applications
- Importing Existing J2EE Applications
- Consuming J2EE Resources
- J2EE and Security Management
- Understanding the J2EE Application Server Runtime Environment
- Ensuring J2EE Compliance
- Refactoring Enterprise Beans

THE PREVIOUS TWO CHAPTERS PROVIDED SOME STRATEGIES for extending web applications with J2EE enterprise-tier technology. This chapter continues the path of those chapters and handles topics such as entity beans, consuming resources, assembling applications from multiple code modules, and verifying the J2EE compliance of applications.

Entity Beans

Beginning with the Enterprise JavaBeans 1.1 specification, entity beans have been a required part of the J2EE platform. Entity beans provide a Java *idiom* (method invocation) for accessing relational functionality in addition to the container benefits provided in the J2EE specification, such as transaction support and security. An entity bean allows persistence to be handled by the container (*container-managed persistence*, or *CMP*) or by the developer (*bean-managed persistence*, or *BMP*). The difference between the two is that with CMP beans you need to define how the Java representation is mapped to the relational model (the container handles the code generation required to make this happen), whereas with BMP beans you must provide both the data representation and the implementation that reflects changes to the Java object model in the database. One common approach to bean-managed persistence is to use JDBC in the enterprise bean lifecycle methods.

A developer starting with an existing relational database must map the relational model currently in the database (if the database is in use by other applications, schema changes typically are not possible) to an object model. There are many possible complex mappings between an object model and the relational database. Relational database views are analogous; some of the same issues may be encountered during the mapping process (for example, a view can be created that cannot be updated, normally because of constraint violations).

Container-managed persistence provides some development advantages over bean-managed persistence. CMP beans allow you to work on an abstract schema, which is the combination of fields and relationships, independent of the underlying mapping to the relational database. The underlying mapping is provided by the application server, through the native object to relational mapping functionality. This capability extends to queries, which are written based on the abstract schema in the Enterprise JavaBeans Query Language (EJB QL). The query language is similar to the query capability provided in SQL.

This separation allows you to provide an object model and implementation that is separate from the mapping, thereby reducing the coupling. Thus, container-managed beans can be developed faster. Some proponents also claim that their runtime performance is better than that of BMP beans because the optimizations can be done in the server.

Bean-managed persistence requires that you implement the life-cycle methods to interact with the persistent storage mechanism. Typically, you would provide and execute SQL queries in the implementation of the life-cycle methods (`ejbStore` would perform an update, `ejbCreate` would perform an insert, and `ejbLoad` would perform a select). The disadvantage of doing JDBC directly in the entity bean is that you do not achieve productivity gains and may not achieve increased performance because of the impedance mismatch between the programming language and a relational database. (Programming languages operate on an object at a time, whereas a relational database can operate on sets of data.) The performance increase may not be realized, because one common mapping is between a row and an object instance. In the entity model, set operations are performed by iterating over a collection of Java objects that cause SQL statements operating on a single row to be invoked. You may be able to incorporate existing tuned queries directly into this model by using a different data representation to enable set-based operations.

NetBeans IDE provides both a top-down and a bottom-up approach for creating a related set of CMP entity beans. The top-down approach first creates the entity beans that describe the abstract schema (fields and relationships representing the data model). The Sun Java System Application Server provides a facility for automatically generating the required database tables. Or you can have the database schema created and use the application server mapping facility. The bottom-up approach generates the beans based on an existing database schema (the generation will produce CMP entity beans).

Creating Entity Beans with the Top-Down Approach

Creating an entity bean from the top down is comprised of the following general steps:

1. Add a bean to your EJB module, using the Entity Bean template in the New File wizard.

2. Select a primary key class for the bean, using the `ejb-jar.xml` file's visual editor.

3. (For BMP beans) Implement the life-cycle methods.

4. (For CMP beans) Add container-managed fields. You can generate such fields by right-clicking the entity bean's "logical" node (under the Enterprise Beans node) in the Projects window and choosing Add | CMP Field or by right-clicking in the bean class in the Source Editor and choosing EJB Methods | AddCMP Field.

5. (For CMP beans) Add container-managed relationships. You can do so in the `ejb-jar.xml` file's visual editor.

6. Add finder methods. You can generate such methods by right-clicking a bean class in the Projects window and choosing Add | Finder Method or by right-clicking the bean class in the Source Editor and choosing EJB Methods | Add Finder Method.

7. Add business methods. You can generate such methods by right-clicking a bean class in the Projects window and choosing Add | Business Method or by right-clicking the bean class in the Source Editor and choosing EJB Methods | Add Business Method.

8. Set up the data source on the application server.

9. (CMP only) If the application server's CMP capability is being used, map the abstract schema specified in the entity bean to a persistence model.

Creating an Entity Bean

NetBeans IDE provides a wizard for creating entity beans in an EJB project (see Figure 10-1).

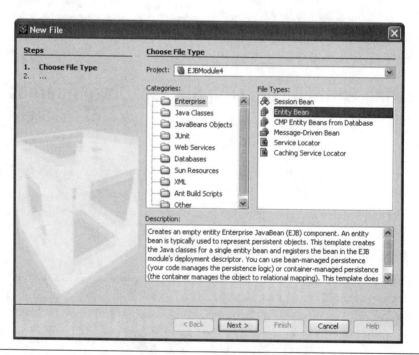

Figure 10-1   New File wizard with the Entity Bean template selected

The wizard collects the minimum information necessary for creation of either a CMP or BMP entity bean. The wizard generates the necessary deployment descriptor entries along with a local home, a local component interface (this provides the ability to perform compile-time checking on the bean class for the component interface methods), a business interface, and a bean class.

The classes are named following the BluePrints recommendations. The component interface will initially be empty, and the home interface will contain the required findByPrimaryKey method. The primary key will default to String, which can be changed later using the visual editor (which is accessible by double-clicking the ejb-jar.xml file, under the Configuration Files node in the Projects window). The visual editor for the deployment descriptor is shown in Figure 10-2.

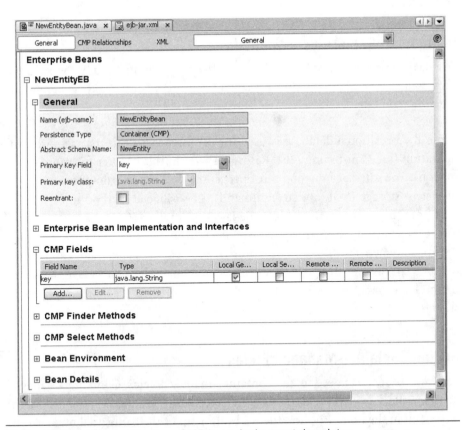

Figure 10-2 Visual editor for a CMP bean deployment descriptor

The deployment descriptor entry includes a display name (using BluePrints recommended naming conventions based on the EJB name). The assembly descriptor also is updated to require transactions for all methods.

Selecting a Primary Key Class

You can select a primary key class for the bean in the deployment descriptor (ejb-jar.xml file). A Java class representing the unique identifier (key) for each entity type must be selected. A Java class must represent the entire key. Compound keys and fields defined as primitive types require creation of wrapper classes. The wrapper class generally overrides equals and hashCode. For CMP beans, this class must also provide public fields with names matching the CMP fields composing the key.

Implementing Life-Cycle Methods

For BMP beans, you need to implement the life-cycle methods. The required work will also be highlighted using TODO comments in the code generated by the bean template.

Typically, a relational database is used for persistence, so this may require configuration (see Consuming J2EE Resources later in this chapter for more information). The ejbStore method must persist the data model from memory to the persistent storage (SQL update command). The ejbLoad method must retrieve data from the persistent model into the Java data model (SQL select statement). The ejbRemove method must remove data from the persistent model (SQL delete statement). Although not required, an ejbCreate statement can be used to add to persistent storage (SQL create statement). The ejbFindByPrimaryKey method is also required, which should determine whether the key is in persistent storage.

Adding Container-Managed Fields

For CMP beans, you need to add container-managed fields. Container-managed fields are the data attributed to this entity. Fields can be added via the EJB Methods menu in the Source Editor, the Add submenu of the contextual menu of the bean's node in the Projects window, or the visual editor for the ejb-jar.xml file. The wizards also provide checkboxes to expose the methods in the local interface.

Adding Container-Managed Relationships

(CMP only) To add container-managed relationships, select the CMP Relationships view in the `ejb-jar.xml` file's editor and then click the Add button to open the Add CMP Relationship dialog box (shown in Figure 10-3). A container-managed relationship represents an association between entity beans. The relationship is managed by the container, which means that adding or removing from one side of the relationship is reflected in the other side.

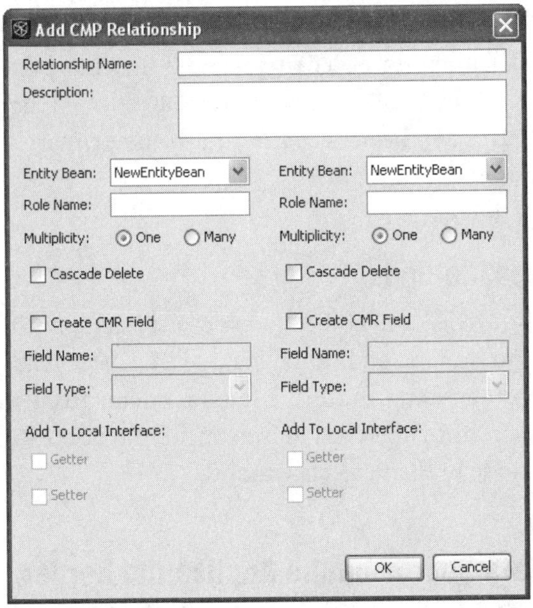

Figure 10-3   Add CMP Relationship dialog box

The Add CMP Relationship dialog box collects the information necessary to generate the necessary deployment descriptor entries and the abstract get and set methods (if navigable).

In the Add CMP Relationship dialog box, the Entity Bean combo box represents the bean on each side of the relationship. The Cascade Delete checkbox enforces referential integrity by removing the dependent bean if the referenced bean is removed. A container-managed relationship (CMR) field (represented as an abstract getter and setter in the bean class) provides the ability to navigate to the other side of the relationship. These fields can be exposed using the Add to Local Interface checkbox.

Adding Finder Methods

Finder methods represent the ability to obtain a set of entity beans based on a set of search criteria. The Add Finder method dialog box can be accessed by right-clicking a bean class in the Projects window (and choosing Add | Finder Method) or the Source Editor (and choosing EJB Methods | Add Finder Method).

The EJB specification requires that a findByPrimaryKey method be present. CMP beans specify an EJB Query Language (EJB QL) query to define additional finder methods. The EJB QL query must return instances of the abstract schema for this EJB. The default abstract schema name is the enterprise bean name, so a typical bean query would be SELECT OBJECT(o) FROM MyAbstractSchemaName AS o WHERE o.color = ?1. BMP beans need to return the primary key (or keys) that meet the search criteria.

Adding Business Methods

Business methods provide the ability to expose services. Entity beans may add business methods to provide additional logic or to expose data. Adding business methods may be done using the EJB Methods menu from the Source Editor contextual menu or from the Add submenu of the contextual menu for the enterprise bean's node in the Projects window.

Setting Up a Data Source on the Application Server

A data source must be set up on the application server. This applies to both BMP and CMP beans. BMP beans may be able to take advantage of the IDE's Use Database enterprise resource capability, whereas CMP beans generally must specify a reference to the application server's CMP resource. (The form varies among application servers but typically is similar to what is done to set up a standard JDBC data source.)

Mapping a Bean's Schema to a Persistence Model

If the application server's CMP capability is being used, the mapping from the abstract schema specified in the CMP entity bean to a persistence model (most commonly a relational database) must be performed. The Sun Java System Application Server provides the ability to create the tables during deployment (so no mapping is necessary in this case). This can be done by specifying the Create Table At Deploy (and, optionally, Drop Table at Undeploy) properties in the IDE's visual editor for the project's `sun-ejb-jar.xml` file, as shown in Figure 10-4.

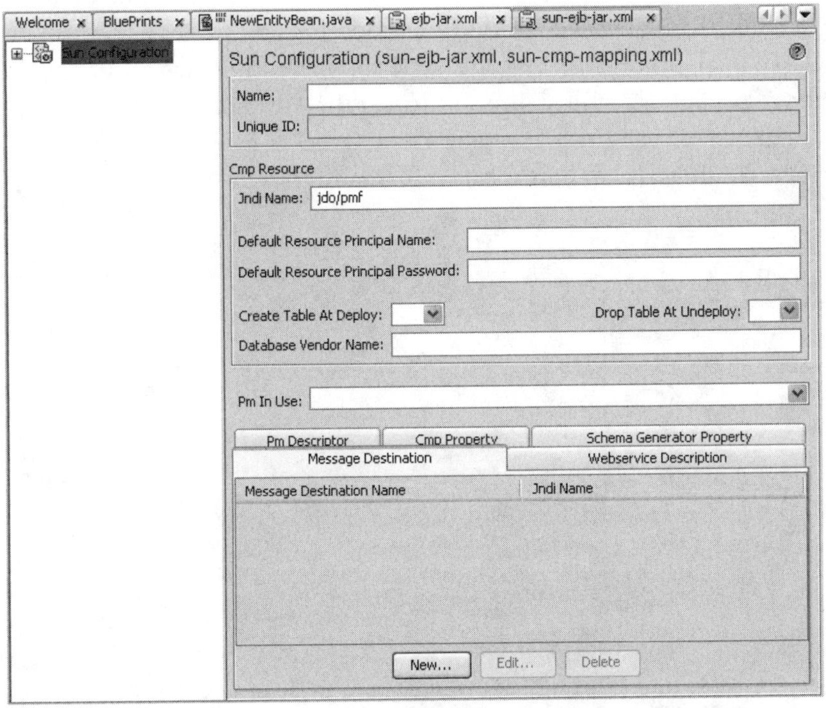

Figure 10-4   Visual editor for the `sun-ejb-jar.xml` file (Sun Configuration panel)

Mapping is done by describing how each CMP field and relationship represents a column in the database. As of the EJB 2.1 specification, this mapping is server specific and, thus, must be performed using the application server editor. When performing the mapping using Sun Java System Application Server 8.1, the first step is to create a database schema file from an existing database. The database schema must be created as a peer to the `sun-ejb-jar.xml` file (which is located in the `src/conf` folder and can be accessed from the Configuration Files node in the Projects window). A database schema object provides an XML snapshot of the database metadata. The application server uses this during design-time mapping as a way to access database metadata (without requiring a live database connection). This file is also passed to the application server during deployment for use during code generation.

Once the database schema object has been created, each CMP bean must specify the database schema which contains the table to which it is mapping. This dialog box is launched by double-clicking the node for the `sun-ejb-jar.xml` file to open its visual editor, selecting the node for the entity bean in the left pane, selecting the Cmp Mapping tab, and clicking the Advanced Settings button. The visual editor with the Cmp Mapping tab selected is shown in Figure 10-5. The Advanced Settings dialog box is shown in Figure 10-6.

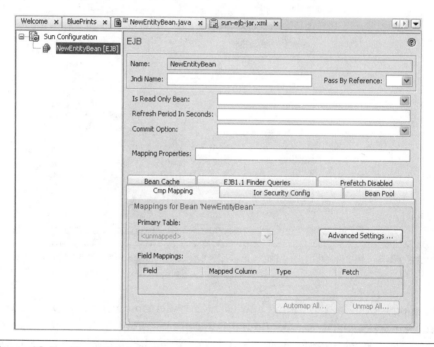

Figure 10-5 Visual Editor for the `sun-ejb-jar.xml` file (EJB panel with Cmp Mapping tab selected)

The final step of mapping CMP and relationship fields from a table can be performed from the Cmp Mapping tab (see Figure 10-7).

The Automap All button automates the mapping between tables and fields. Using this feature provides full automation for most mappings, which can be further customized later (or even removed using the Unmap All feature).

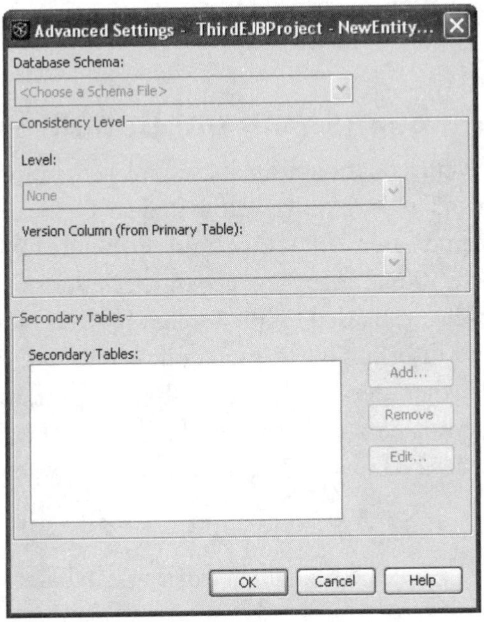

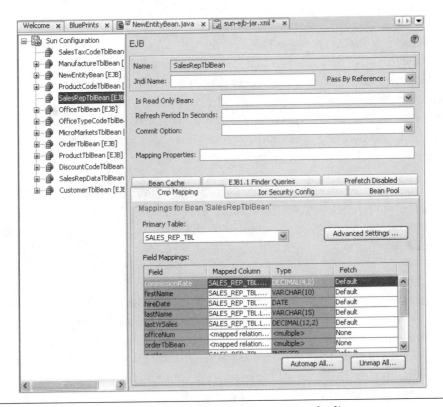

Figure 10-6 CMP Mapping Advanced Settings dialog box

Figure 10-7 CMP mapping in the `sun-ejb-jar.xml` visual editor

Creating Entity Beans with the Bottom-Up Approach

Starting with an existing relational database and generating entity beans that represent a natural mapping is fully automated in NetBeans IDE 4.1. From a single wizard, you can create CMP entity beans, generate CMP fields with types appropriate for the relational mapping, generate relationship fields (along with the relationship cardinality) based on the foreign key and index constraints, and provide the mapping information to the application server (see the top-down approach for details when performed manually). The wizard will detect joined tables, so there may not be a one-to-one mapping between tables and entity beans from the selected database. The wizard will also generate primary key classes if necessary.

To create a set of entity beans based on an existing database:

1. In the Projects window, right-click the node of the EJB module that you want to add the beans to and choose New | CMP Entity Beans From Database.
2. Complete the wizard to create the mappings.

The wizard contains two steps (see Figures 10-8 and 10-9). The first step specifies how to obtain database metadata. The package for the generated Java classes is also required. The wizard also allows default generation of finder methods and exposing the fields in the component interface. Make sure the underlying database process is already started. (If you are using the Pointbase database that is included with Sun Java System Application Server 8.1, you can start it from the IDE via the Tools | Pointbase Database menu item.)

If the Generate Finder Methods for CMP Fields checkbox is selected, a single-argument finder method, along with the corresponding EJB QL query for selecting the collection of entity beans matching the input parameter, is generated for each CMP field.

Selecting the Add CMR and CMP Fields to the Local Interface checkbox will generate a method in the local interface for each CMP and relationship field. This typically is used in conjunction with the transfer object and transfer-object assembler pattern from a session facade to create domain objects based on entity beans. The transfer objects are standard serializable Java classes that represent the data and can be used outside of J2EE components. The transfer object assembler typically is a Java class that can create transfer objects (from an entity bean, in this case). A session facade typically is used to provide a coarse-grained

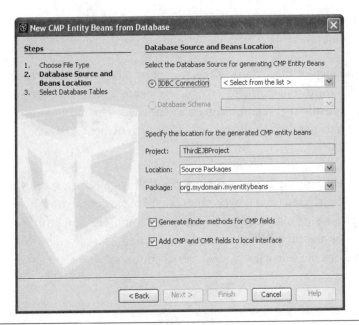

Figure 10-8 Database Source and Beans Location page of the New File wizard for the CMP Entity Beans from Database template

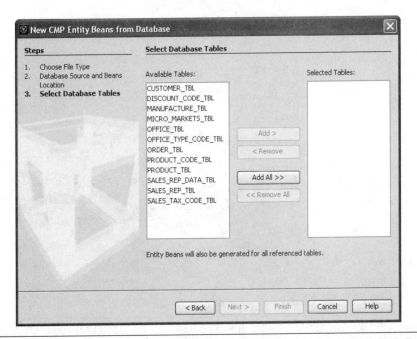

Figure 10-9 Select Database Tables page of the New File wizard for the CMP Entity Beans from Database template

set of services. A session facade can encapsulate entity bean access and reduce coupling (and increase performance) for clients.

The second step of the wizard selects the set of tables to include in the generation. The wizard will perform transitive closure (based on foreign key constraints) to ensure that relationships are generated. The most common scenario is to select a group of logically related beans to generate CMP beans for a single module.

After you select all the tables you need, the IDE will create a set of CMP beans, one per table selected (and maybe others that are part of the transitive closure of the foreign keys/primary keys of the selected table). The Sun Java System Application Server mapping will be correctly configured. You can still tweak it the way you need from the `sun-ejb-jar.xml` visual editor, as shown in Figure 10-10.

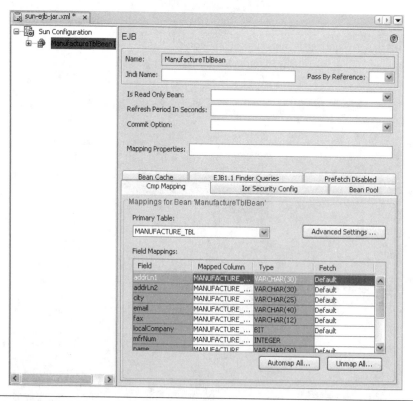

Figure 10-10   Visual editor for the `sun-ejb-jar.xml` file with a CMP bean selected

Assembling J2EE Applications

A J2EE application is a collection of web applications and EJB modules that interact with one another and that can be assembled, deployed, and executed as a unit. NetBeans IDE takes advantage of the capability to declare dependencies between projects in defining a J2EE application project. Previous chapters cover creation of individual web application and EJB Module projects. A NetBeans J2EE Application project aggregates these individual projects.

You can create a J2EE application by opening the New Project wizard and selecting the Enterprise Application template, as shown in Figure 10-11. You can then add individual modules (one IDE project per module) to the J2EE application.

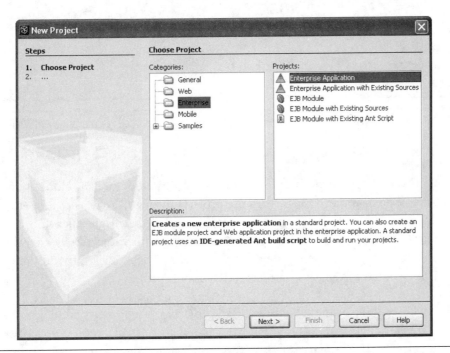

Figure 10-11   New Project wizard with the Enterprise Application template selected

When you are creating a NetBeans J2EE Application project, the Name and Location page of the wizard (shown in Figure 10-12) gives you the option of creating one empty EJB Module project and one simple Web Application project.

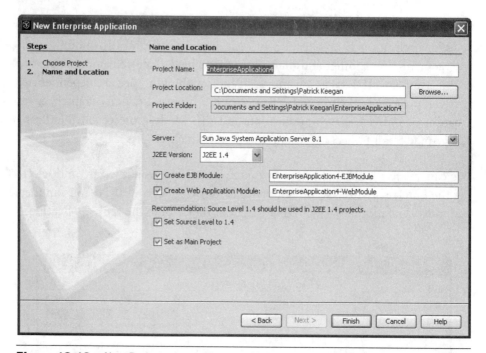

Figure 10-12   New Project wizard, Name and Location page for the Enterprise Application project template

You can later add web application modules and EJB modules to a J2EE Application project (or remove them from the project) through the Project Properties dialog box of the J2EE Application project. To do that, right-click the J2EE application's project and choose Properties. Then, in the Project Properties dialog box, select the Packaging node (see Figure 10-13) and click the Add Project button to add the Web Application or EJB Module project.

You will see three or more NetBeans IDE projects in the Projects window when you are working with a J2EE application (see Figure 10-14): the J2EE Application project itself that exposes the application deployment descriptors (application.xml and possibly sun-application.xml) and then one NetBeans IDE project per module that is part of the application. The J2EE Application project will delegate the build steps for all the submodules and will package the resulting EJB JAR files or Web Archive (WAR) files into a deployable application archive called an EAR (Enterprise Archive) file.

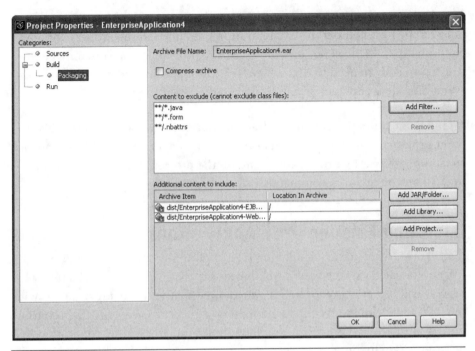

Figure 10-13 Project Properties dialog box for an Enterprise Application project with the Packaging panel displayed

Figure 10-14 Projects window showing an Enterprise Application project that contains an EJB module and a web module (each of which is also an IDE project)

The deployment descriptor for a J2EE application is called `application.xml` (and can be found under the Configuration Files node in the Projects window). NetBeans IDE 4.1 does not provide a visual editor for this file, mainly because you are unlikely to need to edit it. The IDE automatically updates this file whenever a module is added to or removed from the application.

A J2EE application project can be cleaned, built, executed, and deployed like any other projects in the IDE. You can also verify the application's J2EE compliance by running the Verify Project command on the project. Right-click the project's node to see the menu of commands.

Importing Existing J2EE Applications

If you have already started developing J2EE applications outside of NetBeans IDE, it is not too late to switch your development environment to NetBeans IDE. This process will be very easy for you if your source structure already complies with the J2EE BluePrints conventions. It might be a good time to study these conventions and modify your project to follow these guidelines. Your application will be easier to maintain, new developers joining your project will know immediately where things are, and the integration with NetBeans IDE and its powerful build system (entirely based on Ant) will be straightforward.

Importing BluePrints Conventions-Compatible J2EE Application Projects

If you have started your development without NetBeans IDE, and you are following the Java BluePrints conventions for your project structure, you can use the Enterprise Application with Existing Sources template in the New Project wizard (shown in Figure 10-15).

To import an existing enterprise application:

1. Choose File | New Project.
2. In the New Project wizard, select the Enterprise folder, select the Enterprise Application with Existing Sources template, and click Next.
3. In the Name and Location page of the wizard (see Figure 10-16), fill in the Location field with a valid top-level directory containing a BluePrints-compliant J2EE application.

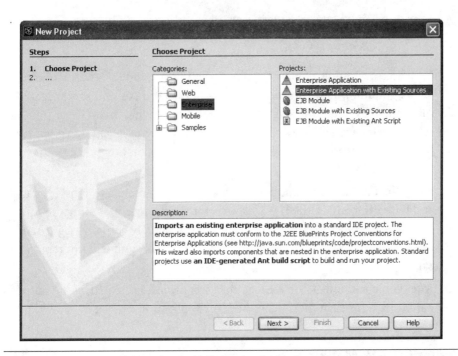

Figure 10-15　New Project wizard with Enterprise Application with Existing Sources template selected

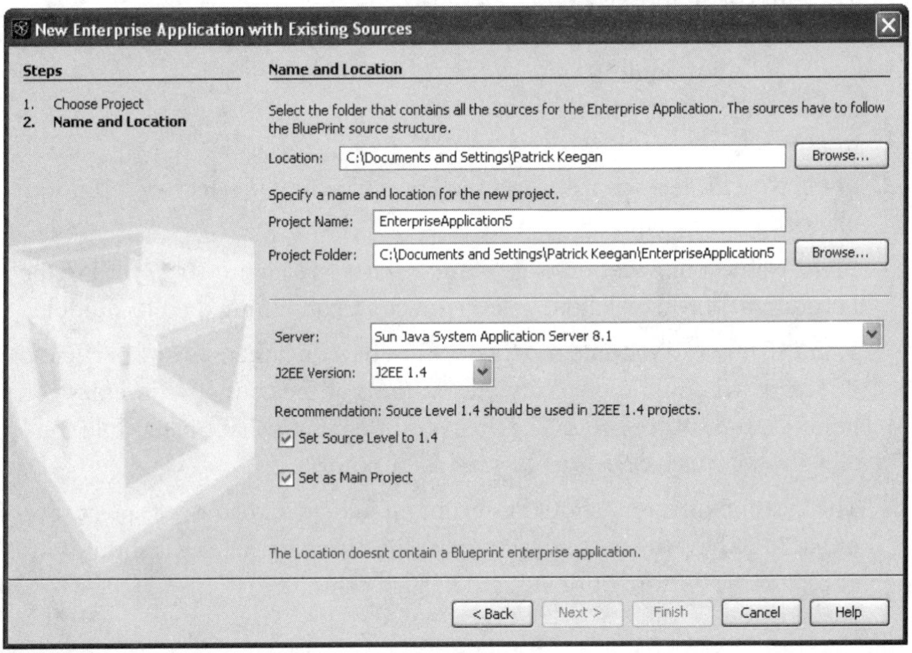

Figure 10-16　New Project wizard, Name and Location page for the Enterprise Application with Existing Sources template

This directory should contain subdirectories for each module (web application or EJB module) that comprises the J2EE application, as well as a `src/conf` subdirectory containing a valid J2EE application deployment descriptor file called `application.xml` (and, optionally, one called `sun-application.xml`). If the Finish button does not get enabled, it means that these conditions are not matched.

4. Fill in the Project Name and Project Folder fields to designate a display name and folder to contain the IDE's settings for the project, including the Ant script. The project folder specified should not already contain a `build.xml` file, because the IDE will generate one automatically and will not replace an existing one.

5. After you click Finish, the J2EE application project is created, as are individual projects for each module in the J2EE application.

Importing EJB Modules

You can also import into the IDE stand-alone EJB modules (similar to how you import Web Application projects) by using the EJB Module with Existing Sources template in the New Project wizard.

To import an EJB module:

1. Choose File | New Project.
2. In the New Project wizard, select the Enterprise folder, select the EJB Module with Existing Sources template, and click Next.
3. In the Name and Location page of the wizard (see Figure 10-17), fill in the Location field with a valid top-level directory containing the EJB module.

   Your existing EJB module source does not have to adhere to any particular directory structure. You specify the locations of the configuration files, libraries, and source roots. The main requirement is that the module contain a valid `ejb-jar.xml` deployment descriptor.

   The location directory should not contain folders named `dist`, `nbproject`, or `build` or have an existing `build.xml` file. Warning messages should appear at the bottom of the wizard in such cases.

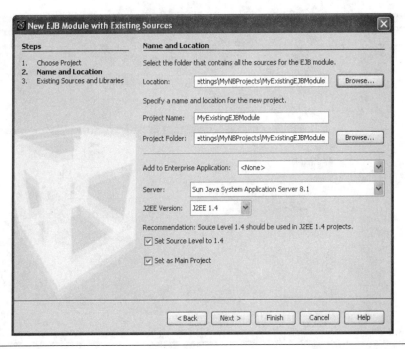

Figure 10-17   New Project wizard, Name and Location page for the EJB Module with Existing Sources template

4. On the Existing Sources and Libraries page of the wizard (shown in Figure 10-18), specify the following properties:

   ▪ **Configuration Files Folder.** Specifies the location of your deployment descriptors and other configuration files. You must have at least a valid `ejb-jar.xml` deployment descriptor to complete the wizard.

   ▪ **Libraries Folder.** Specifies the location of the class libraries that the EJB module depends on. All JAR files in this folder are added to the EJB Module project's classpath and packaged with the module for deployment.

   The IDE scans the folder you designate in the Libraries Folder field only once when you create the project. After the project is created, adding JAR files to this folder outside the IDE does not add them to the module's classpath. You have to add them manually through the Libraries tab of the module's Project Properties dialog box.

5. In the Source Package Folders field, add any source root folders. In the Test Package Folders field, add any test package folders (containing JUnit tests).

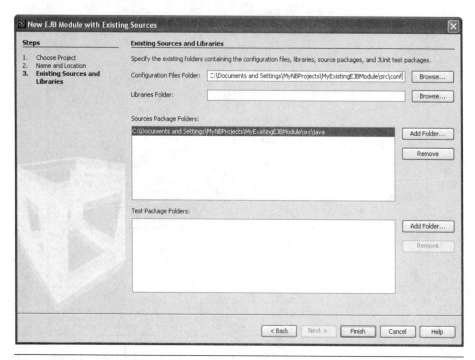

Figure 10-18   New Project wizard, Existing Sources and Libraries page for the EJB Module with Existing Sources template

6. Click Finish. A new NetBeans IDE project is created in the Projects window, and you can start using this EJB Module project like any other IDE project.

The IDE does not convert deployment descriptors from other application servers to Sun Java System Application Server deployment descriptors. An external tool you can use for this purpose, the Sun Java System migration tool, is available free at http://java.sun.com/j2ee/1.4/download.html#migration.

Consuming J2EE Resources

One of the goals of deployment descriptors in the J2EE platform is to provide a standard way of describing external facilities that need to be available for successful execution of the J2EE application. The declaration in the deployment descriptor references the expected interface available and the name used to locate this instance. This binding and declaration mechanism allows the late binding of resources. (In J2EE role terms, the deployer can change the actual resource used without changing the source code or the J2EE-mandated deployment descriptors.)

A *resource* is an external entity required by a J2EE application that is referenced using the standard deployment descriptor. A large number of resources can be used, but some of the most common are JDBC (via the `javax.sql.DataSource` interface), JMS (via the `javax.jms.*` interfaces), and enterprise beans (using the interfaces exposed by the bean developer).

Several steps are required to incorporate a resource into an application:

- Declaration of the resource in the standard deployment descriptor
- Resource setup in the server-specific deployment descriptor, which may also include setup on the server instance itself
- Acquisition of the resource using JNDI
- Using the resource in the programming environment

NetBeans IDE provides commands to automate the use of resources. Typically, you realize that a resource should be used while you are writing Java code. The IDE makes it easy to add a resource as you are coding by providing an Enterprise Resources submenu on the contextual menu in the Source Editor for Java classes contained in enterprise projects (Web Application and EJB Module). See Figure 10-19.

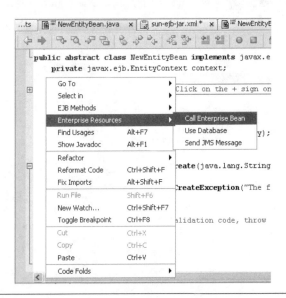

Figure 10-19　Source Editor with the contextual menu open and the Enterprise Resources submenu selected

The Enterprise Resource menu provides a set of commands that automate the use of JMS, JDBC, and enterprise beans. Subsequent sections in this chapter describe what happens when the wizards are invoked and how to use the wizards.

All the actions are able to incorporate the J2EE BluePrints Service Locator pattern, which encapsulates and caches the JNDI initial context lookup. This pattern aggregates all boilerplate lookup code and provides the potential for performance enhancements.

NetBeans IDE provides two different service locator strategies: caching and non-caching. The caching strategy uses the singleton pattern and caches both the initial context and the results from the JNDI lookup. The noncaching locator does not cache the lookup results but instead reuses the initial context. The Service Locator templates are available under the Enterprise node in the New File wizard, as shown in Figure 10-20.

The Service Locator template generates a Java source file that can be further customized. The service locator last used for the project is stored with the project

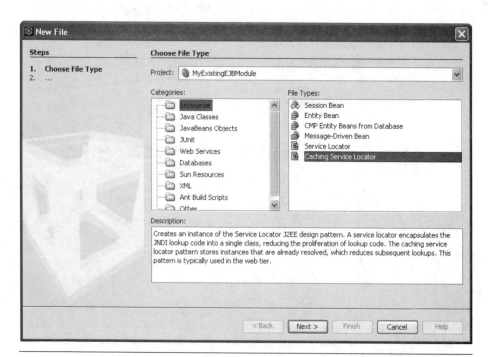

Figure 10-20   New File wizard with the Caching Service Locator template selected

settings, allowing the last locator to be reused easily. The service locator naming conventions provided in the templates are incorporated into the enterprise resource commands; therefore, changing the name of the public lookup methods after generation may require manual intervention following the use of the enterprise resource commands.

The caching service locator strategy is most useful from a web module where resource definitions are shared across the entire module. The singleton pattern can be used effectively in this scenario to reuse lookup instances. In an EJB module, resource declarations are scoped to a single enterprise bean; thus, the singleton pattern is not applicable. An EJB module will commonly use a noncaching service locator.

Using Enterprise Beans

If you want to use an enterprise bean, you must go through the following steps:

1. Declare an `ejb-ref` entry or an `ejb-local-ref` entry (depending on whether the enterprise bean exposes local or remote interfaces) in the deployment descriptor. The deployment descriptor entry will specify the home and component interface, a name used in the JNDI lookup to specify the instance, the type of enterprise bean (either session or entity), and a reference to the actual enterprise bean.
2. Perform a JNDI lookup to obtain an instance of the home interface.
3. Use a create or finder method on the home interface to obtain an instance of the component interface.

The Call Enterprise Bean command (which you can access by right-clicking the Source Editor and choosing Enterprise Resources | Call Enterprise Bean) automates this process. The dialog box shown in Figure 10-21 provides a way to select the enterprise bean to invoke. This dialog further enables you to specify the enterprise bean, the desired lookup strategy, and whether checked exceptions should be converted to runtime exceptions.

Using the Call Enterprise Bean command in an EJB Module project or a Web Application project will result in the following:

- Generation of an `ejb-ref` or `ejb-local-ref` in the deployment descriptor. If this is done from an EJB module, this feature can be invoked directly only

Figure 10-21   Dialog box for the Call Enterprise Bean command

from the bean class. This feature requires that the referenced enterprise bean is in the same deployment unit (either the same module or the same J2EE application) as required by the semantics of the ejb-link (the reference is based on *ModuleName#EjbName* syntax and requires the reference to be collocated).

■ Generation of the lookup code. If a service locator is being used, the generated code delegates the lookup to the locator; otherwise, lookup code is generated. The generated code uses the JDK logging framework to log the exception. The lookup code returns the home interface unless a stateless session bean is referenced, in which case an instance of the component interface is returned.

■ Establishment of a project dependency between the current project and the referenced project as the interfaces from the enterprise beans need to be used during compilation. The interfaces will not be included in the archive of the referencing project but will instead assume that the server supports delegation to the application class loader (for references outside a module). If this is not true, the Java Extension mechanism can be used to add a classpath reference to the EJB module.

Using a Database

The Use Database command automates the process of incorporating a relational database into an application. If you intend to use a database, you must go through the following steps:

1. Declare a `resource-ref` entry in the deployment descriptor. The deployment descriptor entry must specify the resource-type `javax.sql.DataSource`, the ability to share the resource, and the authorization mechanism (typically, the authorization is done by the container).

2. Add code to perform a JNDI lookup to obtain an instance of `DataSource`.

3. Use server specific mechanisms to configure the application server to use the JDBC resource. This typically involves adding the JDBC driver to the server classpath, as well as setting up a connection pool for the JDBC connection describing how to connect (including authentication) to the database.

The Enterprise Resources | Use Database command (available by right-clicking a file in the Source Editor) automates this process. When you choose this command, the Choose Database dialog box (shown in Figure 10-22) appears and prompts you to select the database to use in either a web module or an EJB module. In the dialog box, specify a JNDI name (used as the resource reference name), the connection to use, and whether a service locator should be used or inline code should be generated (lookup code is generated in the current class). The list of connections is the same as what is provided in the Runtime window. The Runtime window provides the ability to edit and query the target database.

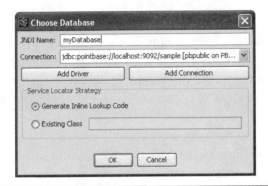

Figure 10-22   Choose Database dialog box

After you fill in the Choose Database dialog box, the following occurs:

- A resource reference is added to the deployment descriptor using the form jdbc/*JNDIName*. Existing resource references are reused if possible (matching is done using the description, which initially is populated via the connection string).

- Code is generated to automate the JNDI lookup, using the specified lookup strategy to obtain the data source.

- If the Add Driver and Add Connection buttons are used, a connection node (and also possibly a driver node) is added to the Runtime window.

- Assuming that you are using the Sun Java System Application Server, the necessary steps to enable successful deployment and execution are performed. (Technically, it's the IDE's Sun Java System Application Server integration plug-in module that provides this support. By the time you read this, there might be IDE plug-in modules to provide equivalent features for different servers.) This might involve creating a connection pool and adding the JDBC driver to the classpath of the application server. The connection pool setup can be configured later in the Server Resources node or via the administrative capability of the server. The Server Resources node enables you to provide version control for and deploy server resources that are required to successfully execute an application. The resources provide all the necessary information to configure the setup. This may include usernames and passwords, so editing these files may be necessary when sharing the application with other team members.

Sending a JMS Message

The Send JMS Message command automates the process of sending a message to a queue or topic. The J2EE 1.4 specification defines the concept of a message destination, which provides a way to specify logical destinations for messages. A message destination allows the decoupling of the message consumer and message producer. The most common scenario is to have a message-driven bean (MDB) linked to the message destination. However, the message destination mechanism allows only the logical message destination to be used by the module sending the message. Although this concept defines a generic linking mechanism, additional information, such as the type of destination (J2EE 1.4 allows other messaging systems to be used), and the message format must be exchanged.

If you want to use JMS, you need to do the following:

- Add a resource reference to declare a `ConnectionFactory`. The connection factory is used to create JMS queue or topic connections.

- Add a message destination reference that declares the message destination type (which must match the type declared for the message destination), the use (the sender will produce messages), and the destination (in the form of a link). The link will be in the format *moduleName#destinationName* and must be included in the same application.

- Add code to send the message. The code to send a message must do a JNDI lookup to obtain the connection factory, use the connection factory to create a session, use the session to create a message producer, use the session to create a message, send the message, and close the session and connection.

The Send JMS Message command automates this process. To use this command, right-click in the Source Editor and choose Enterprise Resources | Send JMS Message. The Select Message Destination dialog box (shown in Figure 10-23) appears, providing a way to select a message destination and to specify whether a service locator should be used or inline code should be generated (lookup code is generated in the current class). Only projects that can supply a destination are shown in the list of projects (Web Application and EJB Module).

Figure 10-23 Select Message Destination dialog box

After you complete the Select Message Destination dialog box, the following occurs:

- A resource reference is added to the deployment descriptor, specifying the intention to use a `ConnectionFactory`. The IDE's Sun Java System Application

Server integration plug-in module shares the connection factory with the message consumer. This can be changed by creating a new `ConnectionFactory`, if desired.

▪ A message destination reference is created and linked to the selected destination. The message type is discovered by determining the message type of the consumer linked to the destination.

▪ A private method providing the code necessary to send a single JMS message (named `sendJMSDestinationName`) is created. This method handles connection, session, and producer creation and destruction. This method accepts a context parameter that allows data to be passed via parameters instead of instance variables, although instance variables can be used as well.

▪ A second private method (`createJMSMessageForDestinationName`) is added to create the message (this is the template pattern) from the supplied session and potentially the context parameter.

J2EE and Security Management

The J2EE platform offers a rich environment for securing web applications, web services, and enterprise beans in a declarative manner by working with application resources and user roles. The two concepts are defined as follows:

▪ Resources are visible or callable features of the applications. For EJB modules, resources are public EJB methods declared on home or remote interfaces. For web modules, resources are URL patterns that are mapped to JavaServer Pages (JSP) files, servlet methods, and other components.

▪ Roles define access privileges and can be associated with one or more users.

J2EE applications are secured by mapping resource to roles. When a resource is called, the caller must supply a role name that is authorized to access the resource. If the caller cannot supply an authorized role, the call is rejected. In J2EE applications, the application server verifies the caller's role before allowing the caller to execute the resource.

The authorized combinations of roles and resources are declared in deployment descriptors. The application server reads them from the deployment descriptors and applies them. This process is known as *declarative security*.

The necessary tasks that you must perform to secure a J2EE application are:

1. Declare the different roles.
2. Specify which roles are permitted to access the resources.

This section describes the different steps to follow to secure a simple web application with NetBeans IDE. For a complete tutorial on J2EE and security, you can refer to the J2EE tutorial at http://java.sun.com/j2ee/1.4/docs/tutorial/doc/Security2.html.

Simple Declarative Security

If you want to secure the access for the web pages exposed within a J2EE application, you need to declare <security-constraint>, <security-role>, and <login-config> elements in the web.xml deployment descriptor (which you can find in the Projects window by expanding the web project's Configuration Files node). The visual web.xml editor does not expose those elements in NetBeans IDE 4.1, so you need to switch to the XML view and add the following elements:

```
<security-constraint>
  <web-resource-collection>
    <web-resource-name>basic security test</web-resource-name>
    <url-pattern>/*</url-pattern>
  </web-resource-collection>
  <auth-constraint>
    <role-name>staffmember</role-name>
  </auth-constraint>
</security-constraint>


<login-config>
  <auth-method>BASIC</auth-method>
  <realm-name>basic-file</realm-name>
</login-config>

<security-role>
  <role-name>staffmember</role-name>
</security-role>
```

These settings protect the access of all the web pages (see the <url-pattern> element), using the BASIC login configuration. The authorized logical user is called staffmember.

Registering Users for an Application Server Instance

To add authorized users to the Sun Java System Application Server, follow these steps:

1. Make sure the server instance is up and running by opening the Runtime window, right-clicking the server instance's node, choosing Start/Stop Server (as shown in Figure 10-24), and then starting the server if it is stopped.

Figure 10-24   Starting the application server from the IDE's Runtime window

2. Right-click the server instance's node and choose View Admin Console. The login page for the Admin Console appears in a web browser.

3. Log into the application server's Admin Console, and enter the username and password of a user in the admin-realm who belongs to the asadmin group. The name and password you entered when installing the server will work. The NetBeans IDE/Sun Java System Application Server bundle uses these default values: admin for the username and adminadmin for the password.

4. In the Admin Console tree, expand the Configuration | Security | Realms node and select the file realm to add users you want to enable to access applications running in this realm.

5. Click the Manage Users button.

6. Click New to add a new user to the realm. In this case, we'll use the username ludo and the password ludo as well. You can also enter a group to which the user belongs, but leave that field blank for this example.

7. Click OK to add this user to the list of users in the realm. Figure 10-25 shows
    the state of the console after entering the user ludo to the realm.

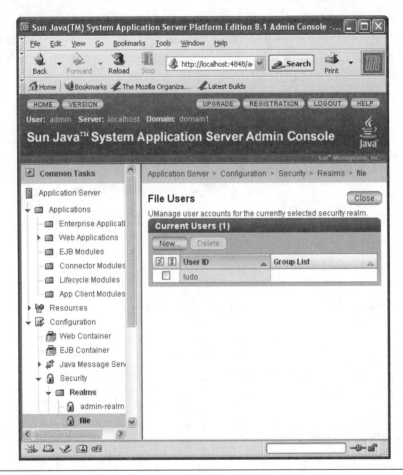

Figure 10-25   Sun Java System Application Server Admin Console after a user account
is created

8. Click Logout when you have completed this task.

Now that you have registered a username for this application server instance,
you can map the J2EE logical security role called staffmember to this physical
user called ludo. To do that, use the IDE's visual editor for the sun-web.xml file:

1. Open the sun-web.xml file from the Projects window by expanding the
    project's Configuration Files node and double-clicking the sun-web.xml node.

2. In the visual editor, expand the Sun Web Application node. If you have declared the `<security-constraint>`, `<security-role>`, and `<login-config>` elements as described in the Simple Declarative Security section on page 269, the `staffmember` node should appear.

3. Select the `staffmember` node, click the Master Roles tab in the right pane of the visual editor, click Add Principal, and type `ludo` in the New Principal Name dialog box. Figure 10-26 shows what the visual editor should look like after you have completed this step.

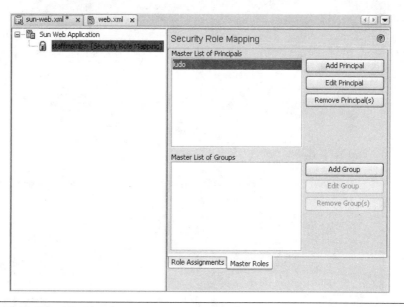

Figure 10-26   Visual editor for the `sun-web.xml` file, Master Roles tab, after the principal `ludo` is added

4. Click the Role Assignments tab, select `ludo` in the Principal Master List, and click the Add button to assign that user to the `staffmember` role. Figure 10-27 shows what the visual editor should look like after you have completed this step.

Now when you run this web application, you are prompted for a username and password when you first try to access the application's welcome (as shown in Figure 10-28). Enter `ludo` as the username and `ludo` as the password, and you should be able to access the requested web page.

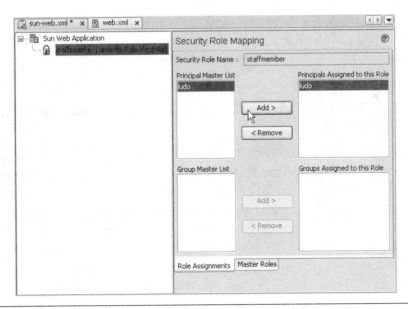

Figure 10-27   Visual editor for the `sun-web.xml` file, Role Assignments tab, after the `staffmember` role is mapped to the user `ludo`

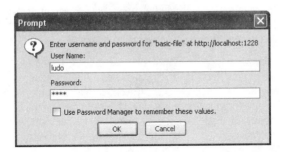

Figure 10-28   Prompt for username and password to access a web application that has security constraints set up

This section is only an introduction to J2EE security settings. Make sure you read the J2EE tutorial document, which covers more advanced security concepts for J2EE applications, such as web-services message protection for service endpoints (WSS in the SOAP layer is the use of XML Encryption and XML Digital Signatures to secure SOAP messages). You can find a complete tutorial at the following URL: http://docs.sun.com/source/819-0079/dgsecure.html#wp14462.

Remember, once you are ready to use more advanced security settings, you can take advantage of the IDE's visual configuration editors (for `sun-ejb-jar.xml` and `sun-web.xml`) to edit these security settings.

Understanding the J2EE Application Server Runtime Environment

The Sun Java System Application Server integrates nicely with NetBeans IDE, via both well-published interfaces (JSR 88) for configuration and deployment and NetBeans IDE extensions called the J2EE Server Integration APIs (see http://j2eeserver.netbeans.org). Although the most complete runtime management tool for the application server is the Admin Console (a management tool in the form of a web page, shown in Figure 10-25 earlier in this chapter), some developer-oriented management features have been exposed from the IDE's Runtime window under the Servers node. From there, for each registered server instance, you can view the server log file (for local servers), launch the Admin Console tool, explore the list of deployed J2EE applications or J2EE resources (and undeploy them), and more.

 If you want to explore the entire content of an application server domain or to see the configuration files, the log files, or the repository of the deployed applications, you can add this domain directory in the IDE's Favorites window.

By default, the Favorites window is not visible within the IDE, but you can display it in the explorer area of the IDE by choosing Windows | Favorites. Then you can right-click the Favorites root node, choose Add to Favorites, and navigate to the application server's domain directory. Once you have added this directory in the Favorites window, you can view those files in the IDE's Source Editor and take advantage of other IDE features such as the Validate XML command, which is useful for validating things such as the `config/domain.xml` file.

Server Log

The Sun Java System Application Server instance container process uses a log file to track system and user messages ranging from severe errors to informational messages describing the current state of the server. The server log file is an important source of information that a J2EE developer needs to use actively during development or deployment and execution of J2EE applications. There is one server log file per instance, usually located under the domain directory in the `logs/server.log` file. NetBeans IDE can display the content of the most recent lines of the server log via the server instance node popup menu called View Server Log. This menu is active only for local server instances, because the IDE needs access to the file.

Server Management

For a registered application server instance, whether the server is local (on the same machine that the IDE is running on) or remote, the IDE offers extensive administration capabilities via the Runtime window tree view (shown in Figure 10-29).

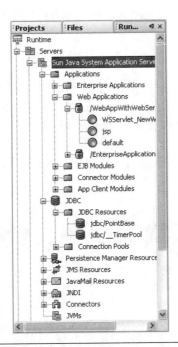

Figure 10-29   Runtime window with the node for a Sun Java System Application Server instance selected

Once the server is running, you can get read/write access to most of the developer-oriented administration parameters, such as:

- The list of J2EE deployed applications, from where you can introspect their properties and undeploy them

▪ The list of registered resources and their properties (JDBC resources, connection pools, Persistence Manager resources, JMS resources, JavaMail resources, JDNI names, and Connector and JVM settings)

Each of these management artifacts is represented as a node. The corresponding commands (Delete, Undeploy, Refresh, and so on) are available as popup menu items (when you right-click the node), and corresponding properties are available via the Properties popup menu item. For other management artifacts, you can always access them by opening the application server's Admin Console (right-click the server's node in the Runtime window and choose View Admin Console). This command opens a web browser that then displays the URL for the administration console.

JVM Options

The JVM parameters of a server instance are among the most important server administration parameters from a developer standpoint. You can access these parameters by right-clicking the server's JVMs node in the Runtime window and choosing Properties. The Properties dialog box for the JVMs node is shown in Figure 10-30.

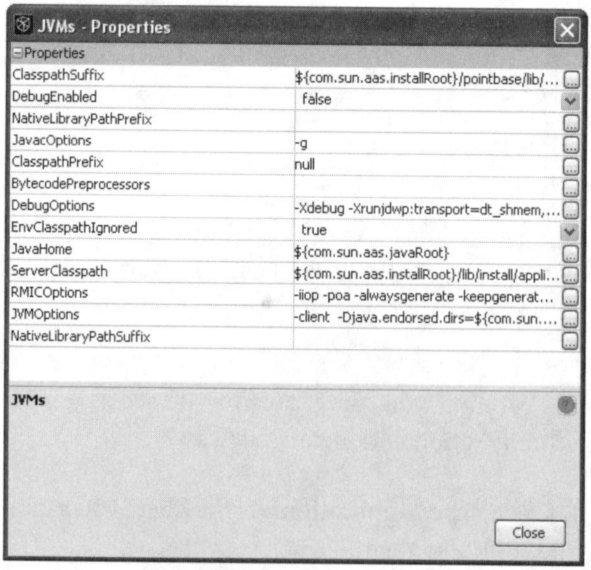

Figure 10-30   Property sheet for the JVMs node for an application server in the Runtime window

Use the `server-classpath` entry (shown as `ServerProperty` in the property sheet) when you want to add shared libraries or JAR files that would be used by all the J2EE applications deployed to this server instance, as well as the necessary JDBC driver JAR files to access databases. Use the `jvm-options` parameter (shown as `JVMOptions` in the property sheet) to define Java options like HTTP proxies or options that would be relevant to the deployed J2EE applications. You can modify the `java-home` entry (shown as `JavaHome` in the property sheet) to change the location of the JDK used by the server instance.

Most of these settings require a server instance restart to take effect. NetBeans IDE can figure out when a local instance has to restart, and at the next J2EE project deployment, execution, or debugging session, the server is restarted automatically. For remote servers, you have to log into the remote machine to perform a server restart, as there is no command (CLI or Admin Console based) to restart a remote server in Sun Java System Application Server 8.1.

JDBC Drivers

Using the Sun Resources template category in the New File wizard (shown in Figure 10-31), you can define J2EE resources such as:

- JDBC connection pools
- JDBC resources
- JMS resources
- JavaMail resources
- Persistence resources

The wizard for the JDBC Connection Pool template (shown in Figure 10-32) is of particular help in improving your productivity. It enables you to create resources, either from live database connections registered within NetBeans IDE or from a predefined list of well-known JDBC drivers—including all the Sun DataDirect drivers for DB2, Oracle, Microsoft SQL Server, and Sybase, as well as drivers for the Pointbase and Apache Derby databases. Note that in the Sun Java System Application Server 8.1 Platform Edition, only the Pointbase driver is provided. The Sun Datadirect drivers are included with the Standard Edition and Enterprise Edition of Sun Java System Application Server 8.1.

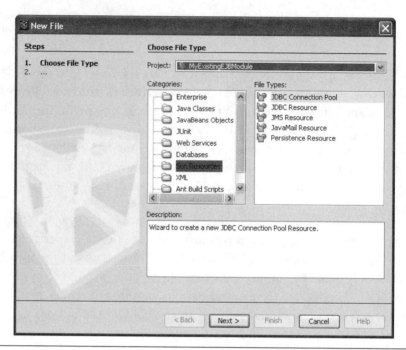

Figure 10-31 New File wizard with the JDBC Connection Pool template selected

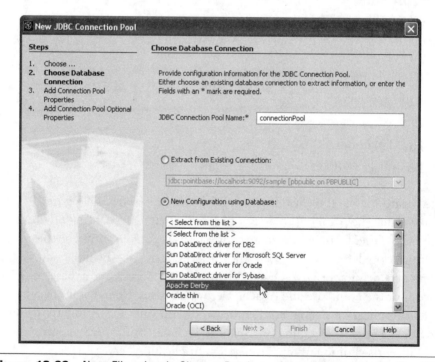

Figure 10-32 New File wizard, Choose Database Connection page for the JDBC Connection Pool template

These server-specific resources are created under the `setup` directory, which in the Projects window is represented as the project's Server Resources node. These server resources are then either automatically deployed to the server whenever the project is executed or manually registered, using the Register menu item, as shown in Figure 10-33.

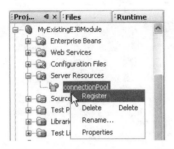

Figure 10-33   Registering a database connection in a project

Double-clicking a server resource node opens the property sheet for this resource (see Figure 10-34), where you can modify all the necessary properties before doing a registration.

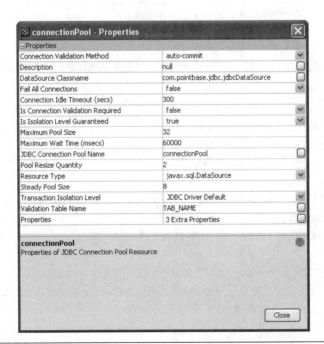

Figure 10-34   Property sheet for a JDBC connection pool

Server Properties

The server's Properties dialog box (shown in Figure 10-35), accessible via the Properties menu item of a server node, allows the editing of the admin username or password, as well as the setting for enabling the IDE's HTTP Monitor. This HTTP Monitor can work only for local application servers.

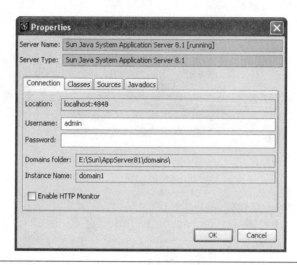

Figure 10-35 Properties dialog box for the Sun Java System Application Server

Using JavaServer Faces Technology in a Web Application

Sun Java System Application Server 8.1 bundles all the latest JavaServer Faces (JSF) APIs and the JSF implementation out of the box, and these libraries are recognized by NetBeans IDE. The JSF config DTDs are also registered in the IDE, meaning that XML code completion and validation are available in the IDE for the JSF config 1.0 and 1.1 XML files.

The JSF libraries are automatically in the web application project classpath when the project targets the Sun Application Server, so that all the classes are available to import and to use from your web application.

Furthermore, the Java BluePrints Solution Catalog is accessible directly through the IDE's Help | BluePrints Solutions Catalog menu item and contains some web tier solutions that incorporate JSF technology, which are installable as IDE projects with one click. Install a solution, run the project, study it, debug it, modify it, and use it as a starting point for your JSF project. See Chapter 7 for more details.

Working with Ant

NetBeans IDE's Ant-based project system (introduced in Version 4.0 and extended in Version 4.1) is perhaps the biggest thing that sets NetBeans apart from other IDEs. All projects created within NetBeans IDE rely on the Ant tool for building. This is also true for the J2EE project types like web applications, EJB modules, and J2EE applications. Therefore, these projects can be built either from the IDE or from outside the IDE using Ant 1.6.2.

The IDE-generated build script also includes targets for executing, debugging, and deploying the application. In NetBeans IDE 4.1, it is not possible to use these targets outside the IDE, because they would require an operational runtime environment. This limitation should go away in NetBeans IDE 4.2.

Another NetBeans IDE advantage is that all of the Sun Application Server 8.1 Ant optional tasks are registered in the IDE. These tasks include

- `sun-appserv-deploy`
- `sun-appserv-undeploy`
- `sun-appserv-instance`
- `sun-appserv-component`
- `sun-appserv-admin`
- `sun-appserv-input`
- `sun-appserv-update`

So if you have existing Ant scripts that are using these Ant task extensions, you can run these `build.xml` files directly from the IDE itself as though you were invoking the Sun Application Server tool `asant` (which itself is a wrapper around Ant to declare these extensions).

For example, if you download all the J2EE samples for the Sun Application Server, all the samples can be built from the IDE using the sample `build.xml` files provided with the sample. You could make the samples visible in the IDE by choosing Window | Favorites, right-clicking the Favorites node, choosing Add to Favorites, and navigating to the directory to display. Once the samples are visible in the Favorites window, you can navigate to a sample's `build.xml` file, right-click it, and choose an Ant target to run.

For more information regarding these tasks, refer to the application server documentation at http://docs.sun.com.

Ensuring J2EE Compliance

The J2EE platform extends the many benefits of the Java language to the enterprise, such as portability, by providing a set of specifications for application servers and an extensive set of compatibility tests. The J2EE platform enables you to run enterprise applications on a variety of J2EE application servers.

The IDE provides a rich environment for developing J2EE applications. But one of your most crucial objectives as a J2EE developer is ensuring that your application is J2EE compliant. By being J2EE-compliant, the application will deploy and run in any J2EE vendor's application server as long as that vendor's application server is compliant with the J2EE specification. To help you ensure that your J2EE application is J2EE compliant, the IDE provides a built-in J2EE verifier. The NetBeans IDE J2EE Verifier is a tool intended to help you test your web application or enterprise application for the correct use of J2EE APIs. In addition, it confirms portability across J2EE-compatible application servers, which helps you avoid inadvertently writing nonportable code.

When the Verifier is invoked in NetBeans IDE, it runs a series of tests against a selected NetBeans IDE project to ensure that the application is J2EE compliant. The output from running the Verifier is displayed in the NetBeans IDE Output window in table form and contains the following information:

- Test Status—pass, fail, or warning
- Test Description—a description of the compatibility test that was run
- Test Result Description—a detailed description of the test result

You can also filter the Verifier output. You can view all compatibility test results, compatibility failures only, or compatibility failures and warnings only.

After you finish developing a web application or enterprise application and before you deploy it, you should run the J2EE Verifier against your project to ensure that you are not using any vendor-specific proprietary extensions to the J2EE platform. Using a proprietary extension will make it difficult to port to other J2EE application servers.

To launch the Verifier against your web application or enterprise application project, you must have your project open in NetBeans IDE. From the Projects window, right-click the main node of the project you want to verify and choose Verify Project. Figure 10-36 shows the contextual menu that is displayed when you right-click a web application or enterprise application project.

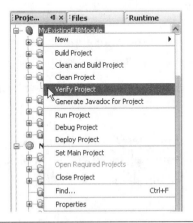

Figure 10-36   From the Projects window, running the Verify Project command for a J2EE application

Once the Verify Project command is chosen, the Verifier window (shown in Figure 10-37) appears at the bottom of the IDE and starts displaying results of the verification.

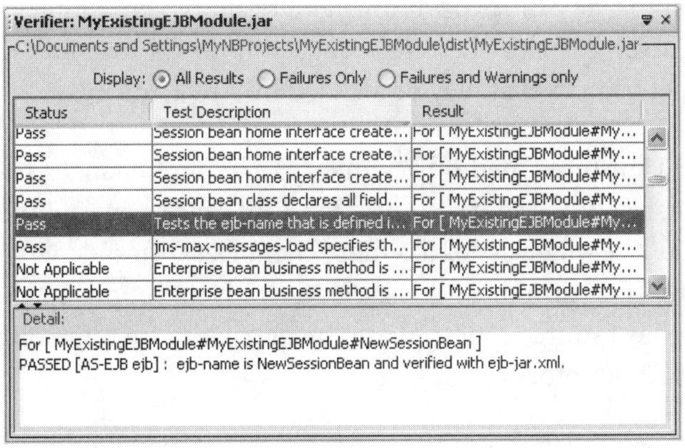

Figure 10-37   Output from the Verify Project command

The results consist of all of the compatibility tests performed against your application. The Verifier lists test status, test description, and a detailed test result. The default for the Verifier results is to display all compatibility tests that fail first, followed by those that have a warning result and then those that have passed. When a row or test is selected in the table, a detailed description of the test result is displayed. Also, the Verifier test results display can be filtered by selecting one of the following radio buttons:

▪ All Results—displays all of the compatibility test results

▪ Failures Only—displays only the compatibility test failures

▪ Failures and Warnings Only—displays both compatibility test failures and warnings

You should fix all compatibility test failures before deploying the application. As you make corrections to your web or enterprise application, you can rerun the Verifier by again right-clicking the project's node in the Projects window and choosing Verify.

Refactoring Enterprise Beans

Software applications evolve over time and require updates, bug fixes, feature enhancements, and so on. To support this type of development activity, Net-Beans IDE refactoring features extend to J2EE applications.

Enterprise beans are among the types of code most likely to need refactoring during an enterprise software application's lifetime. However, refactoring enterprise beans can be very time consuming as a result of the complexity of changes that may be involved with the refactoring, due to the number of classes and deployment descriptors that may be affected by a refactoring.

For example, a business method rename may require changes not only in the EJB class you are editing, but also in a local interface, remote interface, calling classes (such as a servlet class or a remote client class), and deployment descriptors. NetBeans IDE simplifies this task not only by applying the refactoring changes to the Java source code, but also by making those more difficult changes in deployment descriptors.

Following are some of the things you can do when refactoring your J2EE source code.

- Rename an enterprise bean
- Rename a field or method of an enterprise bean
- Change method parameters (including parameter names, parameter types, and method visibility), add method parameters, and remove method parameters
- Encapsulate fields by changing their visibility, adding getter and setter accessors, and determining whether to use accessors even when the field is accessible

NetBeans IDE allows you to review your refactoring changes before committing them. Likewise, the IDE allows you to undo your J2EE refactoring changes after having committed them and even to revert refactoring changes to deployment descriptors.

 If you want to undo a refactoring operation, you must call the Undo command from a Java source file. Though Undo affects deployment descriptors, the command cannot be called from a deployment descriptor.

For complete descriptions of refactoring features, see Refactoring Commands on page 104. For notes on servlet refactoring, see Editing and Refactoring Web Application Files on page 162. Following are some notes regarding the J2EE implications of some of the refactoring operations:

- For CMP beans, the method rename of a selector or finder automatically updates the EJB QL (Enterprise JavaBeans Query Language) statements and query element in the deployment descriptor. However, the IDE does not allow you to change the method name of a mandatory EJB method such as `ejbCreate()`.

  Even in the case where a renamed method was previously overloaded, a new deployment descriptor entry is made for the refactored method name. For instance, updates to deployment descriptors tagged as primary key fields and composite primary key fields as a result of method rename refactoring are supported. Also, a rename of web service endpoint interfaces are handled by NetBeans IDE by updating the appropriate WSDL.

- Even in the case of a CMP bean, a field rename refactoring of a primary key results in field accessors deployment descriptors being updated. In addition, if a relationship field is renamed, the `cmr-field` in the deployment descriptor is updated.

▪ Encapsulating fields refactoring in an enterprise bean class works the same way as in standard classes, with the exception of primary keys in CMP enterprise beans, which cannot be refactored in NetBeans IDE 4.1.

## CHAPTER 11

Developing J2ME Mobility Applications

- Downloading and Installing the Mobility Pack
- Setting Up Mobility Projects
- Creating a Project from Scratch
- Importing a Project
- Physical Structure of Mobile Projects
- Using Mobility File Templates
- Configuring the Project's Classpath
- Debugging Your Project
- Configuring Your Project for Different Devices
- Setting the Active Configuration for Your Project
- Reusing Project Settings and Configurations
- Structuring Project Dependencies
- Managing the Distribution JAR File Content
- Handling Project Resources for Different Configurations
- Writing Code Specific to a List of Configurations
- Using Configuration Abilities
- Creating and Associating an Ability with a Configuration
- Localizing Applications
- Using the MIDP Visual Designer
- Deploying Your Application Automatically
- Incrementing the Application's MIDlet-Version Automatically
- Installing Nonstandard Emulator Platforms
- Using Ant in Mobility Projects
- Using Headless Builds
- Finding More Information

THE NETBEANS MOBILITY PACK CAN SIMPLIFY many aspects of your MIDP development process. It includes, among other things, the MIDP Visual Designer for managing the flow and content of your application screens, an integrated device fragmentation solution with editor support, and an end-to-end build process that can even include deployment of the application to a remote server.

This chapter covers a range of the Mobility Pack functionality and should give you a better understanding of how you can use many of its features. Projects created for NetBeans Mobility Pack share many qualities with general Java projects. You should, therefore, read through Chapter 3, as this section primarily describes the differences between general and Mobility project types.

Downloading and Installing the Mobility Pack

The standard NetBeans IDE 4.1 download does not include support for developing mobile applications. You need to download the Mobility Pack separately and use its "add-on" installer to integrate the Mobility Pack functionality with the NetBeans IDE installation you already have on your system.

For NetBeans IDE 4.1, you should be able to find the Mobility Pack installer on the same download page as the IDE installer.

Once you have downloaded the installer, launch it (in the same way that you launched the NetBeans IDE installer) and complete the wizard. The wizard will help you identify the installation of NetBeans IDE to build on.

Setting Up Mobility Projects

After you have installed NetBeans IDE and the Mobility Pack, creating a new project is your next step in developing a mobile application. The IDE does the following upon creation of a mobility project:

- Creates a source tree optionally containing a simple MIDlet.
- Selects an appropriate emulator platform for your project. Normally, the bundled J2ME Wireless Toolkit platform is selected.
- Sets the project runtime and compile-time classpath.
- Creates a build script that contains commands for running, compiling (including mobile-specific tasks such as preprocessing, preverification, and obfuscation), debugging, and building Javadoc.

Mobility Primer

NetBeans Mobility Pack makes it easy for all programmers to start development for J2ME applications quickly, even if you've had only J2SE programming experience.

If you are trying out mobile application programming for the first time, you can just think of J2ME as having a more limited version of the J2SE API and let NetBeans Mobility Pack take care of the foreign J2ME issues. Though there are more differences than just a smaller API, it's not necessary to know all the intricacies before producing a working mobile application.

To help you get started, here are some terms that are used throughout this document:

- *J2ME*—Java 2 Platform, Micro Edition, is the Java platform meant to run on small devices. Currently, these devices are typically cell phones or PDAs, but J2ME is also used on other embedded systems. A configuration, a profile, and optional packages are what compose a J2ME platform.

- *CLDC*—Connected Limited Device Configuration is a J2ME configuration that is currently most often used on mobile phones. It contains a runtime environment and a core API that are appropriate for the limited processor speed and memory size of mobile devices.

- *MIDP*—Mobile Information Device Profile is the set of APIs that provides higher-level functionality required by mobile applications, such as displayable components *(screens)* and network communication.

- *MIDlet*—A class required by all MIDP applications. It acts as the interface between the application and the device on which it is running. A MIDlet is similar to a main class in a J2SE project.

- *Preverification*—When building an application that runs with CLDC, all compiled classes must be preverified. Preverification is a process that adds annotations used by the CLDC JVM to a class file's bytecode. The preverification process also ensures that the class contains only code that will run on its CLDC version.

- *Device fragmentation*—Term used for the variations between mobile platforms that prevent a single application from automatically running optimally on all phones. These differences can be physical (screen size, screen color depth, available memory, and so on) or software related (available APIs, CLDC/MIDP version, and so on).

- *Preprocessor*—NetBeans Mobility Pack ships with a preprocessor that is used as part of its device fragmentation solution. The preprocessor is an Ant task that runs before files are compiled. It looks for special Java comment tags within the file and adds or removes line comments based on these tags.

- *Obfuscation*—A process that makes class files difficult to reverse-engineer. This is usually accomplished by, at least, replacing names of packages, classes, methods, and fields with short identifiers. This has the result of decreasing the size of your application and, therefore, is an important aspect of the mobile application build process.

If you're interested in learning more, countless online and offline resources are available. A good place to start looking is http://java.sun.com/j2me/.

Creating a Project from Scratch

The process of creating a project from scratch is nearly identical to how it is done with general Java projects:

1. Choose File | New Project.

2. In the Categories tree, select the Mobile folder.

3. Select Mobile Application or Mobile Class Library

   The Mobile Application template provides an option to generate an example MIDlet automatically. The Mobile Class Library does not generate any classes for you.

   The MIDP 1.0 UI, the MIDP 2.0 UI, and the Bluetooth examples use the MIDP Visual Designer.

4. Click Next.

5. Optionally, fill in the following fields in the Name and Location panel of the wizard:

   Project Name. The name by which the project is referred to in the IDE's user interface.

   Project Location. The location of the project on your system.

   The resulting Project Folder field shows the root project directory that contains folders for your sources, build and properties files, compiled classes, and so on.

6. Optionally, deselect the Set As Main Project checkbox if you have another project open that you want associated with the IDE's main project commands (such as Build Main Project).

7. Optionally, if you selected Mobile Application project, you may deselect the Create Hello MIDlet checkbox to avoid generating an example MIDlet. Otherwise, a small sample MIDlet is created that uses the MIDP Visual Designer.

8. Choose the emulator platform you would like your project to use by default. This setting controls your project's classpath as well as which emulator and device are launched when you run your project.

   Note that you can change this setting once the project has been created.

9. Click Finish.

Importing a Project

The J2ME platform supports automatic imports from existing J2ME Wireless Toolkit projects, Sun Java Studio Mobility projects, and projects consisting of stand-alone MIDP sources. When you import projects, the sources remain in their existing locations.

 Unlike with general Java projects, only a single source root is supported for Mobility projects. If the project you are importing has multiple source roots, you have to create one project for each source root and then make dependencies between the projects. This is explained further in Structuring Your Projects in Chapter 3 on page 48.

To create a new NetBeans project from a Sun Java Studio Mobility project or stand-alone sources:

1. Choose File | New Project.
2. In the Categories tree, select the Mobile folder.
3. Select Import Mobility Studio Project or Mobile Project from Existing MIDP Sources, and click Next.
4. In the Imported Sources Location field, enter the folder that contains the default package of your sources (the folder might be called src).
5. In the Imported Jad/Manifest Location field, enter the folder that contains the application's Java Application Descriptor (JAD) file. You can leave this field blank if your project does not have a JAD file.
6. Click Next.
7. Optionally, edit the following fields in the Name and Location panel of the wizard:

   Project Name. The name by which the project is referred to in the IDE's user interface.

   Project Location. The location for the new project.
8. Optionally, deselect the Set As Main Project checkbox if you have another project open that you want associated with the IDE's main project commands (such as Build Main Project).
9. Click Next.
10. Configure the project's default emulator platform.
11. Click Finish.

To create a new NetBeans project from a J2ME Wireless Toolkit project:

1. Choose File | New Project.
2. In the Categories tree, select the Mobile folder.
3. Select Import Wireless Toolkit Project and click Next.
4. On the Specify WTK Project page of the wizard (shown in Figure 11-1), specify the location of your Wireless Toolkit installation directory that contains the project you would like to install.

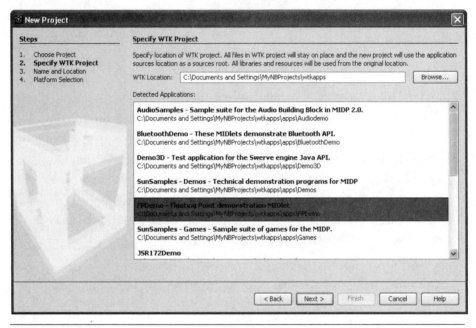

Figure 11-1   New Project wizard, Specify WTK Project page

5. A list of all projects contained in the installation directory is displayed. Highlight the project you would like to import.
6. Click Next.
7. The remaining steps are identical to those listed above. Fill in the Name and Location page and the Platform Selection page of the wizard as described in steps 7 through 11 in the previous procedure.

Two projects that use the same source root should not be open concurrently within the IDE. Though the IDE takes steps to prevent this situation, the projects will become unstable should it occur.

Configuration vs. Configuration

One naming conflict that can cause confusion in this text is that between the NetBeans concept of project configuration and the J2ME concept of device configuration. Because this text focuses on covering NetBeans IDE, the unmodified term *configuration* will henceforth refer to project configurations.

Physical Structure of Mobile Projects

You can examine the physical structure of your Mobile project using the Files window. This window is located, by default, next to the Projects window or accessible via Window | Files in the main menu.

When you create a Mobile project, the IDE creates the same directories and files as those that are created for general Java projects, except that a separate `test` directory is not created. Tests, if generated, are placed in the same packages as the classes they are testing.

The `build` and `dist` folders, created the first time you build the project, are slightly different due to the more complicated nature of the MIDP build process. The following directories are created under `build`:

- `compiled` folder, which contains all compiled classes.
- `preprocessed` folder, which holds preprocessed versions of your source files. The files contained here are different from the original sources only if you are using configurations.
- `obfuscated` folder, which holds the obfuscated versions of your class files.
- `preverified` folder, which holds the preverified versions of your class files. These are the class files that are packaged in your project's distribution JAR file.

These files are maintained both to increase the speed of the build process and to give you information you can use to isolate where in the build process bugs may have been introduced into your application.

The `dist` folder contains your project's distribution JAR file and JAD file.

The NetBeans build process follows Ant standards for management of temporary build classes. This means that only source files with a more recent timestamp than that of the class files in the build directories are automatically rebuilt when the Build command is run. Also, deleting a source file from the project does not automatically delete the associated class files from the build directories. ***Therefore, it is important to clean and rebuild the project after a source file has been removed from the project.***

Using Mobility File Templates

The process of creating files in Mobility projects is identical to that of creating files in general Java projects. Templates for creating MIDP classes can be found under the top-level MIDP category in the New File wizard, as shown in Figure 11-2. You can open the New File wizard by choosing File | New File.

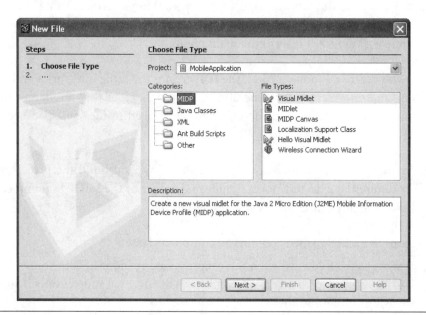

Figure 11-2   New File wizard, MIDP templates

MIDP Canvas

To create a MIPD Canvas:

1. Select MIDP Canvas in the File Types list and click Next.

2. Optionally, modify the following fields in the Name and Location panel of the wizard:

    MIDP Class Name. The name for the new class.

    Package. The package in which the new class is located.

    The resulting Created File field shows the full path location of your new class.

3. Click Finish.

MIDlet

The wizard for creating MIDlet file types differs slightly from that of other file templates in that it also collects information that is used in the application's JAD file.

1. Select one of the MIDlet file types in the File Types list and click Next.
2. Optionally, modify the following fields in the Name and Location panel of the wizard:

    MIDlet Name. This is the value that is shown in the list of MIDlets displayed when starting the application. It can be different from the MIDlet's class name.

    MIDP Class Name. The name for the new MIDlet class.

    MIDlet Icon. The location of this MIDlet's icon. The combo box contains all .png files located in your project.

    Package. The package in which the new MIDlet is located.

    The resulting Created File field shows the full path location of your new class.

3. Click Finish.

 All MIDlets that you add to the project are automatically added to the project's application descriptor.

Localization and Support Class

This is an advanced template that uses configurations; therefore, it is described in Localizing Applications later in this chapter.

Configuring the Project's Classpath

Like most project settings, the classpath used to compile Mobility projects is managed in the Project Properties dialog box. Two panels in particular control the classpath: the Libraries & Resources panel and the Platform panel. In addition to compilation, code completion is controlled by these settings.

Changing the Project's Emulator Platform

The selected emulator platform is used to determine which vendor-supplied libraries are to be used for project compilation. By default, your project is configured to use the latest version of the J2ME Wireless Toolkit. You can modify this using the Platform panel of the Project Properties dialog box:

1. Right-click your project in the Projects window and choose Properties.

2. Select the Platform node in the Project Properties dialog box (as shown in Figure 11-3).

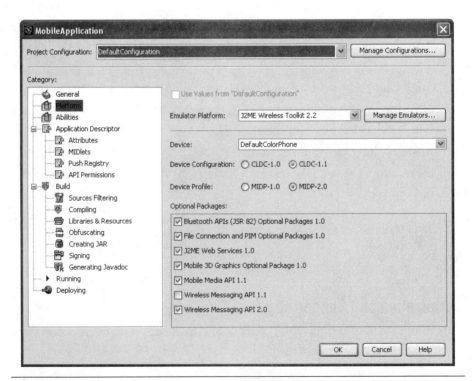

Figure 11-3   Mobile Application Project Properties dialog box, Platform panel

3. Optionally, modify any of the following fields to change which emulator libraries are used to build and run the project:

Emulator Platform. The installed emulator platform you would like to use. This controls which values are available for all following fields.

Device. Selects which device skin to use when launching the application.

Device Configuration. Determines the device configuration. This setting affects your classpath.

Device Profile. Determines the device profile. This setting affects your classpath.

4. **Optional Packages.** Select or deselect any number of the listed packages. Again, this setting affects your project's classpath.

 Sometimes, one device profile or device configuration is disabled when a given emulator platform is selected. This is a result of that emulator platform's response to a Unified Emulator Interface (UEI) query regarding its profile and configuration abilities.

You can still develop an application for the disabled configuration or profile using the selected platform (for example, developing a MIDP-1.0 profile with the WTK2.0 emulator platform). First, ensure that you do not use any invalid code for the desired profile or configuration; then add a MicroEdition-Configuration or MicroEdition-Profile attribute to the project's Application Descriptor. These attributes are managed in the Project Properties dialog box's Attributes panel.

Though NetBeans Mobility Pack ships only with the J2ME Wireless Toolkit, it is also possible to install additional third-party-vendor emulators into the IDE. This is done using the standard Platform Manager, which can be accessed in the standard way from the Tools | Java Platform Manager main menu option or from within the Project Properties dialog box.

1. Right-click your project in the Projects window and choose Properties.

2. Select the Platform node in the Project Properties dialog box.

3. Click Manage Emulators. This opens the Java Platform Manager.

4. Click Add Platform.

5. Navigate to the location of the third-party emulator you would like to install, and click Next. If the emulator platform is detected successfully, the Next and Finish buttons are enabled.

Note that only UEI-compliant emulators are detected. See Installing Non-standard Emulator Platforms later in this chapter to learn how you can install non-UEI-compliant emulators into the IDE.

6. Optionally, click Next to specify the locations of emulator sources and documentation.

7. Click Finish.

Adding JAR Files and Folders to the Classpath

If your project depends on additional APIs or classes that aren't part of the selected emulator platform, you can add them to your project's source path manually. Unlike classpath items for general Java projects, all classes added by this panel are packaged in the project's distribution JAR file. Care must be taken to ensure that all included classes pass preverification.

1. Right-click your project in the Projects window and choose Properties.

2. Select the Libraries & Resources node in the Project Properties dialog box.

3. Click Add Jar/Zip or Add Folder. In the file browser, choose the file or folder containing the classes you would like to include.

4. Click OK to close the Project Properties dialog box.

 If you want to use a library solely for compilation without packaging it with your application, you should make that library an optional API of one of your emulator platforms. See Changing the Project's Emulator Platform earlier in this chapter.

Also, it is important to remember that the preverification process can cause the build process to fail even for projects that compile without problem. All classes in the Libraries & Resources panel must preverify correctly using the selected emulator platform's preverify command for the build process to succeed.

Debugging Your Project

Debugging Mobility projects can be accomplished in the same way as in general Java projects; right-click your project in the Projects node and select the Debug Project command. The emulator opens, and after you select the MIDlet to run on the phone, the program execution stops at any set breakpoints.

Nevertheless, there are some things you should be aware of:

▪ Not all third-party emulators support debugging commands equally well. If you encounter problems like breakpoints being skipped or step-into commands not working, it may be the result of a faulty runtime environment.

- Always remember to disable obfuscation when debugging.
- Method invocation is not supported by the CLDC JVMs, which can affect your debugging experience. For example, adding something like `myObject.toString()` to the watch panel of the debugger will not return a correct result.
- Debugging a mobile application is often slower than debugging J2SE applications.

Configuring Your Project for Different Devices

One of the most problematic aspects of development for Mobility projects is the issue known as device fragmentation. Writing a single application that will run on disparate platforms can be challenging. Differences in physical aspects of the platform, such as screen size and free memory, as well as software issues such as available API's, are some of the reasons why building a single application for multiple devices can require variations in both code and project settings. Fortunately, NetBeans Mobility Pack has built-in support for this issue that simplifies the problem.

The solution is based on the concept of project configurations. You may have noticed that one major difference in the Project Properties dialog box between Mobility and general Java projects is the combo box located at the top of the dialog box labeled Project Configurations. This combo box is the starting point for using the device fragmentation solution. It contains one element for each configuration in your project, as well as an item that creates new configurations.

In general, you should create one configuration for each distribution JAR file you plan on building for your project. So, for example, if you are planning to support three different screen sizes, using two sets of vendor-specific APIs, you would create six configurations.

Creating a Configuration

1. Right-click your project in the Projects window and choose Properties.
2. Click the Manage Configurations button. This opens the Project Configuration Manager dialog box, shown in Figure 11-4.

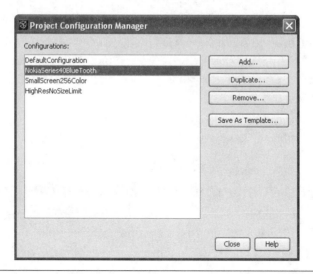

Figure 11-4 Project Configuration Manager

3. Click Add to open the Add Project Configuration dialog box.

4. Enter a name for your new configuration and click OK.

   This name should be an identifier that describes the distribution that this configuration is used for. For example, some descriptive configuration names might be NokiaSeries40Bluetooth, SmallScreen256Color, or HighResNoSizeLimit.

5. Click Add again if you'd like to create another configuration. Otherwise, click Close to close the dialog box.

 Configuration names are just strings and can be set to whatever you'd like. The only restrictions are that they must be valid Java identifiers and that they must not conflict with existing configuration names within the project.

Customizing Configurations

Once you have created your configurations, you may make customizations within the Project Properties dialog box that pertain to only one configuration. There are two basic principles of the configurations within the Project Properties dialog. First, by default, all configurations take the values set for the default configuration. Second, user-added configurations can override the default settings for any panel (other than the General panel) by unchecking the checkbox labeled Use Values from "Default Configuration." Once this checkbox has been unchecked, that configuration uses its own settings for the panel.

The following is an example of changing the default configuration and customizing a single configuration:

1. Right-click your project in the Projects window and choose Properties.
2. Make sure DefaultConfiguration is selected in the Project Configurations drop-down box. In the Emulator Platform drop-down box, select J2ME Wireless Toolkit 2.2, and in the Device drop-down box of the Platform panel, select DefaultGreyPhone.
3. In the Project Configurations combo box at the very top of the Project Properties dialog box, select one of the configurations you created in the previous portion of this section.
4. Select the Platform panel. All controls in this panel should be disabled. This is because the configuration is currently drawing its values from DefaultConfiguration.
5. Deselect the Use Values from "DefaultConfiguration" checkbox. All controls on the panel are now enabled, as they are no longer taking their values from the default configuration.
6. Change the Device combo value to DefaultColorPhone.

    You have now configured the DefaultConfiguration to use the DefaultGreyPhone device and your user-added configuration to use the DefaultColorPhone.

Setting the Active Configuration for Your Project

At any given time, only one configuration is active for your Mobility project. Project settings from the Project Properties dialog box are based on this active configuration.

You can view or set the active configuration in several ways:

-   Right-click the project node in the Projects window and hover over the Set Active Project Configuration menu option. The active configuration is marked by a bullet. You can click any configuration in this list to activate the selected configuration.

■ Right-click the project node in the Projects window and choose Properties. Changing the selected configuration in the Project Configuration combo box activates the newly selected configuration.

■ Use the combo box in the Build toolbar. The selected item in the combo box is the active configuration.

Physical Structure of Mobility Projects with Configurations

Once a project containing multiple configurations has been built, the `build` folder will contain the build directories for the default configuration, and the `dist` directory will contain its distribution JAD file and JAR file. Additionally, the `build` and `dist` directories will contain one subdirectory for each configuration in the project. These subdirectories will hold the build and distribution files for the like-named configuration.

Reusing Project Settings and Configurations

Creating a project with several different configurations and settings within those configurations can be a time-consuming process. If you often want to support the same set of deployment platforms for each application you create, it is useful to reuse those configurations and settings. NetBeans IDE has several features that address this need.

Duplicating Project Settings

If you have configured an entire project that has settings you would like to reuse on a new project, you can do so using the Duplicate Project command.

To reuse a project's settings in another project:

1. Right-click your project in the Projects window and select Duplicate Project.
2. Optionally, update the Project Name and Project Location fields.
3. Select Create Empty Source Root or Copy All Sources, depending on your preference.

    Whenever you select the Copy All Sources option, all files in the original project's source root are copied to the `src` folder contained in the new project. This occurs even when the original project has an external source root.

Your newly created project has all of the settings and configurations from the original project. These may include some settings that are no longer appropriate (for example, JAD file and JAR file name, filtering options, and some JAD file attributes).

Using Project Configuration Templates

Alternatively, you might want just to reuse the settings from one or two configurations. You can do this with configuration templates, which allow you to create new configurations based on the saved settings of other useful configurations. Only the settings from panels that are not taking their values from the default configuration are stored in templates. They are very easy to create:

1. Right-click your project in Projects window and choose Properties.
2. Click Manage Configurations.
3. Highlight the configuration that contains the reusable settings and click Save As Template.
4. In the Save Project As Configuration Template dialog box, enter a name for the template and click Save.

   Templates are uniquely stored in the IDE, so choose a descriptive name.

Now that you have saved this configuration template, it is possible to create new configurations based on it:

1. Right-click your project in the Projects window and choose Properties.
2. Select Add Configuration from the Project Configurations combo box.
3. Select the template you would like to use from the Use Configuration Template combo box.
4. Modify the name of the configuration in the New Configuration Name text box if desired. Click OK.

This template-based configuration has the same settings as the template for each panel of the template that was not using the values from the default configuration.

 Once a template is created, it does not remain synchronized with its original configuration. Also, it is not possible to update existing templates directly. Instead, create a new configuration based on the template, update it, delete the original template, and then save the new configuration as a new template with the original template name.

Structuring Project Dependencies

Unlike other NetBeans project types, Mobility projects are based on the concept of a single source root that results in a single distribution JAR file. It is possible to simulate multiple source roots by setting up one project for each source root and then using project dependencies. It may be helpful to think of the source root containing the MIDlet as the Application project, while all other source roots should be considered Library projects.

 There are no programmatic differences between Library and Application projects other than the option to include a MIDlet when creating an Application project. The differences between project types are purely conceptual in nature.

To structure your project dependencies:

1. Right-click your Application project in the Projects window and choose Properties.
2. Highlight the Libraries & Resources panel in the Project Properties dialog box.
3. Click Add Project.
4. Navigate to the project root of a Library project and ensure that the correct Project JAR file is highlighted in the Select Project JAR Files dialog box.
5. Click Add Selected Project JAR Files.
6. Repeat for each Library project.

If there are interdependencies among the Library projects, these must be set up in the same manner. Note that dependencies may not be circular; if project A depends on project B, project B cannot depend on project A (or any other project that depends on project A).

Using Dependencies with Configurations

If your Library project and Application project make use of project configurations, it is important to take care when setting up the project dependencies. Though it is tempting to assume that the Application project will automatically depend on the correct version of the Library project (based on configuration name matching), this is not the case.

Assume, for example, you are working with an Application project that has configurations named SmallScreen and LargeScreen, and a Library project that has two configurations of the same name. To set up the dependency between the two projects:

1. Right-click your Application project in the Projects window and choose Properties.
2. Select the Libraries & Resources panel in the Project Properties dialog box.
3. Select the SmallScreen configuration from the Project Configuration combo box and then uncheck the Use Values from "DefaultConfiguration" checkbox.
4. Click Add Project.
5. Navigate to the project root of the Library project and highlight the project JAR file that is prefaced with /dist/SmallScreen in the Select Project JAR Files dialog box.
6. Click Add Selected Project JAR Files.
7. Select the LargeScreen configuration from the Project Configuration combo box and then repeat these steps (but highlighting the /dist/LargeScreen distribution JAR file when appropriate).
8. Click OK.

Managing the Distribution JAR File Content

By default, all class files resulting from compilation, as well as all nonsource files contained under the project's source root folder, are placed in the distribution JAR file. All classes and resources specified in the Libraries & Resources panel are also placed in this distribution JAR file.

Your project may contain files under its source root that should not be distributed. These files can be filtered in the following manner:

1. Right-click your project in the Projects window and choose Properties.
2. Select the Sources Filtering panel.
3. Select the default filters provided that are appropriate for your project. Hovering your mouse over the checkbox text displays which regular expression is used to filter files from the distribution JAR file.
4. In the Select Application Packages/Files field, make any necessary adjustments to the files to be distributed. Selected files are distributed.

Deselect a node, and notice that all children nodes are also deselected. If any node is deselected, all of its ancestor nodes are grayed out to indicate a partial selection.

5. Click OK to close the Project Properties dialog box.

The next time you build the project, the selected files and resources will not be added to the distribution JAR file.

Handling Project Resources for Different Configurations

One of the most common causes of device fragmentation is different screen sizes on mobile devices. Disparate screen sizes require different resources, and usually, it is not advisable to include unused resources in the distribution JAR file.

Imagine the scenario where your application has a fixed-size splash-screen image, and you want to include only the correct-size image with each configuration. There are two different methodologies that you can use to manage this problem using NetBeans Mobility Pack. Which method you should use depends on whether you are working with an existing project structure or have the freedom to handle the problem in any way that suits you.

Using Different Resource Locations

One technique is to create size-specific resource JAR files or folders that contain identically named resources. For example, you might have a directory structure like this:

```
/res/small/splashScreen.png
/res/medium/splashScreen.png
/res/large/splashScreen.png
```

Your source code would read simply:

```
Image splashScreen = Image.createImage("splashScreen.png");
```

Then you can modify the Libraries & Resource panel such that each configuration imports only the correct resource file for the screen size on the devices to which it will be deployed.

Using Configuration-Specific Code Blocks and the Filtering Panel

An alternative solution is to have distinctly named resources all contained under the project's source root. So you might have a directory structure something like this:

```
/src/res/splashScreenSmall.png
/src/res/splashScreenMedium.png
/src/res/splashScreenLarge.png
```

Then you would need three configuration-specific code blocks in your source code for the create statement, meaning that your source would look like the code in Figure 11-5.

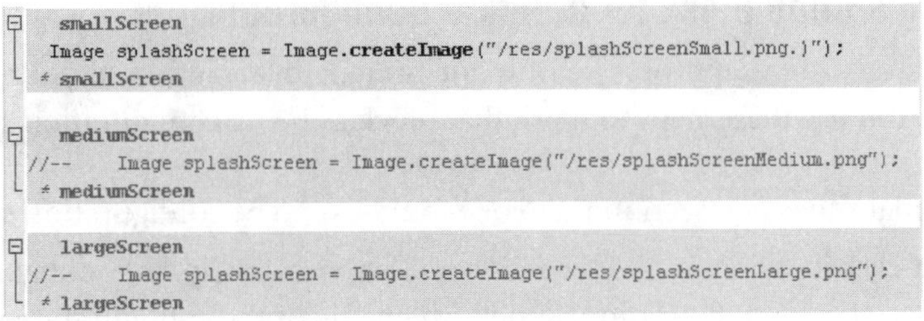

```
   smallScreen
     Image splashScreen = Image.createImage("/res/splashScreenSmall.png.)");
   # smallScreen

   mediumScreen
   //--    Image splashScreen = Image.createImage("/res/splashScreenMedium.png");
   # mediumScreen

   largeScreen
   //--    Image splashScreen = Image.createImage("/res/splashScreenLarge.png");
   # largeScreen
```

Figure 11-5   Example of configuration-specific code blocks in the Source Editor

Finally, the Filtering Sources panel would be modified for each configuration such that only the used resource would be selected in each one.

Both of these solutions result in similar-size application JAR files that include only the used resources. Therefore, it is up to you which technique is best suited to your project structures.

Writing Code Specific to a List of Configurations

Perhaps one of the most uniquely challenging aspects of handling the device fragmentation problem has been managing differences in code between distributions of an application. The NetBeans approach to the problem has been to integrate a preprocessor into the build process that activates or deactivates sections of code based on which configuration is active at compile time.

The NetBeans preprocessor is a low-impact tool that uses Java comments both to define code sections and to activate and deactivate these sections. As such, all files before and after preprocessing can be valid, syntactically correct Java source. This also ensures that the preprocessed files integrate seamlessly with the debugger.

Source files are always saved to the hard drive as though the default configuration were active. This eliminates the VCS conflicts that could otherwise occur due to the local version's having a different active configuration than the VCS version.

A series of context-menu commands exist to assist you in adding these special comments to your source files. These commands are described in the following sections.

Creating a Code Block for a Single Configuration

If a block of code is appropriate only for a single distribution of your application, you can use these steps to mark that block as being configuration specific:

1. Highlight the code section that you would like to be configuration specific.
2. Right-click in the Source Editor and select Preprocessor Blocks | Configuration-Name, where ConfigurationName is the name of the configuration you want to associate with the code section.

Only full lines of text may be associated with a configuration. If you would like to associate only part of a line with the configuration, first break the line into smaller sections and associate the sections appropriately.

This command can also be used to add a configuration to an existing block. Simply right-click inside the block that you would like to modify and select the configuration to add.

Creating a Code Block for Multiple Configurations

If you are a creating or modifying a code block that has multiple identifiers associated with it, it is often easiest to use the Manage Preprocessor Block dialog box. This dialog box allows you to add or remove any number of a block's configurations or abilities.

1. Highlight the code section that you would like to be configuration specific.
2. Right-click the editor document and select Manage Preprocessor Block.

3. In the Manage Preprocessor Block dialog box (shown in Figure 11-6), select the checkbox next to each configuration you would like associated with the code block.

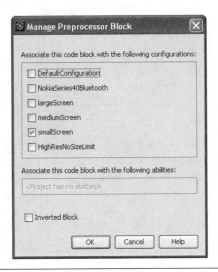

Figure 11-6   Manage Preprocessor Block dialog box

4. Click OK to close the Manage Preprocessor Block dialog box.

Again, this command can be invoked on an existing code block.

Creating an Inverse Code Block for a Single Configuration

The NetBeans preprocessor understands another type of code block definition: the inverse block. Inverse blocks are commented in whenever the project's active configuration is not found in the block's definition.

You can create an inverse block for the active configuration in the following manner:

1. Highlight the code section that you would like to be configuration specific.
2. Right-click in the Source Editor and select Inverted Block (active config name).

Rules That Govern Block Selection

The rules that determine when an existing code block has been selected, or when a new block is created when invoking commands in the Preprocessor Blocks menu, are listed here:

- If the right-click occurs within an existing block, and no text has been highlighted, that block is considered selected.
- If text has been selected when the context menu is opened, and that selection does not overlap with any existing block, any commands create a new block.
- If text has been selected, and it fully encloses (or is fully enclosed by) one code block, that block is considered selected.
- If text has been selected, and it comes into contact with more than one existing block, no blocks are considered selected.
- If text has been selected, and it partially overlaps an existing block, no blocks are considered selected.
- If text has been selected, and it comes into contact with a guarded block, no blocks are considered selected.

Alternatively, you can use the Manage Preprocessor Block dialog box and select the Inverted Block checkbox in addition to the target configurations.

Invoking this command on an existing block will toggle its inverted status.

How to Interpret Code Block Visualization

The visualization of code blocks within the IDE is that of color highlighted sections. This visualization can help you quickly determine some information about code sections:

- Sections that are active for the currently selected configuration are gray. Also, code contained within the section is uncommented.
- Inactive sections are pink. Each line in the code section is prepended with a specially formatted line comment (//--).
- The block identifier that matches the active configuration is colored red.
- The footer line of the preprocessor block is marked with an asterisk (*).

The state of the special comments within the IDE's Source Editor is unimportant, as the preprocessor runs before any compilation command and places the lines of each code block in the correct comment state.

If the special comments within the code blocks become out of sync with the actual state of the code block in the IDE, you can correct them by simply switching configurations. The preprocessor automatically fixes the errors.

Duplicating a Code Block

Sometimes, there is a section of code that must be defined differently for some configurations and that must exist even for configurations that don't explicitly define a code block in the section. An example of this would be if your class definition is fragmented. For example, all of your configurations that will be deployed to Nokia devices might define your Canvas object like this

```
public class MIDPCanvas extends com.nokia.mid.ui.FullCanvas {
```

while the rest of your configurations would just extend Canvas. After adding the appropriate code blocks, you would be left with the code shown in Figure 11-7.

```
public class MIDPCanvas
            NokiaSeries40Bluetooth
        extends com.nokia.mid.ui.FullCanvas
          * NokiaSeries40Bluetooth
            !NokiaSeries40Bluetooth
//-- extends Canvas
          * NokiaSeries40Bluetooth
  {
```

Figure 11-7   Duplicated code blocks in the Source Editor

These types of blocks can be created in one step using the Create If / Else Block context-menu command:

1. Highlight the code section that you would like to be duplicated.
2. Right-click the editor document and select Preprocessor Blocks | Create If / Else Block (*IdentifierName*), where *IdentifierName* is the name of the identifier you want to duplicate the block for.

Two code blocks are created, each containing the highlighted code. The second code block is an inverse block.

You can also use the Create If / Else Block command on existing code blocks. Doing this adds the selected identifier to the code block and then creates a new duplicate block with the selected identifier in its header.

Using Configuration Abilities

Though associating code blocks with individual configurations may be a sufficient solution for some applications, it can sometimes be difficult to maintain. You might find that you are always adding a certain group of configurations to the same code blocks. Or, when adding a new configuration to an existing project, you might find it onerous associating that configuration with each existing and appropriate code block.

In reality, code blocks are usually defined to address some specific feature of the platform to which that code will be deployed; and often, several deployment platforms share the same features and, thus, the same code blocks. To address these problems, configurations have the concept of abilities.

Abilities are identifiers that can be associated with code blocks in much the same way that configuration names are. Configurations can then be associated with as many abilities as desired. Once this is done, activating a configuration uncomments any code block containing either the configuration or any of its associated abilities.

For example, you might be creating an application with six different distributions. In your source, you create some code blocks that handle calls to a vendor-specific Bluetooth implementation. Three of your target distribution platforms will have that specific Bluetooth API available. Rather than list in each code block those three configuration names, you would instead associate that code block with an ability called VendorSpecificBluetoothAPI. Then you associate it with the three configurations that support the Bluetooth API.

This makes maintenance much easier for existing code blocks. Now, if you decide to support a new device that has a certain ability, you can simply attach all appropriate abilities to the new configuration. Then it will automatically be compatible with all existing code blocks.

As such, it is almost always preferable to use abilities when creating code blocks rather than simply configurations. The only cases for using pure configuration names are when you are never planning on supporting more than a few plat-forms for a given application or when the code block is really specific to only one deployment platform.

Creating and Associating an Ability with a Configuration

To create and associate an ability with a configuration:

1. Right-click your project in the Projects window and choose Properties to open the Project Properties dialog box.

2. Select the Abilities panel.

3. From the Project Configuration drop-down box, select the configuration you would like to associate with the new ability.

4. Uncheck the Use Values from "DefaultConfiguration" checkbox (if you did not select DefaultConfiguration in the previous step).

5. Click the Add Ability button to bring up the Add Ability dialog box, shown in Figure 11-8.

Figure 11-8   Add Ability dialog box

6. If the ability you want to attach to the configuration is not in the Abilities list box, click the New Ability button and continue to the next step. Otherwise, select the ability or abilities you would like to attach and click OK.

7. Enter a name for your new ability. Ability names, like configuration names, can be any valid Java identifier strings. They should be as descriptive as possible, as they must be unique among all other abilities and configurations in the project.

8. Click OK to close the New Ability dialog box.

9. The newly created ability is listed and selected in the Abilities list box. If you are satisfied with the new ability, click OK to close the Add Ability dialog box.

10. Click OK to close the Project Properties dialog box. Your configuration is now associated with the newly created abilities.

Once an ability is associated with at least one configuration in the project, that ability will appear in the Preprocessor Blocks contextual menu in the Source Editor. Abilities can be treated exactly like configurations with regard to creating or modifying preprocessor blocks.

The list of abilities contained in the Abilities List view of the Add Ability dialog box contains all the abilities that are attached to configurations in any project that the IDE is currently aware of. The IDE is aware of more projects than those that are open, so don't be surprised if you see some abilities there that don't belong to any open project.

There is no Remove Ability button in the Add Ability dialog box, because it simply displays all abilities that are associated with any configuration.

Localizing Applications

In the mobile development world, there are many different ways of handling localization or translation of your product into different languages. The official support within the NetBeans Mobility Pack is based on the concept of using bundled `message.property` files. The messages file, as well as a small support class that uses it, can be generated for you automatically by the Localization Support Class template:

1. In the Projects window, right-click the package you would like to contain your LocalizationSupport class and select New | Localization Support Class. If that option is not available, select File/Folder.

   Alternatively, select File | New File (Ctrl-N) from the main menu.

2. Select the MIDP node in the Categories list box and then Localization Support Class in the File Types list, and click Next.

3. Optionally, fill in the following fields in the Name and Location panel of the wizard:

   Class Name: The generated class' name.

   Messages Bundle Name: The name of the message bundle.

   Package: The package in which to create the files.

   Default String Value: The value that is used if a property is not found in the message bundle.

   Error Message: The error message that is displayed when there is a problem loading the message bundle.

4. Click Finish to create the files in the locations displayed in the Created Class File and Created Bundle File fields.

The automatically generated support class should now appear in your project and can be modified as desired. The following process outlines how an existing application can be localized using the support class:

1. All hard-coded text strings from your application should be added to the created `message.properties` file using the following format:

   `PROPERTY_NAME=My Translatable Text String`

2. The strings in your source files should then be replaced with code like this:

   `LocalizationSupport.getMessage("PROPERTY_NAME")`

3. Once all strings have been added to the `message.properties` file, right-click it's node in the Projects window and choose Add Locale.

4. Select a locale that you want to support from the Predefined Locales list box, or use the combo boxes at the top of the form to define a new locale.

5. Click OK.

6. Expand the `message.properties` node in the Projects window and double-click the newly added locale.

7. Translate all properties into the appropriate language.

8. Repeat these last five steps until all supported languages have been added.

This technique uses the `microedition.locale` property of the phone to determine which version of the `message.properties` file should be used. If the region is not found, the default bundle is used.

If you prefer, you can force a particular region to be used by calling the following code before using `LocalizationSupport.getMessage()`:

```
LocalizationSupport.initLocalizationSupport("en_US")
```

In this case, the `en_US` version of the `message.properties` file is always used. Forcing a region is useful when you are planning on supporting only one language per distribution JAR file. The Filtering panel should be used to ensure that only the used properties file is bundled with the application.

Using the MIDP Visual Designer

NetBeans Mobility Pack includes the MIDP Visual Designer to assist with the creation of MIDlets. This full-featured designer allows you to create your application's flow rapidly and modify the screen content of standard MIDP 1.0 or MIDP 2.0 components using an intuitive GUI. See the Understanding the Flow Designer and Understanding the Screen Designer sections later in this chapter for an overview of the tool and the following sections for some common task descriptions.

Creating a New Visual Design

To create a new visual design:

1. In the Projects window, right-click the package you would like to contain your visual design and select New | Visual Midlet. If that option is not available, select File/Folder.

   Alternatively, select File | New File (Ctrl-N) from the main menu.

2. Select the MIDP node in the Categories list box and then Visual MIDlet or HelloMIDlet.java in the File Types list, and click Next.

3. Select the MIDP version for your MIDlet to use (according to the version supported by the device you are developing for) and click Next.

4. Fill out the fields as described in Using Mobility File Templates earlier in this chapter, and click Finish.

Your visual design opens in the Flow Design view. If HelloMidlet was selected, the MIDlet will already contain a TextBox screen that displays the text "Hello, World!"

Adding Objects to the Component Palette

User-defined screens and items can be added to the component palette for use with the designer. Though the screen editor does not allow editing of all attributes of user-added components, they can still be used with the Flow Designer:

1. Ensure that the class you want to use is on your project's classpath.
2. Click the ▣ button at the top of the component palette. This opens the MIDP Palette Manager dialog box.
3. Click Add from Project.
4. Select the project that contains the object you want added to the component palette and click Next.
5. Select all the objects to add, using the Found MIDP Classes list.

   All classes inheriting from `Displayable` or `Item` on the selected project's classpath are shown in the list.
6. Optionally, use the Add to Category combo box to select the palette category to which the object will be added, and click Finish.
7. Click Close.

Your component(s) will now be available in the chosen category whenever you open the Visual Designer. This is true for any project you open. As such, it is possible that a class in the component palette won't be on your project's classpath.

Building a Small Application with the Visual Designer

The following steps illustrate how to create the skeleton of a two-screen application that could be used to send an SMS:

1. Create a new visual design document and click the Flow Design button in the designer toolbar.
2. Click and drag the TextBox from the Screens group in the component palette to the Flow Designer.
3. Click and drag the transition source labeled Start Point on the Mobile Device screen to your newly added TextBox.

   Your first screen has now been added. If you run the application at this point, the application will start with a text field, with no commands associated with it.

4. Click and drag the OK command from the Commands group in the component palette to your TextBox screen. Now add an Exit command to the same screen.

5. Click and drag an Alert from the Screens group in the component palette to the Flow Designer.

6. Double-click the new Alert screen. It will open in the Screen Designer.

7. Click the Device screen where it reads <Enter Text>. This text box will now be editable. Enter the message "SMS Sent" and press Ctrl-Enter to save your changes.

8. Use the combo box at the top of the Screen Designer to switch to the TextBox screen, as shown in Figure 11-9.

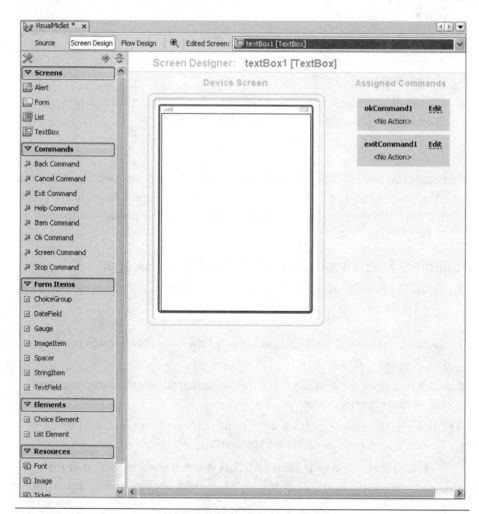

Figure 11-9 Visual Designer with a TextBox screen added

9. Click in the text box and delete the `<Edit Text>` string. Again, press Ctrl-Enter to save your changes.

10. Use the property editor to set the Title property to `"Enter SMS text:"`.

11. Click the Flow Design button in the toolbar to return to the Flow Design view.

12. Click and drag the transition source labeled okCommand from the TextBox screen to the Alert screen.

13. Click and drag the transition source labeled exitCommand from the TextBox screen to the Mobile Device screen.

    The Form Designer should now look similar to what is shown in Figure 11-10. If you were to run the application at this point, it would begin with a text

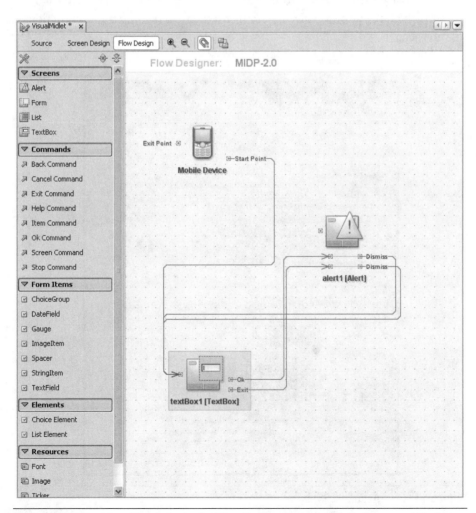

Figure 11-10   Visual Designer in the Flow Design view and an alert screen added

box screen and OK and Exit options on its soft keys. Pressing the OK soft key would bring you to the alert screen. Pressing the Exit soft key would exit the program.

14. Use the Inspector view to select the okCommand that is located under the TextBox screen node.

15. In the Properties panel, click in the Action property's value field to open the Action dialog box.

16. In the Action dialog box, enter sendSMS in the Pre-Action User Code field, as shown in Figure 11-11, and click OK.

    This action generates a method stub called sendSMS. This is where you could place the code that would handle sending an SMS. It is called each time the OK button is clicked, and if it returns False, the transaction does not occur.

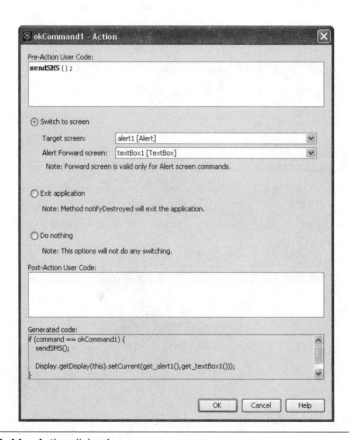

Figure 11-11   Action dialog box

17. Click the Source button in the Visual Designer toolbar to view the source for your application. The main code generated by the Visual Designer is folded. You should also see the sendSMS method. You can enter code here for SMS handling, if you like.

You have now created a very simple MIDP application.

Understanding the Flow Designer

The Flow Designer visually represents the different paths that can be taken between your application's different screens. Using this view, you can add or remove screens, as well as the transitions between them. It is also possible to modify the properties of the screens and transitions.

The Flow Designer is composed of four parts: the component palette, the Inspector, the Flow Design panel, and a property sheet. Following is a quick overview of these panels, as well as their respective abilities.

Component Palette

The component palette (shown in Figure 11-12) contains groupings of all Java objects that can be added to your application with the designer. If an object does not exist in the component palette, it cannot be added to the application using the Flow Designer.

The following categories are used:

- **Screens:** Contains items for creating Alert, Form, List, and TextBox components.
- **Commands:** Contains an item for each command type defined in javax.microedition.lcdui.Command. Commands are used as sources for transactions between screens.
- **Form Items:** Contains items that can be added to screens.
- **Elements:** Contains elements that can be added to List and ChoiceGroup components.
- **Resources:** Resources that can be used by other items. Includes Font, Image, and Ticker.
- **Custom Components:** Any custom components that you have added to the palette.

All groups can be expanded or collapsed individually by clicking the header bar containing the group name. The groups can be collapsed or expanded simultaneously by clicking the ⚛ (collapse all) or ⚛ (expand all) button at the top of the palette.

Figure 11-12   Component palette

Inspector

The Inspector (shown in Figure 11-13) displays all objects that have been added to the visual design in a tree formation. The root node of the tree is the MIDP Design node, with child nodes for Screens, Commands, and Resources. Any objects from these groups that have been added to the design appear under their respective group header nodes.

If a node represents an object that can have action commands associated with it, it has an Assigned Commands group node containing each assigned action. Similarly, objects that support elements or items contain an Elements or Items group.

Selected objects in the Inspector are highlighted in the Screen Designer or Flow Designer view (if the object appears in the currently active design view). Additionally, the object's properties are displayed in the Property Sheet view.

Right-clicking a component node opens a menu consisting of standard node commands (Rename, Cut, Copy, Paste, Delete, Move Up, Move Down, and Properties).

Right-clicking the Action Command, Elements, or Items node opens a menu containing actions for adding a new node to the list or changing the order of the list.

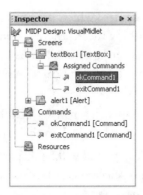

Figure 11-13   Inspector

Property Sheet

A standard property sheet is visible when the designer is open. This property sheet shows the editable properties for any object selected in the Designer or Inspector view.

The property sheet contains all MIDP2 properties for the selected object. Additionally, there are some items specific to the source code and components, as described here:

- **Instance Name:** The name of the object.
- **Action Source:** When a transition is selected that is initiated with a command, this property appears. It defines which command object to use as the transaction source.
- **Lazy Initialized:** Checkbox that determines when the component is initialized. If true, it is initialized when the MIDlet's `startApp()` method is invoked. Otherwise, it is initialized the first time the component is needed.
- **Pre-Callback Method:** A method is created by this property value that is called before the component is initialized. Used only when Lazy Initialize is selected.
- **Post-Callback Method:** A method is created by this property value that is called after the component is initialized. Used only when Lazy Initialize is selected.
- **Action:** Property that appears when an action command is selected. A special property editor is used to set this value.
- **Radio Buttons:** Used to control which screen is shown when this transaction occurs. Selecting nothing means there is no target. Selecting Exit means the application will end when the transition is followed. Selecting Switch enables the target screen drop-down box, which can be used to select a new screen.
- **Target Displayable:** Contains all screens available in the visual design. The selected screen is the one displayed when the command is invoked.
- **Forward Displayable:** Select what will be displayed after an alert. Appears only when a connection is selected that targets an alert.
- **Callback Validation Method Name:** Entering a value in this field creates a method by that name in the source. This method returns a `Boolean`. If the return value is `True`, the forward action will occur; otherwise, it is skipped.
- **Post-Callback Method Name:** Entering a value in the field creates a method by that name in the source. This method is called after the display is updated to the new value.

Additional properties are determined by what is supported by the associated object.

Several property types have special editors associated with them:

- **String Editor:** A dialog box opens, containing a text box. Values entered in this text box are used as the property value. If the Use as Custom Code Expression checkbox is selected, the value entered in the text box is used as though it were Java code rather than as a static string. So, for example, entering `getTitle()` in an alert's Title property when Use as Custom Code Expression is selected causes that component to be constructed with code like this:

```
alert = new Alert(getTitle(), "text", get_image2(), AlertType.INFO)
```

The user must implement a `getTitle()` method for the component to work properly.

- **Image Dialog:** Used to set the resource path for image resources.

  The Select Image list contains all images that will appear in the project's distribution JAR file. As shown in Figure 11-14, selecting an image displays a preview of the image, as well as the dimensions, file size, and name of the file. Clicking OK sets the property to the path of the selected image.

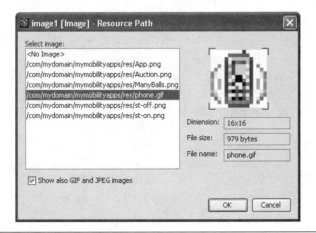

Figure 11-14   Image dialog box

- **Constraints:** Selecting the Constraints property on TextBox objects opens the Constraints dialog box. Use the radio button to specify the restrictive constraint setting and the checkboxes to specify any additional constraint modifiers.

- **Font:** Editing the Font property on Font resources opens the Font dialog box. This dialog box allows you to specify which font to use. Selecting Custom from the main radio button enables the dialog box's font checkboxes; otherwise, the default or system font is used.

- **Layout:** Editing the Layout property of any Form item opens the Layout dialog box. This dialog box allows you to specify properties that determine how the item will appear within the form.

Flow Designer

The main screen of the Flow Designer uses drag-and-drop to add and connect components in the MIDlet. All designs contain a Mobile Device element that represents the MIDlet's start point.

Displayable components (screens) can be dragged from the component palette and dropped onto the Design screen. After a screen has been added, appropriate commands, elements, items, and resources can be added to it by dragging the object from the component palette and dropping it on the screen.

Transition sources are displayed on the right side of the component to which they are attached. These are used to create transitions to different screens by selecting the transition source and dragging to the target screen. The connection is visualized in the design as a line.

Transitions can also be selected. Doing so paints the transition in a different color and displays the transition sources' properties in the property sheet.

Selecting a screen node highlights all transitions to and from that screen in a different color. Double-clicking a screen opens it in the Screen Design view.

Toolbar

The toolbar of the Flow Designer has only two items:

- Snap to Grid: Toggles between displaying and hiding a dotted grid on background of the designer page. Also determines whether screens snap to set locations or can be moved with complete freedom.

- Realign Components: Realigns all existing screens to a grid pattern.

Understanding the Screen Designer

The Screen Designer allows you to customize screens that have been added to the visual design. It contains two main sections: Device Screen and Assigned Commands, which will be discussed here.

Device Screen

The device screen simulates how the screen will appear on a real device. All elements, items, and resources (components) appear in the order in which they are listed in the Inspector view. Components can be dragged to new locations in the Inspector to change display order.

Hovering over a component highlights it with a dashed line. Clicking the component selects it and highlights it with a solid line. Clicking editable areas within a selected component (as shown with a moving dashed line) allows inline editing of the selected area. Noneditable sections of components cannot be modified inline but usually can still be selected. As always, properties of the selected object appear in the property sheet.

New components can be dragged and dropped directly to the desired location of the device screen. Only components that are valid for the screen type are added. Appropriate elements and items can be added to existing components (for example, Choice Element objects can be added to existing Choice Group objects). Trying to add a component not supported by the screen/object shows a standard Not Allowed icon.

Right-clicking the device screen and selecting Set Screen Size brings up a dialog box in which you can set the height and width of the device screen in pixels. Clicking the ▦ (Activate Viewport) button simulates how the screen will appear on a device that has these dimensions. The ▲ and ▼ buttons move this view up and down the design.

Assigned Commands

This portion of the Screen Designer shows all transition sources attached to the screen by the user. The box may be selected to see the transaction source's properties in the properties dialog box. Additionally, you can open the transaction target in the Screen Designer by clicking its name in each of these command boxes.

This list has a subsection for item commands as well. These commands appear only when you are editing a form screen; one Item Command box is displayed for each assigned item command. They function in the same way as normal Assigned Commands boxes.

Toolbar

The Screen Design toolbar has a combo box containing all screens added to the visual design. Selecting a screen from this combo box displays the screen in the Screen Designer.

Also in the toolbar is a Zoom icon. This simply increases the viewable size of all components in the screen within the IDE.

Deploying Your Application Automatically

NetBeans Mobility Pack provides you the ability to deploy your application. There are several methods of deployment, including simply moving the JAR file to a specified location on the local machine or using various protocols to move the file to a remote server. These options are specified in the Deploying panel of the Project Properties dialog box.

1. Right-click your project in the Projects window and choose Properties.
2. Select the Deploying node in the Category tree (as shown in Figure 11-15).
3. In the Select Deployment Method combo box, select the method you would like to use.
4. Optionally, set MIDlet-Jar-URL to a value other than the default (which is simply the JAR file name) by deselecting the Override JAR URL in JAD checkbox and entering a new value in the text field.

The remainder of the form is based on which deployment method you have selected above.

Copy

Use the Target Directory field to specify where the distribution JAR and JAD files should be copied.

FTP

1. Enter the server location in the Server field.
2. Optionally, use the Target Directory field to enter the remote directory to which the JAR file and JAD file should be copied.

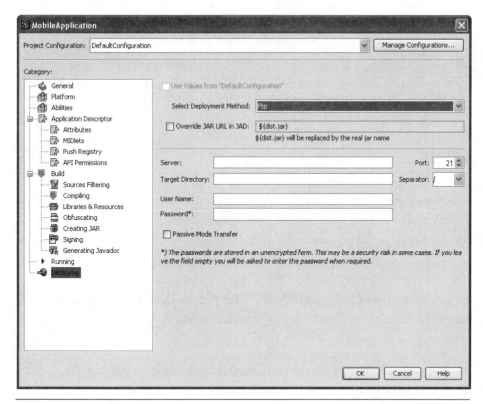

Figure 11-15   Project Properties dialog box, Deploying panel

3. Enter the remote server's port in the Port field.

4. In the Separator field, specify the path separator used on the server.

5. Enter the remote username in the User Name field.

6. Optionally, select the Passive Mode Transfer checkbox. The Passive Mode Transfer checkbox is used to toggle between passive and active FTP mode. If you are having trouble connecting to your FTP server, and you are behind a firewall, you should select this checkbox.

SCP

1. Enter the server location in the Server field.

2. Check the Trust All Unknown Hosts checkbox to bypass the requirement that the host appear in your machine's known hosts file (which is normally located at `${user.home}/.ssh/known_hosts`).

3. Optionally, enter the remote directory to which the JAR and JAD files should be copied in the Target Directory field.

4. Enter the remote server's port in the Port field.

5. Enter the remote username in the User Name field.

6. Select the Use Password Authentication radio button or, if you use public/ private key authentication, select the Use Authentication Key radio button. If you select Use Authentication Key, enter the location of your private key in the Key File field.

WebDAV

1. Enter the server location in the Server field.

2. Optionally, enter the remote directory to which the JAR and JAD files should be copied in the Target Directory field.

3. Enter the remote server's port in the Port field.

4. Enter the remote username in the User Name field.

Once you have set up this panel, right-click your project in the Projects window and select the Deploy Project command to deploy the project.

Incrementing the Application's MIDlet-Version Automatically

The IDE has a built-in method that allows you to auto-increment the MIDlet-Version attribute in the JAR file each time you deploy the application. This can be useful, as some physical devices have a Check for Updates function for installed applications. If you increment the value, this device function automatically detects a new version when you deploy the application.

Deploying with an incremented value can be done in the following manner:

1. Right-click your project in the Projects window and choose Properties.

2. Highlight the Attributes node in the Project Properties dialog box.

3. Select the MIDlet-Version record and click Edit.

4. Enter `${deployment.number}` in the Value field.

5. Click OK.

Installing Nonstandard Emulator Platforms

This section describes the process by which you can use an emulator platform installed on your system that is not automatically recognized by the Java Platform Manager. Platforms are not automatically detected if they do not comply with the Unified Emulator Interface (UEI) specification. This specification defines queries that allow external tools to determine the capabilities of the emulator (for example, supported MIDP and CLDC versions). Though most modern emulators are written in accordance with this standard, it can still be useful to use the older, non-UEI-compliant emulators.

 This is an advanced topic and requires manual modification of NetBeans system files. Modifying or creating these files incorrectly can cause instability within the IDE.

When platforms are added to the IDE via the Platform Management dialog box, an XML platform descriptor file is generated and stored in your NetBeans user directory (*userhome*\config\Services\Platforms\org-netbeans-api-java-Platform) directory. The userhome directory is located by default at C:\Documents and Settings*username*\.netbeans for Windows machines and /home/*username*/.netbeans for Linux machines.

 Emulators that are not UEI-compliant can sometimes be installed in the J2ME Wireless Toolkit as a device. Once installed in the J2ME Wireless Toolkit, the device appears in the Devices combo box of the Platforms panel when that platform is selected.

Though the Nokia 7210 can be installed in this manner, it is still used here as an example illustrating how platform descriptor files can be manually created or edited.

As an example, the Nokia 7210 emulator is not UEI compliant but is one of the remaining MIDP 1.0 Nokia emulators available for development. To install this platform, you can create and save the following platform descriptor file in the previously mentioned directory:

```
<?xml version='1.0'?>
<!DOCTYPE platform PUBLIC '-//NetBeans//DTD J2ME PlatformDefinition 1.0//
  EN' 'http://www.netbeans.org/dtds/j2me-platformdefinition-1_0.dtd'>
<platform name="Nokia_7210"
    home="C:\Nokia_7210" type="CUSTOM" displayname="Nokia 7210"
    srcpath=""
    docpath="${platform.home}/docs/api,${platform.home}/
        docs,${platform.home}/docs/NokiaUI,${platform.home}/docs/
        tooldocs"
```

```
    preverifycmd="&quot;{platformhome}{/}bin{/}preverify&quot;
        {classpath|-classpath &quot;{classpath}&quot;}
         -d &quot;{destdir}&quot;&quot;{srcdir}&quot;"
    runcmd="&quot;{platformhome}{/}bin{/}7210.exe&quot;
        &quot;{jadfile}&quot;"
    debugcmd="java -classpath
        &quot;{platformhome}{/}tools{/}emulator.jar&quot;
        -Demulator.home=&quot;{platformhome}&quot;
        com.nokia.phone.sdk.Emulator
        -classpath &quot;{platformhome}{/}lib{/}classes.zip&quot;
        -debugger -dbg_port {debugaddress} -port 2800
        &quot;{jadfile}&quot;">
    <device name="Nokia_7210"
        securitydomains="real_life,manufacturer,trusted_3rd_party,
        untrusted,custom,minimum" description="Nokia 7210 Emulator">
        <configuration name="CLDC" version="1.0" displayname="CLDC"
            classpath="${platform.home}/lib/classes.zip"
            dependencies="" default="true"/>
        <profile name="MIDP" version="1.0" displayname="MIDP"
            classpath="${platform.home}/lib/classes.zip" dependencies=""
            default="true"/>
    </device>
</platform>
```

 A DTD for the XML format can be found at http://www.netbeans.org/dtds/j2me-plat-formdefinition-1_0.dtd and contains useful information to assist in creating these descriptor files.

There are several things to notice in platform descriptor. First, items surrounded by {} are replaced with runtime values when any action is taken using the platform. Second, if quotation marks are required around any parameters at runtime, those quotes should be added to the platform descriptor file as ".

The file begins with a standard XML header:

```
<?xml version='1.0'?>
<!DOCTYPE platform PUBLIC '-//NetBeans//DTD J2ME PlatformDefinition 1.0//
    EN' 'http://www.netbeans.org/dtds/j2me-platformdefinition-1_0.dtd'>
```

Following the header is the platform element. This is the primary element of the document, and it takes the following attributes:

- name: identifies the platform within the IDE. This must be a unique identifier.
- home: the folder in which the platform is installed.

- type: distinguishes between UEI and non-UEI platforms. Valid values are UEI-1.0, UEI-1.01, and CUSTOM. Values specified in runcmd, preverifycmd, and debugcmd are used only if type is set to CUSTOM.

- preverifycmd: defines the command line used when running preverification. The following properties can be used and have the following values:

  platformhome: contains the value of the platform home directory

  srcdir: location of the src files for preverification

  destdir: location where the preverified files should be placed

  classpath: the device's classpath

  / : value of File.separator

- runcmd: defines the command line used when starting the emulator. The following properties can be used and have the following values:

  platformhome: value of the platform home directory

  device: unique identifier for the device currently selected for this platform

  jadfile: the relative path of the project JAD file

  jadurl: the URL for the JAD file when using OTA execution

  securitydomain: value defining the security domain during execution

- debugcmd: defines the command line used when debugging in the emulator. This command has the same list of arguments as runcmd, with the addition of:

  debug: a switch indicating whether debugging has been launched

  debugaddress: the port at which the debugger will attach

  debugtransport: the method of connection with the debugger

  debugserver: the value of debug server

  debugsuspend: the value of debug suspend

With this information, it is possible to create the platform tag header

```
<platform name="Nokia_7210_MIDP_SDK_v1_0"
```

The platform should have a unique name. It is often sufficient to use the platform home directory name:

```
home="C:\Nokia_7210" type="CUSTOM" displayname="Nokia 7210"
```

home should be set to the parent directory of the platform. `type` is set to `CUSTOM`, as this is a non-UEI emulator type. `displayname` can be any identifier and is the value displayed in the Platform combo box in the Platform panel of the Project Properties dialog box.

```
srcpath=""
```

Sources are not included with this emulator, so this attribute can be set to the empty string.

```
docpath="${platform.home}/docs/api,${platform.home}/
        docs,${platform.home}/docs/NokiaUI,${platform.home}/docs/
        tooldocs"
```

All directories under platform home that contain a Javadoc `index.html` page are included on the doc path. This setting determines what Javadoc documentation will be available within the IDE when this platform is selected.

```
preverifycmd="&quot;{platformhome}{/}bin{/}preverify&quot;
        {classpath|-classpath &quot;{classpath}&quot;}
         -d &quot;{destdir}&quot;&quot;{srcdir}&quot;"
```

`preverifycmd` executes the `preverify.exe` that resides in the platform's `bin` directory. The platform classpath, `src`, and `dest` locations are all passed to the `preverify` command as defined by the command itself. Note that the command's `-nonative` and `-nofinalize` arguments can also be used, should they be required.

```
runcmd="&quot;{platformhome}{/}bin{/}7210.exe&quot;
        &quot;{jadfile}&quot;"
```

`runcmd` executes the 7210 executable file contained in the platform's `bin` directory. The only passed argument is the `jadfile` location, which the emulator then uses to launch the application.

```
debugcmd="java -classpath
        &quot;{platformhome}{/}tools{/}emulator.jar&quot;
        -Demulator.home=&quot;{platformhome}&quot;
        com.nokia.phone.sdk.Emulator
        -classpath &quot;{platformhome}{/}lib{/}classes.zip&quot;
        -debugger -dbg_port {debugaddress} -port 2800
        &quot;{jadfile}&quot;">
```

debugcmd is atypical, as it requires the emulator to be launched using the emulator.jar file rather than the 7210 executable file. This is the only way of starting the emulator such that it is aware of the debugger port that NetBeans will use to attach to it. This is the last attribute of the platform element.

Enclosed within the platform container are device elements for each device supported by the platform. The following attributes are supported by the device element:

- name: identifies the device within the IDE. This should be unique within the platform container.
- securitydomains: comma-delimited list of the security domains defined for this device. Example value: untrusted,trusted,minimum,maximum.
- description: the value that appears in the Device combo box in the Platform panel of the Project Properties dialog box.

So you can create the following device element for the Nokia 7210:

```
<device name="Nokia_7210"
        securitydomains="real_life,manufacturer,trusted_3rd_party,
        untrusted,custom,minimum" description="Nokia 7210 Emulator">
```

The device name is what will be displayed in the Device combo box in the Platform panel of the Project Properties dialog box when the containing platform is selected in the Emulator Platform combo box.

The device element must contain a configuration and a profile element. Both of these have the same set of attributes:

- name: identifies the version of configuration or profile. CLDC should be the value for the configuration element and MIDP for the profile element.
- version: the version number of the configuration or profile.
- displayname: an expanded description of the name field.
- classpath: a comma-delimited list of JAR and .zip files that make up the configuration or profile.
- dependencies: a comma-delimited list of dependencies. For example, MIDP 1.0 profile might have dependencies="CLDC > 1.0".

The Nokia 7210 emulator supports MIDP 1.0 and CLDC 1.0, so the following elements can define its abilities:

```
<configuration name="CLDC" version="1.0" displayname="CLDC"
    classpath="${platform.home}/lib/classes.zip"
    dependencies="" default="true"/>
<profile name="MIDP" version="1.0" displayname="MIDP"
    classpath="${platform.home}/lib/classes.zip" dependencies=""
    default="true"/>
```

Once the file has been created and saved in the appropriate location, restart Net-Beans IDE. Your newly created platform will now be available for selection in the Platform panel of the Projects Properties dialog box.

Using Ant in Mobility Projects

As with general Java project types, Mobility project-related commands are controlled by an automatically generated Ant script. This Ant script is named `build.xml` and is located directly in your project's home folder. Examining this file reveals that it, by default, simply imports the project's `build-impl.xml` file. The relationship between these two files is important to understand if you would like to modify the build process in some way. Feel free to modify `build.xml` however you like, but do not change `build-impl.xml`. `build-impl.xml` may be regenerated by the IDE, so changes you make to this file can be lost.

 Should your `build-impl.xml` file become corrupted, you can force it to be regenerated by deleting it and closing and then reopening the project.

Adding functionality to the NetBeans build process can be accomplished by overriding the targets defined in the `build-impl.xml` file that run both before and after the main build targets. These are described in detail in each project `build.xml` file.

It is also acceptable to override the main project targets if you are interested in completely changing the behavior of the build script. These main targets are invoked by the similarly named project commands within the IDE.

Mobility Ant Library

Mobility Pack ships with a special Ant library responsible for handling J2ME-specific tasks. This library can be freely shared, and is located at *NetBeansHome*/mobility/modules/org-netbeans-modules-kjava-antext.jar.

Tasks that exist in the Mobility Library are listed here, along with descriptions of what they can do. Each task is listed along with its attributes and nested elements. Required elements are bolded.

- ExtractTask: extracts specified JAR and .zip files to a given location.

  *ClassPath: the archives to extract as a full path.

  *ClassPathRef: the archives to extract as a reference to an existing Ant object.

  *Nested ClassPath: the archives to extract specified with a nested Classpath element.

  Dir: the target directory for extraction.

  ExcludeManifest: specifies if the META-INF/Manifest.mf files should be excluded from extraction. Defaults to False.

  * one of the class path attributes must be defined.

- JadTask: support for updating existing JAD file with correct JAR size and URL information. Also provides supports for JAR file signing.

  JadFile: location of the source JAD file.

  JarFile: location of the source JAR file.

  Output: destination JAD file. If unspecified, the source location is used.

  Url: value to be set for the MIDlet-Jar-URL property.

  Encoding: the encoding used for the JAD file. Defaults to UTF-8.

  Sign: set to True if signing should be used. Defaults to False.

  *KeyStore: location of the KeyStore file.

  KeyStoreType: use to set the keystore type explicitly. Valid settings are Default and PKCS12. If not set, the extension of the keystore file is used to determine the type.

  *KeyStorePassword: the keystore password.

  *Alias: the owner of the private key to be used for signing.

  *AliasPassword: the password to access the alias' private key.

  *Required if Sign is True.

- ObfuscateTask: support for obfuscation using the ProGuard obfuscator.

  SrcJar: location of source JAR file to be obfuscated.

DestJar: destination of the obfuscated JAR file.

ObfuscatorType: specifies which obfuscator to use. In NetBeans IDE 4.1, the only acceptable value is ProGuard or NONE. If NONE is selected, SrcJar is simply copied to the DestJar location.

ClassPath: classpath required by SrcJar classes. Can be specified using nested classpath instead.

ClassPathRef: classpath for SrcJar classes specified as Ant reference.

*ObfuscatorClassPath: classpath for the obfuscator.

*ObfuscatorClassPathRef: classpath for obfuscator as Ant reference.

*Nested ObfuscatorClassPath: classpath for the obfuscator as a nested element.

Exclude: a comma-separated list of classes that should not be obfuscated.

ObfuscationLevel: integer value specifying level of obfuscation. Valid values are 0 through 9, with the default 0.

ExtraScript: string containing any additional obfuscation commands.

*Obfuscator classpath must be set using one of these methods.

The exact commands used by different obfuscation levels can be seen within the IDE. Simply open the Project Properties dialog box and select the Obfuscating panel. Changing the obfuscation level on the slider displays the script commands in the Level Description panel.

- PreverifyTask: support for preverification.

SrcDir: location of classes to be preverified.

DestDir: destination directory for preverified classes.

PlatformHome: home directory of the emulator platform to be used for preverification.

PlatformType: controls the format of the preverification command line used. Valid values: UEI-1.0, UEI-1.0.1, or CUSTOM. The default value is UEI-1.0.1.

Configuration: the configuration to use for preverification. Valid values: CLDC-1.0 and CLDC-1.1. Ignored when PlatformType is set to CUSTOM.

ClassPath: classpath for sources in SrcDir. Can also be defined using nested elements.

ClassPathRef: classpath for sources in SrcDir as an Ant reference.

CommandLine: command line to be used for preverification. Required when PlatformType is CUSTOM.

- RunTask: support for running and debugging an application.

*JadFile: location of target application's JAD file. Required when **JadUrl** is not set.

JadUrl: URL for application's JAD file when using OTA execution.

PlatformHome: location of emulator platform used for execution.

PlatformType: controls the format of the execution command line used. Valid values: UEI-1.0, UEI-1.0.1, or CUSTOM. The default value is UEI-1.0.1.

Device: target emulator platform device.

ExecMethod: determines if OTA or Standard execution is used. Ignored if JadUrl is not set or PlatformType is CUSTOM.

ClassPath: classpath for sources in SrcDir. Can also be defined using nested element.

ClassPathRef: classpath for sources in SrcDir as Ant reference.

SecurityDomain: security domain in which execution takes place.

Debug: set to True to run in Debug mode. The default value is False.

DebugAddress: should just be the port number to use for attaching to the debugger.

DebuggerAddressProperty: the address to which the debugger tries to connect.

DebugTransport: specifies the transport type to use for debugging. Default is dt_socket.

DebugServer: specifies whether emulator should run in server mode. The default is True.

DebugSuspend: specifies whether emulator should wait for connection before starting the application. The default is True.

*CommandLine: command line for running emulator. Required when PlatformType is CUSTOM.

Using Headless Builds

Because the IDE's project commands are based on Ant scripts and properties files, you can run these targets from outside of the IDE as *headless builds*. Headless builds for Mobility projects operate under the same principles as for general Java projects. See Running a Project from Outside of the IDE in Chapter 3 for more information.

Computers with NetBeans IDE

Assuming that the project has already been opened in NetBeans on the target computer and no reference problems exist, any Ant target can be invoked from within the project directory. For example, typing `ant jar run` at a command line will compile, package, and execute the project.

As always, Ant properties can be set by using the `-D` switch. Examine your project's `build.properties` file to see which properties can be set. Normally, this is used to activate a certain configuration. For example, the following line will run the project using the `BigScreenConfig`:

```
ant -Dconfig.active=BigScreenConfig run
```

Computers without NetBeans IDE

Running NetBeans projects on computers that have no NetBeans installation is somewhat more complicated. It is strongly recommended that projects be opened within NetBeans, as then the IDE can be used to configure the project to work on the new machine. But if this is not possible, you should take the following actions to set up the project:

- You must have access to the Mobility Ant Library, as described in Using Ant in Mobility Projects earlier in this chapter.
- Create a `/private` subdirectory in `nbproject` containing a file called `private.properties`. This file should match the properties file located in the NetBeans user's `/private` directory for the same project. Update the hard path references to refer to local locations.
- Create a `build.properties` file somewhere on the local machine. This file should be similar to the one located on the NetBeans user's `{user home}/` `build.properties` file. It should contain all properties (with correct path information) that refer to libraries or emulator platforms used by the project in question.

Once these files have been created, the headless build can be invoked similarly to how it is started on machines with NetBeans IDE installed. The only difference is that the `user.properties.file` should be set to point to the `build.proper-ties` file created above. So, for example,

```
ant -Duser.properties.file=C:\{path}\build.properties jar
```

will build the distribution JAR files of the project. Make sure to use a fully qualified path to the `build.properties` file.

Finding More Information

The following online resources might be useful to you if you would like to learn more about NetBeans, NetBeans Mobility Pack, or J2ME technology in general:

- NetBeans download page:

  http://www.netbeans.org/downloads/index.html

- Mobility Pack home page:

  http://developers.sun.com/prodtech/javatools/mobility/index.jsp

- NetBeans IDE articles:

  http://www.netbeans.org/kb/index.html

- J2ME documentation:

  http://java.sun.com/j2me/docs/index.html

- J2ME technical articles and tips:

  http://developers.sun.com/techtopics/mobility/reference/techart

- Java Mobility forums:

  http://forums.java.sun.com/category.jspa?categoryID=22

- Developer Network Mobility Program:

  http://sun.com/developers/mobility_program

CHAPTER 12

Integrating Existing Ant Scripts with the IDE

- Creating a Free-Form Project
- Mapping a Target to an IDE Command
- Setting Up the Debug Project Command for a General Java Application
- Setting Up the Debug Project Command for a Web Application
- Setting Up Commands for Selected Files
- Setting Up the Compile File Command
- Setting Up the Run File Command
- Setting Up the Debug File Command
- Setting Up the Debugger's Apply Code Changes Command
- Changing the Target JDK for a Free-Form Project
- Making a Custom Menu Item for a Target
- Debugging Ant Scripts

THE USER INTERFACE FOR STANDARD PROJECTS in NetBeans IDE is designed to handle common development scenarios, to be easy to use, and to encourage good programming practices (such as modular design with no circular dependencies). It is particularly well suited to creating projects from scratch.

However, the standard user interface does not cover all scenarios, particularly for projects originally developed in other environments. If this is your case, you can take advantage of the IDE's tight integration with Ant to customize the IDE to work with your existing Ant build script.

If you already have your own build script and do not want to (or cannot) re-create it through the IDE, you can set up the IDE to use that build script by creating a free-form project. Free-form projects also might be preferable to standard projects if you create multiple outputs from individual source roots or if there is anything too restrictive in standard projects.

 Before committing to using your existing build script with the IDE, carefully consider whether you really need to use your own Ant script, and make sure that it is not possible to replicate your existing build processes with a combination of standard IDE projects, because standard IDE projects will likely be easier to maintain on a long-term basis.

The IDE's project system is based on Ant to the degree that even incremental commands (such as for compiling a single file) and other commands that you might specifically associate with IDE use (such as debugging) are defined in the build script. Build targets for these commands are generated by default in standard projects but not in free-form projects. In free-form projects, it is left up to you to write the targets in whatever way will work with your project.

Using a build script that was created outside of the IDE entails the following steps:

- Creating a project in the IDE using one of the free-form (With Existing Ant Script) templates.
- Mapping key existing build targets to the IDE commands that correspond to them (such as for compiling and running applications and running tests). You can create these mappings in the New Project wizard as you set up the project or later in the Project Properties dialog box.

- Registering classpath items (such as external source roots or JAR files) in the New Project wizard (when creating the project) or in the Project Properties dialog box (after creating the project) so that IDE-specific features such as code completion and refactoring work correctly.

- Creating new build targets for commands that are IDE-specific and creating mappings to these targets in the project's `project.xml` file. For some commands, the IDE helps you by offering to generate a target (and the mapping in the `project.xml` file) when you first run the given command in the IDE, but you might have to modify the target to get it to work correctly for your project. For other commands, you might have to write the target from scratch and manually create the mapping in the project's `project.xml` file. In NetBeans IDE 4.1, the IDE offers to generate targets and mappings for the Debug Project and Compile File commands but leaves it to you to create targets for commands such as Run File, Test File, and Debug File. Most likely, post-4.1 versions of the IDE will offer target generation for the latter commands.

Creating a Free-Form Project

1. Choose File | New Project.

2. Select a project category (such as General, Web, or Enterprise) and then select the With Existing Ant Script template for that category.

3. In the Name and Location page of the wizard, fill in the Location field with the folder that contains the various elements of your project, such as your source folder, test folder, and build script.

   If the build script is at the top level of the folder that you have specified, the rest of the fields are filled in automatically. If the build script is not found, fill in the Build Script field manually.

   Note that for NetBeans IDE 4.1, the folder for your compiled classes should also be in this folder. If it isn't, some editing features, such as refactoring, might not work correctly. This should be fixed in releases after NetBeans IDE 4.1.

   If you wish, you can change the other fields, such as Project Folder (which determines where the IDE stores metadata for the project).

4. In the Build and Run Actions page, specify targets for the listed IDE commands so that the IDE knows which target in your script to run when you

choose the command in the IDE. You can click the combo-box arrow next to each command to select from a list of all targets in the build script, or you can type a target in the combo box manually. If the IDE finds a likely target for the command, it is filled in automatically, though you can change it if you like. If you leave any of the commands blank, you can later fill them in manually outside of the wizard.

If the build script imports targets from other build scripts, those targets are not shown in the combo-box list, though you can type one of those targets manually.

Not all available IDE commands are given here. You can provide mappings for other IDE commands (such as Compile File) directly in the `project.xml` file. See Mapping a Target to an IDE Command later in this chapter.

5. (For Web projects only) In the Web Sources page, specify the folder that contains your web pages, fill in the context path for the application, and mark the J2EE Specification level.

6. In the Source Package Folders page, specify all of the folders that contain your top-level packages. For example, if the package structure of one of your source roots begins with `com`, choose the folder that contains `com` (such as `src`).

   Similarly, if you have any test packages, you can specify them here in the Test Package Folders area.

   On this page, also be sure to set the Source Level to the appropriate JDK version. Even if this is already accounted for in your Ant script, you need to set the source level here so that IDE-specific features, such as proper Source Editor syntax highlighting and code completion, work correctly.

7. In the Java Sources Classpath page (and, for Web projects, also in the Web Sources Classpath page), specify any libraries or sources that each source root is compiled against. Doing this hooks up IDE features such as code completion and refactoring to your project. You do not have to specify the JDK on this page.

Most of the fields in the template wizard are also editable in the Project Properties dialog box, so you do not have to fill in each value immediately. For example, if you still have to write a target for an IDE command, you can later map the target to the command in the Build and Run pane of the Project Properties dialog box. To open the Project Properties dialog box, open the Projects window, right-click the project's main node, and choose Properties.

Mapping a Target to an IDE Command

When you use the Java Project With Existing Ant Script project template, the New Project wizard enables you to map specific build targets to IDE commands, including the following:

- Build Project
- Clean Project
- Generate Javadoc
- Run Project
- Test Project

You can also use the Project Properties dialog box (Build and Run page) to map targets to these commands. Other commands (such as Debug Project, Compile File, Run File, Debug File, and Apply Code Changes) need to have targets created for them and then be mapped in the `project.xml` file if you want them to work in the IDE.

If you let the IDE generate an Ant target for a command, the IDE handles this mapping automatically. In NetBeans IDE 4.1, the IDE offers to generate targets for the Debug Project and Compile File commands the first time you run those commands. In future versions of the IDE, target generation will be offered for other commands as well.

See Table 12-1 for a list of commands that you can map to your build script. The IDE Action column gives the code name for the command that you use when mapping a build target to the command.

The next several topics provide examples of how to create Ant targets for specific commands and then map them to the IDE.

The IDE comes bundled with XML schemas for the `project.xml` files and automatically validates them every time you edit and save them. If you make invalid changes to a `project.xml` file, the IDE reports the errors in the Output window.

If you would like to inspect the schemas yourself, you can view them online. See Table 12-2 for a list of the schemas used.

Table 12-1   IDE Commands and Corresponding Action Names Used in the `project.xml` File

Command	IDE Action
Build Project	`build`
Clean and Build Project	`rebuild`
Compile Selected Files	`compile.single`
Clean Project	`clean`
Run Project	`run`
Run Selected File	`run.single`
Redeploy Project (for web applications)	`redeploy`
Test Project	`test`
Test File	`test.single`
Debug Test For File	`debug.test.single`
Debug Project	`debug`
Debug File	`debug.single`
Apply Code Changes	`debug.fix`
Step Into	`debug.stepinto`
Generate Javadoc	`javadoc`

Table 12-2   Free-Form Project Schema

Schema	Description
http://www.netbeans.org/ns/freeform-project/1.xsd	Defines the `<general-data>` part of the `project.xml` file for all free-form project types.
http://www.netbeans.org/ns/freeform-project-java/1.xsd	Defines the `<java-data>` part of the `project.xml` file for all free-form project types.
http://www.netbeans.org/ns/freeform-project-web/1.xsd	Defines the `<web-data>` part of the `project.xml` file for web applications.

Setting Up the Debug Project Command for a General Java Application

To get debugging to work with a free-form project, you need to:

- Make sure that the target you use for compiling specifies `debug="true"` when calling the `javac` task.

- Create a mapping in the IDE between the project's sources and the project's outputs so that the debugger knows which sources to display when you are stepping through the running program.

- Add a target to your Ant script for the command, making sure that all necessary path elements for the command are defined, either in the build script or in a .properties file that is called by the script.

Mapping the Project's Sources to Its Outputs

In NetBeans IDE 4.1 free-form projects, the IDE does not automatically know which sources are associated with compiled classes that you run. Therefore, to get the IDE's debugging features to work, you need to create this mapping between the sources and the outputs.

To map a free-form project's sources to its outputs:

1. In the Projects window, right-click the project's node and choose Properties.
2. In the Project Properties dialog box, select the Output node.
3. In the right pane, click the Add JAR/Folder button and navigate to the folder or JAR file that contains the compiled classes corresponding to the source root selected in the Source Packages Folder field.

   If you have multiple source roots, repeat this step for each source root listed in the Source Packages Folder field.

 When you create your debug target, the outputs you specify here will need to be referenced as part of the classpath attribute of the jpdastart (or nbjpdaconnect) task.

Creating the Debug Target

You can have the IDE generate a debug target for you by running the Debug Main Project command (assuming that you have set the free-form project as your main project) or the Debug Project command and then clicking the Generate button in the dialog box that appears.

When you generate the target, it appears in a file called ide-file-targets.xml, which imports your main build script. This enables you to have IDE-only targets separate from other targets but still allows the IDE-specific targets to reference targets and properties in your main build script.

If you have already have the Run Project command mapped, the generated Debug Project target should look something like the following:

```
<target name="debug-nb">
    <nbjpdastart addressproperty="jpda.address" name="ProjectName"
        transport="dt_socket">
        <classpath path="build"/>
    </nbjpdastart>
    <java classname="MainClass" classpath="build" fork="true">
        <jvmarg value="-Xdebug"/>
        <jvmarg value="-Xnoagent"/>
        <jvmarg value="-Djava.compiler=none"/>
        <jvmarg value="-Xrunjdwp:transport=dt_socket,
            address=${jpda.address}"/>
    </java>
</target>
```

In many cases, the generated target will work without modification. If the target does not work or does not work the way you want it to, you can modify it by hand. See Table 12-3 for further details and some things to look out for.

If you have generated the debug target without having previously designated a run target in the project, the generated target will have some gaps that you need to fill in. Such a target might look something like the following:

```
<target name="debug-nb">
    <path id="cp">
      <!-- TODO configure the runtime classpath for your project here: -->
    </path>
    <nbjpdastart addressproperty="jpda.address" name="Notepad"
transport="dt_socket">
        <classpath refid="cp"/>
    </nbjpdastart>
    <!-- TODO configure the main class for your project here: -->
    <java classname="some.main.Class" fork="true">
        <classpath refid="cp"/>
        <jvmarg value="-Xdebug"/>
        <jvmarg value="-Xnoagent"/>
        <jvmarg value="-Djava.compiler=none"/>
        <jvmarg value="-
Xrunjdwp:transport=dt_socket,address=${jpda.address}"/>
    </java>
</target>
```

Table 12-3   Details of the Debug Target for a General Java Application

Target, Task, Attribute, or Property	Description
netbeans.home	Ant property that is loaded by any instance of Ant that runs inside of the IDE. The if="netbeans.home" attribute ensures that the target is run only if it is called from within the IDE. This attribute is not included in the generated debug target but might be useful in other targets that you include directly in your build script.
nbjpdastart	A special task bundled with the IDE to debug programs within the JPDA debugger.
addressproperty	An attribute of nbjpdastart that defines the property that holds the port that the debugger is listening on. (The IDE automatically assigns the port number to the property.) The value of the property that is defined there (in the case of the examples given on the previous page) is passed as the value for the address suboption of the -Xrunjdwp option.
transport	An attribute specifying the debugging transport protocol to use. You can use dt_socket on all platforms. On Windows machines, you can also use dt_schem.
classpath	An attribute of both the nbjpdastart and the java tasks that represents the classpath used for debugging the application. When generating the debug target, the IDE fills in the classpath provided by the Run Project target, if possible.
sourcepath	An optional attribute of nbjpdastart used to specify the explicit location of source files that correspond to JAR files in your classpath. If you have associated your sources with JAR files in the Output panel of the project's Project Properties dialog box or in the IDE's Library Manager, you should not need to set this attribute. This attribute is not included in the generated target.
fork	Attribute of the java task that determines whether the debugging process is launched in a separate virtual machine. For this target, the value must be true.
classname	Attribute of the java task. It points to the class that the debugger executes. For the Debug Project target, this attribute should be the fully qualified name of the main class of the project. When generating the debug target, the IDE fills in the classname provided by the Run Project target, if possible.
jvmarg	Parameter of the java element for providing arguments to the JVM. The arguments provided in the example are typical for debugging J2SE applications with the JPDA debugger.

The TODO comments mark places where you need to fill in the runtime classpath and the project's main class. For the main class, enter the fully qualified class-name. For the classpath, you could place pathelement elements within the provided path element. For example you could use the location attribute of pathelement to specify the location of folders relative to your project directory (usually, the one that contains the build.xml file), as in the following sample:

```
<path id="cp">
    <pathelement location="libs">
    <pathelement location="classes">
</path>
```

If your project is more complex, you can nest path elements, where the path attribute of pathelement references a different path element, as in the following example:

```
<path id="run.classpath">
    <pathelement path="${javac.classpath}">
    <pathelement path="${build.classes.dir}">
</path>
```

Setting Up the Debug Project Command for a Web Application

To get debugging to work with a free-form web project, you need to:

- Make sure that the target you use for compiling specifies debug="true" when calling the javac task.

- Create a mapping in the IDE between the project's sources and the project's outputs so that the debugger knows which sources to display when you are stepping through the running program.

- Add a target to your Ant script for attaching the debugger to a running web application, making sure that all necessary path elements for the command are defined, either in the build script or in a .properties file that is called by the script.

- Make sure your web server is started in debug mode.

- Make sure your web application is already deployed. (To be able to deploy your application with the IDE's Run Project command, you need to have a target in your build script for deploying your web application and have that target mapped to the Deploy command. You can provide this mapping in the wizard when creating the project or on the Build and Run page of the Project Properties dialog box.)

You can have the IDE generate a debug target for you by running the Debug Main Project command (assuming that you have set the free-form project as your main project) or the Debug Project command and then clicking the Generate button in the dialog box that appears.

When you generate the debug target, it appears (along with four supporting targets) in a file called `ide-file-targets.xml`, which imports your main build script. This enables you to have IDE-only targets separate from other targets but still allows the IDE-specific targets to reference targets and properties in your main build script.

The generated targets should look something like the following:

```
<target name="-load-props">
    <property file="nbproject/debug.properties"/>
</target>
<target name="-check-props">
    <fail unless="jpda.session.name"/>
    <fail unless="jpda.host"/>
    <fail unless="jpda.address"/>
    <fail unless="jpda.transport"/>
    <fail unless="debug.sourcepath"/>
    <fail unless="client.url"/>
</target>
<target depends="-load-props, -check-props" name="-init"/>
<target depends="-init" if="netbeans.home" name="debug-nb">
    <nbjpdaconnect address="${jpda.address}" host="${jpda.host}"
        name="${jpda.session.name}" transport="${jpda.transport}">
        <sourcepath>
            <path path="${debug.sourcepath}"/>
        </sourcepath>
    </nbjpdaconnect>
    <antcall target="debug-display-browser"/>
</target>
<target name="debug-display-browser">
    <nbbrowse url="${client.url}"/>
</target>
```

In addition, a file called debug.properties is generated. This file should look something like the following:

```
jpda.session.name=My_Project
jpda.host=localhost

# Sun Java System Application Server using shared memory (on Windows)
# jpda.address=localhost4848
# jpda.transport=dt_shmem

# Sun Java System Application Server using a socket
# jpda.address=9009
# jpda.transport=dt_socket

# Tomcat using shared memory (on Windows)
# jpda.address=tomcat_shared_memory_id
# jpda.transport=dt_shmem

# Tomcat using a socket
jpda.address=11555
jpda.transport=dt_socket

src.folders=src
web.docbase.dir=web

# you can change this property to a list of your source folders
debug.sourcepath=${src.folders}:${web.docbase.dir}

# Client URL for Tomcat
client.url=http://localhost:8084/myproject

# Client URL for Sun Java System Application Server
# client.url=http://localhost:8080
```

You should be able to get the generated target to work merely by making appropriate edits to the debug.properties file. This target can be used in your project with some customizations to fit your environment. See Table 12-4 for further details on the debug.properties file and Table 12-5 for details on the debug targets.

Table 12-4 Details of the debug.properties File for a Web Application

Debug Property	Description
jpda.session.name	The name that appears in the Sessions window when you debug the application.
jpda.host	The hostname of the machine that the debugged application is running on.
jpda.address	The port that the debugger is listening on.
jpda.transport	The JPDA debugging transport protocol to use. You can use dt_socket on all platforms. On Windows machines, you can also use dt_schem, though the IDE and the debugged application would both have to be running on the same machine.
src.folders	The location of your Java source files.
web.docbase.dir	The location of your web root.
debug.sourcepath	The location of the sources to be referenced when debugging. By default, the value is a reference to the src.folders and web.docbase.dir properties.
client.url	The web page to be opened in the default browser that is specified by the IDE.

Table 12-5 Details of the Debug Target for a Web Application

Target, Task, Attribute, or Property	Description
depends	Attribute where you specify targets that need to be run before the current target is run.
netbeans.home	Ant property that is loaded by any instance of Ant that runs inside of the IDE. The if="netbeans.home" attribute ensures that the target is run only if it is called from within the IDE.
nbjpdaconnect	A special task bundled with the IDE to enable attaching the JPDA debugger to a running application.
host	An attribute of nbjpdaconnect that specifies the hostname of the machine that the debugged application is running on. In this example, the jpda.host property is used. The value of this property is defined in the debug.properties file that is referenced by the build script.

(continued)

Table 12-5   Details of the Debug Target for a Web Application (*Continued*)

Target, Task, Attribute, or Property	Description
`address`	An attribute of `nbjpdaconnect` that specifies the port that the debugger is listening on. In this example, the `jpda.address` property is used. The value of this property is defined in the `debug.properties` file.
`transport`	An attribute specifying the JPDA debugging transport protocol to use. You can use `dt_socket` on all platforms. On Windows machines, you can also use `dt_schem`, though the IDE and the debugged application would both have to be running on the same machine.
`classpath`	An optional attribute of `nbjpdaconnect` that represents the classpath used for debugging the application.
`sourcepath`	An attribute of `nbjpdaconnect` used to specify the explicit location of source files that correspond to JAR files in your classpath.
`nbbrowse`	Element that specifies a web page to be opened in the default browser that is specified by the IDE. In this example, the `client.url` property is used. The value of this property would need to be defined elsewhere in the build script or in a `.properties` file that is referenced by the build script.

Setting Up Commands for Selected Files

To get file-specific commands (such as Compile File, Run File, and Debug File) to work in the IDE, you need to do the following:

▪ Add a target to your Ant script for the command, making sure that all necessary path elements for the command are defined, either in the build script or in a `.properties` file that is called by the script. In NetBeans IDE 4.1, you can have the IDE generate a target for the Compile File command, but you have to write the others from scratch.

▪ Map the target to the IDE through the project's `project.xml` file, and include a `context` element to provide the IDE a way of passing the currently selected files to the Ant script. If the IDE generates the target for you, it performs this step for you as well.

- Define any properties that are needed in the project's `project.xml` file, either in the `project.xml` file or in a properties file that is referenced from the `project.xml` file.

See the next few topics for examples of how to set up the commands.

Setting Up the Compile File Command

To be able to compile selected files in a free-form project in the IDE, you need to create an Ant target for the command.

Generating a Skeleton Target for Compile File

You can create this target by right-clicking a `.java` file and choosing Compile File. The IDE then offers to create a target for you. If you click Generate, the IDE generates a skeleton target in the `ide-file-targets.xml` file and creates a mapping in the `project.xml` file between the target and IDE command. The target might look something like this:

```
<target name="compile-selected-files-in-src">
    <fail unless="files">Must set property 'files'</fail>
    <mkdir dir="build"/>
    <javac destdir="build" includes="${files}" source="1.5"
        srcdir="src">
        <classpath path="resources"/>
    </javac>
</target>
```

In this example, the `files` property picks up the files that you have selected in the IDE. The value of `files` is passed from the `project.xml` file when you choose the Compile File command. If no files are selected in the IDE when Compile File is chosen (and, therefore, no value is passed to `files` from the `project.xml` file), the target does not complete successfully.

In NetBeans IDE 4.1, the IDE also offers to generate the Compile File target for you the first time you try to choose Compile Package on a package. However, the generated target does not actually work on packages. To compile a package, you can use the Ctrl or Shift key to select all of the classes in the package and then right-click and choose Compile Files.

Syntax for Mapping Targets to Commands

Targets in your build script are mapped to IDE commands in the `project.xml` file via the `<action>` element. These mappings are entered into the `project.xml` file automatically when you specify targets for commands (in the New Project wizard or the Project Properties dialog box) or when you have the IDE generate a target for you. If you write a target from scratch, you have to enter the mapping manually.

See Table 12-6 for a description of the parts of the `<action>` element in the `project.xml` file.

Table 12-6 Details of the `project.xml` `<action>` Element

Target, Task, or Property	Description
`context`	Parameter that the IDE uses to collect information about the files that the command is to be run on.
`property`	Parameter that defines the name of the property that is passed the names of the currently selected files in the IDE when the command is chosen. A target can then reference this property to determine what files to run the command on. For example, the target that you can have the IDE generate for the Compile File command references the `files` property to determine which files are to be compiled.
`folder`	Parameter that enables you to specify the directory in which the `filesselected-compile` target is enabled. In the `compile-selectedfiles-in-src` example on the previous page, the value is provided as a reference to the `src` property.
`pattern`	Parameter that contains a regular expression to limit the kinds of files that the target can be run on. In this example, only files with the `.java` extension are passed to the target.
`format`	Parameter that specifies the form in which the selected files are passed to the target. Possible values for this element are `relative-path`—passes the filename with its path relative to the folder specified by the `folder` element `relative-path-noext`—like `relative-path` except that the filename is passed without its extension `java-name`—like `relative-path-noext` except that periods (.) are used instead of slashes to delimit the folders in the path `absolute-path`—passes the filename with its absolute path `absolute-path-noext`—like `absolute-path` except that the filename is passed without its extension
`arity`	Parameter that specifies whether single or multiple files can be passed to the target. Possible values are `<separated-files>delimiter</separated-files>`—Multiple files can be passed. `<one-file-only>`—Only one file can be passed.

Handling Properties in the `project.xml` File

In the example above, the `src` property is referenced from the `project.xml` file. This property needs to be defined, either in a file referenced by the `project.xml` file or directly in the `project.xml` file.

In the `project.xml` file, properties are defined in the `<properties>` element, which belongs between the `<name>` and `<folders>` elements. Within the `<properties>` element, use the `<property>` element and its `name` attribute to define an individual property, or use the `<property-file>` element to designate a .`properties` file. Note that this syntax is different from Ant's syntax for defining properties.

After completing the New Project wizard, where you have specified the build script to use, something like the following is generated in your `project.xml` file:

```
<properties>
  <property name="project.dir">C:\MyNBProjects\SampleFreeForm</property>
  <property name="ant.script">${project.dir}/build.xml</property>
</properties>
```

You can add more property or property file references within the `<properties>` element. Because the `src` property in this example is likely a property that can also be used in your build script, it might be useful to set the property in one place and let both the build script and `project.xml` file use it. A reference to a .`properties` file from the `project.xml` file would look something like the following line:

```
<property-file>${project.dir}/MyProject.properties</property-file>
```

File paths that are referenced from the `project.xml` file are relative to the project folder. For path references to work the same for both the `project.xml` file and the build script, the build script needs to be in the project folder (which is actually the folder that *contains* the `nbproject` folder).

If the build script is in a different folder, you might solve the path discrepancy by moving the `project.dir` property in the example above to a properties file that is common for both the `project.xml` file and build script, and use that property in the values of other properties that you define for your classpath, source path, and so on. For example, you could create a property to specify the location for compiled class files and give it the value `${project.dir}/build/classes`.

Setting Up the Run File Command

To be able to run a selected file in a free-form project in the IDE, you need to create an Ant target for the command and then map that target in the project's `project.xml` file.

 If you are using a post-4.1 version of NetBeans IDE, try to run the Run File command before writing a target. The IDE might offer to generate the target for you, which could save you some time.

Creating the `run-selected-file` Target

Following is a sample target for running selected files:

```
<target name="run-selected-file"
    depends="compile-selected-files-in-src"
    description="Run Single File">
    <fail unless="selected-file">Must set
            property 'selected-file'</fail>
    <java classname="${selected-file}">
        <classpath refid="run.classpath"/>
    </java>
</target>
```

In this example, the `selected-file` property picks up the file that you have selected in the IDE. The value of `selected-file` is passed from the `project.xml` file when you choose the Run File command.

This example also assumes that you have a working `compile-selected-files-in-src` target (like the example in Setting up the Compile File Command earlier in this chapter), though it is also possible to have the target depend on a different compile target you have set in your script.

The example uses the `refid` attribute to reference a run classpath that must be defined elsewhere in the script, with `run.classpath` specified as the `id` attribute of a `path` element. For example, `run.classpath` could be defined as in the following snippet:

```
<path id="run.classpath">
    <pathelement path="${javac.classpath}">
    <pathelement path="${build.classes.dir}">
</path>
```

The paths for javac.classpath and build.classes.dir would need to be defined in their own path elements. If the path element needs to reference a physical location, the location attribute could be used to specify a directory relative to the Ant project's base directory. For example:

```
<path id="build.classes.dir">
    <pathelement location="classes">
</path>
```

Mapping the `run-selected-file` Target to the IDE Command

1. In the Files window, expand the project's folder, expand the nbproject folder, and then open the project.xml file.

2. Within the <ide-actions> element, add a mapping for the Run File command. The mapping might look something like the following example:

```
<action name="run.single">
    <target>run-selected-file</target>
    <context>
        <property>selected-file</property>
        <folder>${src.dir}</folder>
        <pattern>\.java$</pattern>
        <format>java-name</format>
        <arity>
            <one-file-only/>
        </arity>
    </context>
</action>
```

See Table 12-6 for a description of the parts of the <action> element in the project.xml file. See Handling Properties in the project.xml File earlier in this chapter for information on calling properties from the project.xml file.

Setting Up the Debug File Command

To be able to debug a selected file in a free-form project in the IDE, you need to write an Ant target for the command and then map that target in the project's project.xml file.

Creating the `debug-selected-file` Target

Following is a sample target for debugging a selected file:

```
<target name="debug-selected-file"
    depends="compile-selected-files-in-src" if="netbeans.home"
    description="Debug a Single File">
    <fail unless="selected-file">Must set
            property 'selected-file'</fail>
    <nbjpdastart name="${selected-file}" addressproperty="jpda.address"
            transport="dt_socket">
        <classpath refid="run.classpath"/>
        <sourcepath refid="debug.sourcepath"/>
    </nbjpdastart>
    <java fork="true" classname="${selected-file}">
        <jvmarg value="-Xdebug"/>
        <jvmarg value="-Xnoagent"/>
        <jvmarg value="-Djava.compiler=none"/>
        <jvmarg
         value="-Xrunjdwp:transport=dt_socket,address=${jpda.address}"/>
        <classpath refid="run.classpath"/>
    </java>
</target>
```

In this example, the `selected-file` property picks up the file that you have selected in the IDE. The value of `selected-file` is passed from the `project.xml` file when you choose the Debug File command.

This example also assumes you have a working `compile-selected-files-in-src` target (like the example in Setting up the Compile File Command earlier in this chapter), though it is also possible to have the target depend on a different compile target you have set in your script.

The example uses the `refid` attribute to reference two path elements (`run.classpath` and `debug.sourcepath`) that need to be defined elsewhere in your build script. For example, `run.classpath` could be defined as in the following snippet:

```
<path id="run.classpath">
    <pathelement path="${javac.classpath}">
    <pathelement path="${build.classes.dir}">
</path>
```

The paths for `javac.classpath` and `build.classes.dir` would need to be defined in their own path elements. If the path element needs to reference a physical location, the location attribute could be used to specify a directory relative to the Ant project's base directory. For example:

```
<path id="build.classes.dir">
    <pathelement location="classes">
</path>
```

Refer to Table 12-3 for a description of the various parts of the target.

Mapping the debug-selected-file Target to the IDE Command

1. In the Files window, expand the project's folder, expand the nbproject folder, and then open the project.xml file.

2. Within the <ide-actions> element, add a mapping for the Debug File command.

The mapping might look something like the following example:

```
<action name="debug.single">
    <target>debug-selected-file</target>
    <context>
        <property>selected-file</property>
        <folder>${src.dir}</folder>
        <pattern>\.java$</pattern>
        <format>java-name</format>
        <arity>
            <one-file-only/>
        </arity>
    </context>
</action>
```

See Table 12-6 for a description of the parts of the <action> element in the project.xml file. See Handling Properties in the project.xml File earlier in this chapter for information on calling properties from the project.xml file.

Setting Up the Debugger's Apply Code Changes Command

To be able to use the debugger's Apply Code Changes feature in a free-form project, you need to write a special Ant target for the command and then map that target in the project's `project.xml` file. The Ant target needs to call the IDE's custom `nbjpdareload` task, which the IDE uses to reload the fixed code into the debugged program's JVM. See Fixing Code During a Debugging Session in Chapter 5 for information on using Apply Code Changes.

Creating the debug-fix Target

Following is a sample target for running the Apply Code Changes command:

```
<target name="debug-fix" description="Reload Fixed Code Into the
Debugger">
    <javac srcdir="${src.dir}" destdir="${classes.dir}" debug="true">
        <classpath refid="javac.classpath"/>
        <include name="${selected-file}.java"/>
    </javac>
    <nbjpdareload>
        <fileset dir="${classes.dir}">
            <include name="${selected-file}.class"/>
        </fileset>
    </nbjpdareload>
</target>
```

In this example, the `selected-file` property picks up the file that you have selected in the IDE. The value of `selected-file` is passed from the `project.xml` file when you choose the Run | Apply Code Changes command.

The example uses the `refid` attribute to reference the `javac.classpath` path element, which needs to be defined elsewhere in your build script. For example, `javac.classpath` could be defined as in the following snippet:

```
<path id="javac.classpath">
    <pathelement location="libs">
</path>
```

Mapping the debug-fix Target to the IDE Command

1. In the Files window, expand the project's folder, expand the `nbproject` folder, and then open the `project.xml` file.

2. Within the `<ide-actions>` element, add a mapping for the Apply Code Changes command.

The mapping might look something like the following example:

```
<action name="debug.fix">
    <target>debug-fix </target>
    <context>
        <property>selected-file</property>
        <folder>${src.dir}</folder>
        <pattern>\.java$</pattern>
        <format>relative-path-noext</format>
        <arity>
            <one-file-only/>
        </arity>
    </context>
</action>
```

Changing the Target JDK for a Free-Form Project

If you want to set a target JDK for your project that differs from the JDK that the IDE is running on, you must specify the JDK version in *both* of the following places:

- The Ant script for any pertinent tasks, such as `javac`. This ensures that the built targets (and the IDE commands that call them) work correctly.
- The Project Properties dialog box for the project. This ensures that IDE-specific functions, such as code completion and the Javadoc popup, work correctly.

For the `javac` task, you could do this by including the `source` and `target` options when you call `javac`. For example, the call to the task might look something like the following example. The `javac.source` and `javac.target` properties would need to be specified elsewhere in the script or in a `.properties` file with the values set to the appropriate JDK version (for example, 1.3, 1.4, or 1.5).

```
<javac srcdir="${src.dir}" destdir="${classes.dir}"
        debug="true" source="${javac.source}"
        target="${javac.target}"
    <classpath refid="javac.classpath"/>
</javac>
```

To change the target JDK in the project's properties:

1. In the Projects window, right-click the project's node and choose Properties.
2. In the Project Properties dialog box, select the Java Sources node and select the target JDK from the Source Level combo box.

Making a Custom Menu Item for a Target

If your build script has a target that does not exactly correspond to any of the available menu items, you can create a custom menu item for it. The menu item is then available when you right-click the project's node in the Projects window.

To create a custom menu item for a target:

1. In the Projects window, right-click the project's node and choose Properties.
2. In the Project Properties dialog box, select the Build and Run node.
3. Click the Add button next to the Custom Menu Items table to add a blank row to the table.
4. Fill in the target name in the Ant Target column and the name for the menu item in the Label column.

Debugging Ant Scripts

If you need to troubleshoot an Ant script, or you just would like a tool to help you make sense of a working script, you can use the IDE's new Ant Debugger module. The module essentially plugs into the IDE's visual debugging framework, provides most of the debugging features you are used to for Java files, and applies those features to Ant scripts. For example, you can

- Use the Step Into, Step Over, Step Out, and Continue commands to trace execution of the script or a specific target. This feature is particularly useful to help you untangle the order in which nested targets (and even nested scripts) are called.
- Use the Call Stack window to monitor the current hierarchy of nested calls.
- Set breakpoints.
- View the values of properties in the Local Variables window.
- Set a watch on a property.

The Ant Debugger (see Figure 12-1) is not included in the standard NetBeans IDE 4.1 download, but you can add it to your installation through the IDE's Update Center. Choose Tools | Update Center and then go through the wizard to pick and download the module. When presented with a list of update centers in the wizard, first look in the Beta update center.

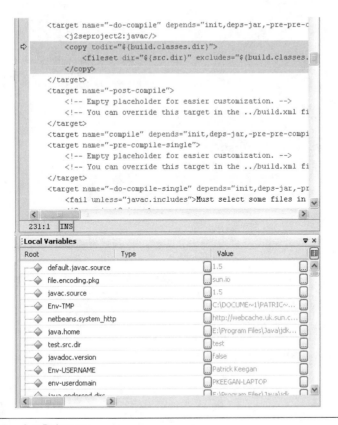

Figure 12-1 Ant Debugger

Most likely, the module will be a standard part of the NetBeans IDE release in versions after 4.1.

Once the Ant Debugger module is installed, to start debugging a build script:

1. Open the Files window and navigate to the build script.
2. Right-click the build script, and choose Debug Target and then the name of the target you want to debug.

   The program counter goes to the line where the target is declared and stops. Then you can step through the target with any of the normal debugging commands.

APPENDIX

Importing an Eclipse Project into NetBeans IDE

A

- Getting the Eclipse Project Importer
- Choosing Between Importing with and Importing without Project Dependencies
- Importing an Eclipse Project and Preserving Project Dependencies
- Importing an Eclipse Project and Ignoring Project Dependencies
- Handling Eclipse Project Discrepancies
- Handling Eclipse Project Reference Problems

IF YOU HAVE PROJECTS THAT YOU HAVE STARTED DEVELOPING in Eclipse, you can easily migrate those projects to NetBeans IDE. The Eclipse Project Importer automates the importing of Eclipse projects by processing the Eclipse project metadata and mapping it directly to new NetBeans projects. For NetBeans IDE 4.1, this module works for Eclipse 3.0 (and compatible) projects and is available through the IDE's Update Center. For subsequent releases of NetBeans IDE, the Eclipse Project Importer probably will be part of the standard IDE.

The NetBeans Eclipse Project Importer not only identifies and automatically fixes Eclipse project discrepancies, but also identifies erroneous Eclipse project references and suggests corrective actions to resolve them once the project has been imported into NetBeans. The NetBeans Eclipse Project Importer is also very flexible, because you can select projects from an Eclipse workspace where project dependencies are automatically identified and marked for importing if such project dependencies exist. In addition, the NetBeans Eclipse Project Importer lets you select individual Eclipse projects for importing into NetBeans without specifying the location of the Eclipse workspace.

This appendix describes how to import projects both from Eclipse workspaces and from specific Eclipse projects.

Getting the Eclipse Project Importer

The NetBeans Eclipse Project Importer is an optional module for NetBeans IDE 4.1, so it is not in the standard download.

To download and install the Eclipse Project Importer module, launch NetBeans IDE and choose Tools | Update Center from the main menu. In the Update Center, navigate to and select the Eclipse Project Importer module, click the arrow button to add the module to the list of modules to download, and then complete the wizard.

Once you have downloaded and installed the Eclipse Project Importer module, you are ready to begin migrating an Eclipse project to NetBeans IDE.

Choosing Between Importing with and Importing without Project Dependencies

As mentioned earlier, NetBeans IDE's Eclipse Project Importer provides two options for importing Eclipse projects into NetBeans.

One option is to select Eclipse projects from an Eclipse workspace, where project dependencies can be automatically identified, marked, and selected by NetBeans IDE's Eclipse Project Importer. This option preserves project dependencies and consequently makes it very easy to import Eclipse projects that have dependencies on other Eclipse projects. The NetBeans Eclipse Project Importer automatically determines the project dependencies for you. You can also use this option to import an Eclipse project that has no additional project dependencies.

The other option for importing Eclipse projects imports only the specified project and ignores any project dependencies that may exist with other Eclipse projects. This option is best suited for situations in which you do not have an Eclipse workspace but do have access to an Eclipse project.

 In most cases, you should use the option to import Eclipse projects using an Eclipse workspace so that project dependencies are preserved. The option to import Eclipse projects directly while ignoring project dependencies is most applicable when an Eclipse workspace is no longer available as a result of an action such as an Eclipse IDE uninstall that resulted in an Eclipse workspace removal.

Importing an Eclipse Project and Preserving Project Dependencies

This section describes the procedure necessary to import an Eclipse project from an Eclipse workspace. When using this option to import Eclipse projects, the NetBeans Eclipse Project Importer automatically determines any project dependencies and imports those projects as well.

To initiate an import of an Eclipse project along with any additional dependent projects, choose File | Import Project | Eclipse Project in NetBeans IDE. From the Import Eclipse Project wizard, specify the location of the Eclipse workspace you wish to import from. An example is shown in Figure A-1.

Once you have specified the location of the Eclipse workspace, click Next to display the Project to Import portion of the Import Eclipse Project wizard. This

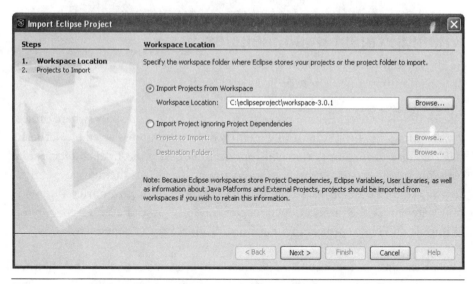

Figure A-1   Import Eclipse Project wizard, Workspace Location panel

portion of the wizard asks you which Eclipse projects you would like to import and where to create the imported project(s) for NetBeans.

If you choose a project for import that has dependencies to other projects, the NetBeans Eclipse Project Importer automatically determines this and marks those dependent projects for import also. In the example in Figure A-2, Main-Project was initially selected, but because MainProject depends on Helper-Project, HelperProject is also marked for importing.

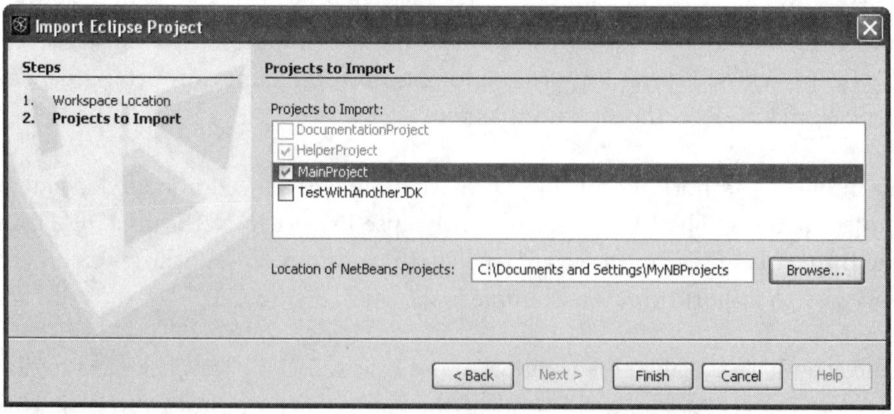

Figure A-2   Import Eclipse Project wizard, Projects to Import panel

To complete the Import Eclipse Project wizard and complete the importing of the Eclipse project(s) into NetBeans, click the Finish button.

If NetBeans discovers discrepancies in the Eclipse project(s) while processing the Eclipse project information and believes that it can resolve those discrepancies automatically, the NetBeans Eclipse Project Importer displays a warning dialog box, showing any Eclipse project discrepancies it has found and the corrective action NetBeans has taken. If you see this dialog box, no additional work is required. For more information on Eclipse project discrepancies, see Handling Eclipse Project Discrepancies later in this appendix.

If the NetBeans Eclipse Project Importer discovers problems in an Eclipse project, such as a project resource that could not be found, NetBeans displays a warning dialog box, along with appropriate actions for you to take to resolve these reference problems once the project has been imported. This dialog box presents a guide to correcting problems that have been detected in the Eclipse project that the NetBeans Eclipse Project Importer cannot correct itself. For more information on Eclipse project reference problems, see Handling Eclipse Project Reference Problems later in this appendix.

If the NetBeans Eclipse Project Importer has found no project reference problems in the Eclipse project you are importing, you can begin using NetBeans IDE on your newly imported Eclipse project(s). For instance, you can immediately begin using the IDE's Projects window to traverse the imported project(s), or you can begin running the newly imported Eclipse projects by right-clicking the newly imported project's node in the Projects window and selecting Run Project from the contextual menu.

Importing an Eclipse Project and Ignoring Project Dependencies

This section describes the procedure necessary to import an Eclipse project when an Eclipse workspace is not available or when you want to import a specific project and ignore project dependencies. When using this option to import Eclipse projects, the NetBeans Eclipse Project Importer ignores any project dependencies that may exist between projects.

To initiate an import of an Eclipse project and ignore any project dependencies that may exist, choose File | Import Project | Eclipse Project in NetBeans IDE. In the Import Eclipse Project wizard (shown in Figure A-3), select the Import Project Ignoring Project Dependencies radio button, and specify the Eclipse project to import and the destination folder where the project should be imported.

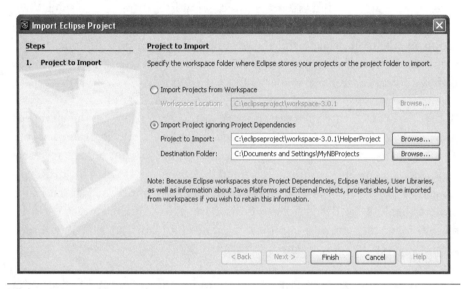

Figure A-3   Import Eclipse Project wizard, Project to Import panel

Once you have specified the location of the Eclipse project to import and the destination folder, click Finish to complete the project import.

If NetBeans IDE discovers discrepancies in the Eclipse project while processing the Eclipse project information and believes that it can resolve those discrepancies automatically, the NetBeans Eclipse Project Importer displays a warning dialog box (like the one in Figure A-4), showing any Eclipse project discrepancies it has found and the corrective action NetBeans has taken. If you see this dialog box, no additional work is required. For more information on Eclipse project discrepancies, see Handling Eclipse Project Discrepancies later in this appendix.

If the NetBeans Eclipse Project Importer has discovered problems in your Eclipse project, such as a project resource that could not be found, NetBeans displays a Reference Problems warning dialog box (like the one in Figure A-5), along with appropriate actions for you to take to resolve these Eclipse project reference problems once the project has been imported into NetBeans. This dialog box is presented so that you may correct problems that have been detected in the Eclipse project while the NetBeans Eclipse Project Importer is processing the Eclipse project information. For more information on Eclipse project reference problems, see Handling Eclipse Project Reference Problems later in this appendix.

If the NetBeans Eclipse Project Importer has found no project reference problems in the Eclipse project you are importing, you can begin using NetBeans IDE on your newly imported Eclipse project, so long as you do not have other dependent projects that must be imported. If there are no additional project dependencies for the project you have just imported, you can immediately begin using the IDE's Projects window to traverse the imported project(s), or you can begin running the newly imported Eclipse projects by right-clicking the newly imported project's node in the Projects window and selecting Run Project from the contextual menu.

Handling Eclipse Project Discrepancies

If the NetBeans Eclipse Project Importer identifies Eclipse project discrepancies while importing an Eclipse project, a warning dialog box is displayed, explaining the Eclipse project discrepancies discovered, along with the action NetBeans will take. You do not need to take any additional action when this warning dialog box appears. See Figure A-4 for an example of this warning.

Figure A-4   Notification of inconsistencies in the imported Eclipse project that NetBeans has corrected

Handling Eclipse Project Reference Problems

If the NetBeans Eclipse Project Importer identifies an Eclipse project reference problem while processing an Eclipse project, a warning dialog box is displayed. This dialog box reports the project reference problem and suggests the corrective action you should take. Figure A-5 shows an example of this warning dialog box.

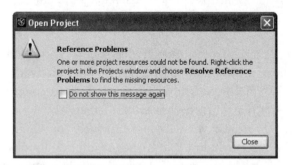

Figure A-5   Notification of reference problems in the imported project that you must resolve after closing the dialog box

To resolve these detected Eclipse project reference problems, go to the NetBeans Projects window, right-click the project that has just been imported, and select Resolve Reference Problems from the contextual menu (see Figure A-6).

Figure A-6   Contextual-menu item for resolving reference problems in an imported Eclipse project

After you select Resolve Reference Problems, the Resolve Reference Problems dialog box (shown in Figure A-7) is displayed, identifying what NetBeans has found for Eclipse project reference problems.

The NetBeans Resolve Reference Problems dialog box describes the Eclipse project reference problems the NetBeans Eclipse Project Importer has found in the imported Eclipse project, along with a suggested solution. To resolve the discovered Eclipse project reference problem(s), simply click the Resolve button. Although the NetBeans Eclipse Project Importer cannot automatically resolve all problems it has found with Eclipse projects, it does give you suggested solutions as to how to resolve the Eclipse project reference problems it has found.

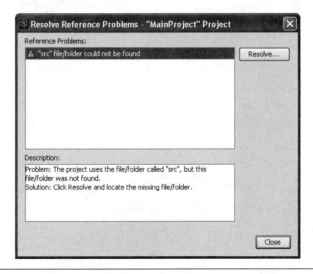

Figure A-7   Resolve Reference Problems dialog box

Index

LEAD or FOLLOW, IT'S
YOUR CHOICE

Check out Sun Microsystems Press Special offers and take advantage of Sun product, technology, training, and service discounts today!

To see the latest developer promotions, go to *sun.com/alldev_bookpromo* and check back as new offers will be updated frequently.

Offers available to qualified customers in the USA and Canada

BOOKS ONLINE
ENABLED

THIS BOOK IS SAFARI ENABLED

INCLUDES FREE 45-DAY ACCESS TO THE ONLINE EDITION

The Safari® Enabled icon on the cover of your favorite technology book means the book is available through Safari Bookshelf. When you buy this book, you get free access to the online edition for 45 days.

Safari Bookshelf is an electronic reference library that lets you easily search thousands of technical books, find code samples, download chapters, and access technical information whenever and wherever you need it.

TO GAIN 45-DAY SAFARI ENABLED ACCESS TO THIS BOOK:

- Go to **http://www.phptr.com/safarienabled**
- Complete the brief registration form
- Enter the coupon code found in the front of this book on the "Copyright" page

If you have difficulty registering on Safari Bookshelf or accessing the online edition, please e-mail customer-service@safaribooksonline.com.